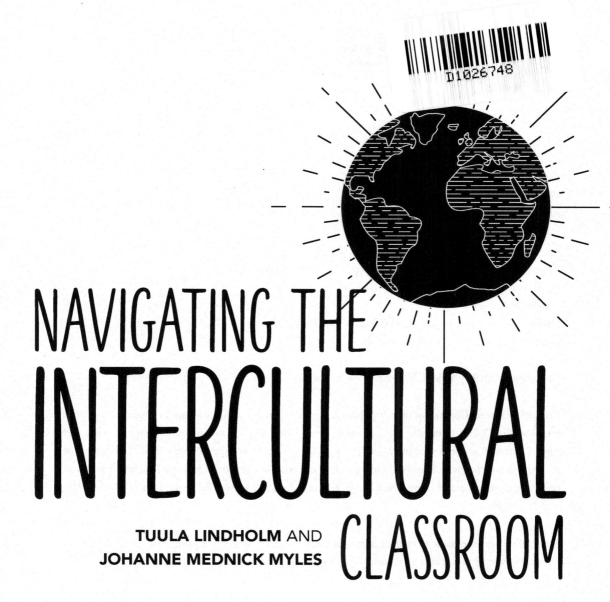

NAVIGATING THE INTERCULTURAL CLASSROOM

TUULA LINDHOLM AND
JOHANNE MEDNICK MYLES

FOREWORD BY **DARLA DEARDORFF**

tesol press

NAFSA.

www.tesol.org/bookstore

TESOL International Association
1925 Ballenger Avenue
Alexandria, Virginia, 22314 USA
www.tesol.org

Director of Publishing and Product Development: Myrna Jacobs
Copy Editor: Tomiko Breland
Cover: Citrine Sky Design
Interior Design and Layout: Capitol Communications, LLC
Printing: Gasch Printing, LLC

ISBN 978-1-945351-26-6
eBook ISBN 978-1-945351-27-3
Library of Congress Control Number 2018958336

A copublication of TESOL International Association and NAFSA: Association of International Educators

FOREWORD

As many ESOL educators have likely observed, language and culture, and in particular intercultural competence, are often addressed separately in the ESOL classroom, many times with only surface-level treatment of these crucial topics (Deardorff and Bowman, 2011). This is cause for concern when considering the key role intercultural communicative competence (ICC) plays in determining the degree of success in interactions, since language alone is not sufficient in guaranteeing success. The integration of language and intercultural competence is urgently needed in the ESOL classroom as students learn to not only navigate a new language, but also the cultural contexts within which to use the language. Thus, ICC plays a key role in determining the degree of success in interactions, since language alone is not sufficient in guaranteeing such success. *Navigating the Intercultural Classroom* not only addresses this need, but excels at discussing practical ways in which intercultural competence can be developed by providing an informative guide for ESOL teachers, administrators and curriculum developers on the integration of language and intercultural competence within the ESOL classroom. Authored by two experienced ESOL professionals who recognize the integral relation between language and intercultural competence, the premise of this book rests in the acknowledgment of intercultural communicative competence development as a process of inner growth and awareness—for both students and teachers.

Over the last several years in particular, with all the research and scholarly efforts around intercultural competence development and assessment, one question persists: How exactly can intercultural competence be developed?" A number of scholars have attempted to answer this question. For example, J. Bennett (2009) outlines a four step process that involves "fostering attitudes that motivate us, discovering knowledge that informs us of our own and others' cultural positions, assessing the challenge and support factors that affect our adaption and developing skills that enable us to interact effectively and appropriately" (p. 125). Other scholars describe three key themes in intercultural competence development: 1) the acquisition of a combination of specific knowledge, skills and attitudes; 2) a recognition of the developmental nature of intercultural competence (meaning a progression from more ethnocentric world views toward a more global mindset); and 3) a focus on the process of learning (Gregersen-Hermans and Pusch, 2012, pp. 23–24). Within these discussions, there is often a lack of focus on language within intercultural competence development. A major strength of this book, then, is that it goes beyond theoretical discussions of intercultural competence to concrete integration of ICC in the *language* classroom through its inclusion of practical examples, engaging activities, and real-life case studies.

Clearly, much work has evolved around intercultural competence in the last decade (see Appendix B in this text), including my research which resulted in the first grounded research-based ICC frameworks (Deardorff, 2006, 2009; Deardorff and Arasaratnam-Smith, 2017). Within this work, it is important to recognize that intercultural competence development is a lifelong process (Deardorff, 2009), so it becomes important for ESOL teachers to guide students toward integrated intercultural/language learning that will carry their students through a myriad of diverse life experiences, ideas which this book was designed to engage.

Navigating the Intercultural Classroom promises to make a significant contribution to the body of work that seeks to, in the words of the authors, "develop both the consciousness and the practical skills required for teachers" to prepare their students to live and work in an increasingly diverse society.

Darla K. Deardorff
Duke University

References

Bennett, J. (2009). Cultivating intercultural competence: A process perspective. In D. K. Deardorff (Ed.), *The Sage handbook of intercultural competence*. Thousand Oaks, CA: Sage.

Berardo, K. and Deardorff, D. K. (2012). *Building cultural competence: Innovative activities and models.* Sterling, VA: Stylus.

Deardorff, D. K. (2006). The identification and assessment of intercultural competence as a student outcome of internationalization at institutions of higher education in the United States. *Journal of Studies in International Education* 10:241–266.

Deardorff, D. K. (2009). *The Sage handbook of intercultural competence.* Thousand Oaks, CA: Sage.

Deardorff, D. K. and Arasaratnam-Smith, L. (2017). *Intercultural competence in higher education: International approaches, assessment, application.* London: Routledge.

Deardorff, D. K. and Bowman, K. (2011). *Beneath the tip of the iceberg: Improving English and understanding of US cultural patterns.* Ann Arbor: University of Michigan.

Gregersen-Hermans, J. and Pusch, P. (2012). How to design and assess an intercultural learning experience. In K. Berardo and D. Deardorff (Eds), *Building cultural competence: Innovative activities and models.* Sterling, VA: Stylus.

Mompoint-Gaillard, P. and Lazar, I., (2015). *TASKs for democracy: 60 activities to learn and assess transversal attitudes, skills, and knowledge.* Strasbourg: Council of Europe. Retrieved fromt http://www.coe.int/t/dg4/education/pestalozzi/Source /Documentation/Pestalozzi4_EN.pdf

CONTENTS

Preface vii

Chapter 1   Intercultural Communication and Teaching
Culturally Diverse Learners 1

Chapter 2   The Role of Intercultural Communicative Competence
in Language Teaching and Learning............................. 41

Chapter 3   Teacher as a Cultural Informant and Classroom Strategist 83

Chapter 4   English for Academic Purposes Programs and
Cultural Expectations... 107

Chapter 5   Employment Preparation Programs and
Cultural Integration.. 127

Chapter 6   Technology and Computer-Mediated
Intercultural Communication 155

Conclusion 171

Appendix A   Understanding Cultural Preferences 173

Appendix B   Models of Intercultural Competence........................... 179

Appendix C   Six Principles of Culture....................................... 185

Appendix D   Observing and Analyzing Cultural Behaviors 187

Appendix E   Communication in the Workplace 193

PREFACE

When we, Tuula and Johanne, came together to write this book, both of us recognized that we would face challenges in how to write about the complex connections between intercultural communication and language teaching. We realized that, in many ways, we had been writing parts of this book in our heads throughout our second language teaching careers. On the surface, practitioners in English to speakers of other languages (ESOL), English as a second language (ESL)/English language development (ELD), bilingual, and dual language programs (referred to in this book as "ESOL programs" for brevity) know that language is infused with culture because language conveys meanings that are inseparable from the cultural context in which it is used. When we are English language teachers in the classroom, we are also cultural informants to our students; the resources we use and our interactions with the students convey meanings that are both linguistic and cultural. As authors, we acknowledge that the study of intercultural competencies in communication stands alone as a separate discipline and is not commonly associated with the study of second language acquisition or with the training of ESL/ELD, bilingual, and dual language teachers (subsequently referred to as "English language teachers," for brevity).

The objective of the book is to explore the connections between two disciplines: English language teaching in ESOL programs *and* intercultural competence and training. Though we are not experts in the field of intercultural communication, we are experienced teachers and curriculum writers who have been thinking, researching, and discussing this topic with our colleagues for decades. We would prefer not to see culture and intercultural communication remain an elephant in the classroom. Instead, we hope to contribute to the body of work that seeks to develop both the consciousness and the practical skills required of teachers to navigate the increasingly intercultural English learning classroom. We, as English language educators, have the responsibility to inform our students and to address the myriad needs they have to adjust and adapt to a new culture.

Culture is commonly associated with nationality, ethnicity, and race. The current research and understanding of culture is, however, much broader. To paraphrase one of the researchers in this field, culture is viewed as a dynamic, elastic concept that is changing and subject to multiple interpretations by various sociocultural groups (Ting-Toomey & Chung, 2012). Any English language teacher who has taught in ESOL programs knows how to correct the speech and writing errors associated with speakers of Arabic, Mandarin, and other languages used in their context. What these educators may not be as familiar with is how every aspect of their identity—of both the teachers and students—is influenced by the region or city they live and/or grew up in and their families, education, socioeconomic background, faith, age, gender, and sexual orientation, among other factors. Culture, in its broader meaning, is therefore a framework of values, attitudes, traditions, beliefs, and standards of behavior that regulate social groups and individuals.

What does it mean, then, to become an effective communicator and to develop intercultural communication competencies? We claim that it requires awareness and knowledge about cultures and cultural practices and customs. Because language is the conveyor of culture, language teaching provides a great platform to explore and understand intercultural communication. We are not suggesting that English language teaching and classroom practices shift the focus away from language teaching but that we, as teachers, curriculum developers, and practitioners, begin to incorporate and address the intercultural dimensions of communication that the students need to know to become successful communicators.

Here are a few main principles to keep in mind in designing curriculum and intercultural communication activities. They are adapted from *The 6 Principles for Exemplary Teaching of English Learners* developed by TESOL International Association (2018). Educators need to

- respect, affirm, and promote students' home languages, cultural knowledge, and experiences;
- learn about students' cultural and geographic backgrounds and seek to understand how their backgrounds have influenced their cultural beliefs and behaviors;
- be mindful of situations that require an intercultural perspective to fully understand the message;
- celebrate multilingualism, multiculturalism, and diversity; and
- guide students to be "interculturalists" and global citizens.

We are including ourselves and our teaching experiences in the chapters with examples that illustrate the ongoing learning that continues to be part of our communication across cultural divides with our students. The overall contexts most familiar to us are North American adult education ESOL, English for academic purposes programs, and other specialized English programs at the postsecondary level. Though we have both taught in ESOL programs, our focus here is to explore intercultural communication and the development of these competencies in contexts in which the students are international students in U.S. and Canadian institutions, and immigrants and newcomers who are settling in and becoming integrated in their communities and the local workforce. These communities include those in Australia, England, Scotland, Wales, Northern Ireland, and other countries in which English is the dominant language spoken in social, educational, and workplace cultural contexts.

INTERCULTURAL COMPETENCE AND INTERCULTURAL COMMUNICATIVE COMPETENCE

Because the terms *intercultural competence* (IC) and *intercultural communicative competence* (ICC) are often used interchangeably and as abstract concepts, their meanings are very much related, and readers may be confused about their meaning and use. Arasaratnam (2016) points out that "the multiplicity in nomenclature of intercultural competence has been one of the factors that have irked researchers who seek conceptual clarity" (p. 3).

To be brief, IC is a broad area of research and practice that has evolved and grown quickly in our increasingly globalized world. IC is the term commonly used in intercultural training programs for exchange and study abroad students, as well as research in the fields of social psychology, sociology, anthropology, and education. As a result, models and definitions of IC are highly diverse and dependent on a particular discipline and frame of reference. However, a commonly referenced definition is the one by Spitzberg and Chagnon (2009), who define IC as "the appropriate and effective management of interaction between people who, to some degree or another, represent different or divergent affective, cognitive, and behavioral orientations to the world" (p. 7). In other words, IC can be defined as "complex abilities that are required to perform effectively and appropriately when interacting with others who are linguistically and culturally different from oneself" (Fantini, 2009, p. 458). For our purposes, the *effective* part refers to the view of the ESOL learner's performance in their new cultural setting, and the *appropriate* part refers to how native English speakers perceive this performance.

For many years, communicative competence in English has been the primary goal of ESOL education. Although there are different but closely related definitions of communicative competence, to put it simply, communicative competence can be defined as what a speaker needs to know to communicate in socially appropriate ways within a particular context and speech community. Richard-Amato (2010) explains Canale's 1983 model of communicative competence as consisting of four interrelated competencies: grammatical, sociocultural, discourse and strategic. Despite understanding and applying components of communicative competence and recognizing its formidable influence on communicative language teaching, Byram (2009, 2013) claims that ICC more effectively recognizes the importance of language *and* culture in second and foreign language acquisition. He argues that given the rise of globalization, new technologies, and large-scale immigration, both teachers and learners now need to be acutely aware of other people's cultures as well as their own. As such, the introduction of IC to complement communicative competence in the form of ICC has more accurately refined the notion of what it means to be a competent communicator (Byram, 2013).

According to Byram (2009), ICC consists of linguistic competence, sociolinguistic competence, and discourse competence. IC, however, consists of three components (knowledge, skills, and attitudes) and is supplemented by five competences: (1) intercultural attitudes/curiosity/openness, (2) knowledge, (3) skills of interpreting and relating,

(4) skills of discovery and interaction, and (5) critical cultural awareness. He also emphasizes that although these five competences are strongly interrelated, it is the first competence, the *attitude* of the person communicating with people of another culture that is the basic competence. In other words, without attention to attitude, the four other competences cannot in actual fact be developed. In short, ICC incorporates both an understanding of the nature of communication across cultures and the development of communicative competence. Byram (2009) highlights that the development of ICC includes a combination of communicative competence and IC, a claim that is particularly relevant to the focus of our book.

We refer to IC when presenting research that specifically addresses IC and to ICC when the focus is English language acquisition; therefore, in our book we wish to draw attention to the formidable place of culture learning in the ESOL classroom.

Each chapter of this book begins with a section on Theoretical Perspectives, which outlines current theory and research in the field. The Classroom Best Practices section includes examples of activities and approaches that we have found helpful in teaching. We have also included examples of intercultural activities that teachers can use and modify for their student and classroom contexts to provide more focused practice. The Case in Point section presents case studies related to a particular pedagogical issue in which culture has played a significant role.

The Appendixes contain additional resources for educators to consult as further background information about ICC. For example, Appendix A is a chart of key cultural dimensions that illustrate a spectrum of preferences that all of us have learned as part of our own cultural socialization. The challenges English language teachers face is to learn to understand the preferences of others who do not share the same cultural background.

Whether you are an English language classroom teacher in an ESOL program, an administrator, or a curriculum developer, we are convinced you will find this book to be engaging and informative. It will provide you with theoretical knowledge and practical classroom strategies that will help you to facilitate learners' acculturation process and optimize their ICC. You will also be made aware of your own cultural orientation through tools that foster experiential learning and self-reflection. Most important, this book bridges the gap between the field of intercultural communication and training and the field of adult English language teaching and learning.

References

Arasaratnam, L. (2016). Intercultural competence. Oxford research encyclopedia of communication. Retrieved from http://communication.oxfordre.com/view/10.1093/acrefore/9780190228613.001.0001/acrefore-9780190228613-e-68#acrefore-9780190228613-e-68-bibItem-0078

Byram, M. (2009). The intercultural speaker and the pedagogy of foreign language education. In D. Deardorff (Ed.), *The Sage handbook of intercultural competence* (pp. 321–332). Thousand Oaks, CA: Sage.

Byram, M. (2013). Intercultural communicative competence in foreign language education: Questions of theory, practice and research. *The Language Learning Journal, 41*(3), 251–253.

Fantini, A. (2009). Assessing intercultural competence: Issues and tools. In D. Deardorff (Ed.), *The Sage handbook of intercultural competence* (pp. 456–476). Thousand Oaks, CA: Sage.

Richard-Amato, P. (2010). *Making it happen. From interactive to participatory language teaching.* White Plains, NY: Pearson Longman.

Spitzberg, B. H., & Chagnon, G. (2009). Conceptualizing intercultural competence. In D. K. Deardorff (Ed.), *The SAGE Handbook of Intercultural Competence* (pp. 2–52). Thousand Oaks, CA: Sage.

TESOL International Association. (2018). *The 6 principles for exemplary teaching of English learners: Grades K–12.* Alexandria, VA: Author.

Ting-Toomey, S., & Chung, L. C. (2012) *Understanding intercultural communication.* New York, NY: Oxford University Press.

INTERCULTURAL COMMUNICATION AND TEACHING CULTURALLY DIVERSE LEARNERS

OVERVIEW

> *Home has really less to do with a piece of soil than, you could say, with a piece of soul.*
>
> —Pico Iyer (2013)

For most immigrants, "home" is a more complex and ever-changing phenomenon than just a place of residence or settlement; home is also an inner sense of belonging to one culture while learning to live and settle in another. Granted, immigrant experiences can be very different; they can involve both happy and unhappy memories. Nevertheless, the English to speakers of other languages (ESOL) student may not yet fully understand the process of adapting to a new home and navigating between or even among cultures. English language teachers simultaneously validate deep feelings their students have about their origins and introduce these students to a new language and culture.

Intercultural work is often referred to as work that involves crossing borders, bridges, or territories, three common "journey" metaphors that imply a transformation of some kind. We inherently possess diverse cultural orientations to the world, which cause us to interpret events differently. Exploring intercultural differences, even the slightest of differences, such as the way someone looks or doesn't look you in the eye, can evoke different emotional and physical responses. English language teachers shift and enter different mindsets and worldviews when they teach students with different cultural backgrounds, values, and life experiences. However, with curiosity, knowledge, and experience, educators learn to accommodate differences and adapt their lessons accordingly. For example, you might decide to have gender-based groupings because some members of the class may feel uncomfortable conversing in mixed company. The fact is that interacting with students is a two-way street; though ESOL learners must acquire English language skills along with intercultural communicative competence (ICC) to become successful participants in their new world, English-speaking students and teachers must also acquire such competence.

Our responsibility as English language teachers, then, is to facilitate these entrances or crossings and learn from them in ways that bring meaning to our work. In the end, we want to feel confident that our students can become well-adapted citizens, having a voice and actively engaging in community and civic society.

This chapter introduces the concept of culture, cultural identity and embedded behaviors, stereotyping cultural behaviors, and the challenges ESOL learners have in acculturating to their new environment.

THINKING ABOUT THE TOPIC

Understanding who our students are, their cultural backgrounds, and their countries of origin can help us as English language teachers apply appropriate methodology and choose classroom activities that can help our students acculturate to their new surroundings. Following are some questions you can ask yourself to get you started:

- How do I go about understanding cultural behaviors that go beyond cooking food, dancing, or celebrating festivals?

- How can I avoid making overgeneralizations and stereotyping my students' behaviors?

- What is intercultural competence and what models have been developed?

- What can I do in the classroom to facilitate the acculturation process?

- Is culturally authentic behavior really a practical goal? What are the barriers?

THEORETICAL PERSPECTIVES

What Is Culture?

We all know that culture influences our behavior. Whether we are shopping for groceries or visiting a doctor or celebrating a birthday, the way we physically move or enter into a conversation is for the most part determined by the culture in which we were raised and live. Although layered and rather complex, we can say that culture is a way of life of a people, consisting of what Spitzberg and Chagnon (2009) refer to as "enduring, yet evolving intergenerational" (p. 6) behaviors, attitudes, beliefs, values, rituals/customs, language, and knowledge that are passed on through various forms of communication. It also includes clusters of expected rules and meanings associated with specific social and professional activities and morally acceptable behavior that take place in education, workplace, medical, and family contexts. *Enduring* and *evolving* are key words here. Cultural traditions and rituals are passed on from generation to generation, yet, whether deliberate or accidental, they change with the times. Think about *cultural hybridization*, which refers to the blending or fusion of cultural elements, such as forms of behavior, music, food, and language from different cultures that are constantly changing in a globalized world.

It should be emphasized that culture is never static. It is dynamic and forms the basis of self-identity and community. Particular styles and values might be central to a cultural group's beliefs; however, individuals may change their cultural identities as they learn about others' attitudes, values, and traditions. In a similar vein, a person might choose to abandon some of the cultural beliefs that were important elements of their upbringing. A variety of experiences or circumstances can influence an individual's cultural beliefs. For example, they might find themselves in a peer group that practices different traditions or have the experience of moving (or fleeing involuntarily) from one country to another. In short, culture informs the way people understand themselves and others. As author Jen told Haupt (2013) in an interview, "We are made by culture, but we make culture too."

We are all human beings possessing similar behaviors. Some obvious examples are that if we are hungry, we gravitate toward food because we cannot survive without it, and if we are sleepy, we all go to bed. Nevertheless, as individuals, we may eat different foods and require different amounts of sleep to function productively in our lives. At the individual level, we are all unique in some way; that is, we have different personalities, although our nature, or way of behaving, may be similar to a parent or relative as revealed in the comment, "She is so much like her grandmother." Our personality can be both inherited and learned through, for example, personal experiences. Laroche and Yang (2014) point out that culture lies somewhere between what we consider universal and what we consider individual; it is culture that "makes us more similar to one group of people than other groups of people" (p. 9). In other words, if culture is a collective phenomenon and learned in one's social environment, "it is the collective programming of the mind that distinguishes one group or category of people from others" (Hofstede, Hofstede, & Minkov, 2010, p. 6). One of the challenges we face when confronted with cultural differences is to decide in the moment if a behavior is universal, individual, or cultural.

We can also look at culture from different vantage points and perspectives, ranging from corporate culture to high culture and from local culture to global culture. Global culture reveals a world becoming more culturally diffused and standardized, especially through technology and mass media. The global village is indeed alive and well as aspects of culture, such as celebrity watching and Facebook postings, become more commonplace on an international scale. However, it is important to realize that local cultures are still very vibrant, well defined, and well established. Cultural behaviors also include unconscious aspects that are not freely chosen or easily modified—ways of being in the world that entail deep affective commitments that people do not readily relinquish. For this reason, ESOL learners tend to remain faithful to their culture of origin as they grapple with understanding and applying their knowledge of the cultural practices and behaviors characteristic of their new home.

Culture and Identity

Cultural identity is closely related to the dynamic nature of culture. If we view identity as being multiple, flexible, and dynamic, then we can understand that it is entirely possible to operate across cultural boundaries. Cultural identity comprises a variety of features, such as gender, ethnicity, national origin, level of education, family dynamics, social class, sexual orientation, values, beliefs, and language use, all of which distinguish one cultural group from another and influence how one interprets or lives in a culture (Nieto, 2010). All these attributes play a role in how people lead their lives and behave in social situations. People also create their multiple identities in different ways. For example, a married Iranian doctor who is a woman with children may identify herself first and foremost as an Iranian woman while a person with the same background may primarily identify herself as a doctor, with various combinations thereof.

How people from different cultural groups interact and share experiences with each other influences culture and identity as well. For example, young people, especially those of many diverse ethnic and racial backgrounds, living in urban United States communities may assume different identities as they relate to, for example, a blend of Hispanic, African American hip hop, working class, and gay culture. If they have Caribbean heritage, they may speak patois, a vernacular form of English spoken in the region, along with the English they learned at school. The concept of intersectionality recognizes that no one person has a singular identity; we are all influenced by the history, politics, power, and ideology that dictate oppression or privilege in a society. As a theory, intersectionality is used to analyze how social and cultural categories overlap and intertwine. As for communication,

> Intersectionality suggests that for dialogue between cultural groups to take place, and perhaps be successful, such groups need to recognize how their identities have historical legacies, power differentials, and political conse-quences that could aid or impede relations between them. Paying attention to privilege and oppression associated with intersectional identities makes the work of creating intercultural dialogue more demanding but potentially more fulfilling to the parties involved. (Yep, 2015, p. 1)

Being aware of intersectionality with your ESOL learners can help you to understand their behavior and their physical and emotional well-being from a more holistic point of view. Creating opportunities for intercultural dialogue and relationship building is the key to fostering understanding.

In addition to the notion of intersectionality, the "third space" or "third place" has been applied to helping us understand cultural combinations, especially when it comes to communication and language use. The term recognizes the fact that one's cultural orienta-tion is complex, deeply ingrained, and multifaceted. According to cultural critic Bhabha (2011), the third space is an in-between place in which creative forms of cultural iden-tity are produced. Cultural difference is built into the very condition of communication because of the necessity to interpret, not just to send and receive messages. Bhabha (2011) goes on to say that the intervention of a third space also challenges our perception of view-ing culture as fixed and unifying. For example, signs and symbols (e.g., pictures, gestures, and objects that carry a particular meaning by individuals who are immersed in a particular culture) can very easily be appropriated, copied, and read in new and different ways by oth-ers not from that culture.

Kramsch (2009) explains that according to Bhabha, we cannot be conscious of our interpretive strategies at the same moment that we activate them because such discourses (ways of organizing meaning that take into account the links between language and culture) are historically embedded in our minds and expressed unconsciously. As a result, when we are interacting with someone from another culture, there is a discontinuity in the traditionally continuous time of a person's discourse practices. For example, an ESOL learner living in the United States might not have the same subconscious discourse related to American history as a Native American would. Understanding someone from another culture requires an effort of translation (language and culture) from one perspective to the other and finding some sort of commonality or harmony after initial discomfort and frustration. To acquire that understanding, learners need to consciously occupy a position where they see themselves both from the inside and from the outside, what Kramsch (2009) calls a third place of symbolic competence that focuses on the process of meaning-making. The third place develops its own unique culture as ESOL learners engage critically in coming to an understanding of English-speaking culture and their ongoing role in it. Sounds a bit complicated, eh? Fortunately, we have language to help us in this process.

Language and Cultural Identity

Language is our vehicle of expression and interaction. Through communication, we preserve and convey our cultural identity. People identify themselves and get identified through the language they use when they talk about their work, family, cultural background, affiliations, attitudes, and values. Words also take on different meanings based on the social status and power relationships between speakers (Think of the CEO of a company in conversation with the janitor of the office building). These meanings, in turn, are deeply connected to the social, cultural, political, and historical contexts in which a conversation takes place. For example, when young people use slang with their friends in the street or argue intelligently with their professors in university, they display different identities and signal different group memberships. Multiethnic and multilingual ESOL learners are especially conscious about grappling with intersecting identities as they continue to be attentive to racial, linguistic, and cultural factors in and out of school where the majority culture is normalized and affirmed (Núñez, 2014). In other words, these students must think about the implications of their culture, language, and race or ethnic group in an unfamiliar culture, whereas for students who are right at home in the culture, such thoughts might rarely cross their minds, if at all (Harklau, 2007).

In short, even when we talk about our own culture, we need to realize that there are numerous subgroups in our society that may be different from one another *and* from the majority. Clearly, we all belong to multiple cultural circles that may define us in variable, even contradictory ways.

Culturally Embedded Behaviors

We learn our native or first language and culturally embedded behaviors through a socialization process that begins at a young age by, to put it simply, observing and copying the behavior of adults around us and through informal and formal education channels. Enculturation is a process by which people acquire acceptable norms, values, and behaviors appropriate to the culture in which they are living. Parents, relatives, teachers, and peers all influence and shape the learning process, deliberately, such as in a school setting, or inadvertently, such as on the playground. Successful enculturation results in individuals having competence in the language, values, and rituals of a particular culture.

Much of our enculturation into social and culturally determined routines and practices happens unconsciously. We may exert our individuality by rebelling against conformity, but we are still part of that cultural milieu. The thing is, once those initial behaviors and worldviews are fairly well established, which is around puberty, it becomes increasingly difficult to see things any other way. As a result, exposure to another language and culture provides our ESOL learners with several coping challenges but also the opportunity to see (and feel) the world with new eyes.

Unless we find ourselves in a cultural context different from the one in which we were raised, it is difficult to understand our own behaviors. (A fish in water is commonly used to illustrate this challenge; a fish is not aware that it lives in water until it jumps out.) However, the behavior of someone who experienced a different kind of socialization can be unsettling if it goes against actions we believe are appropriate to a particular social context. For example, the simple act of paying the exact price for clothing as listed on the tag may seem universal until a shopper decides to bargain, which is perfectly acceptable behavior in many countries. For another example, if you were raised in a culture that makes arguments in a deductive, linear style of logic (If A is true, and B is true, then C must be true), you may never be aware of that deductive, linear approach to argumentation unless you are immersed in a culture (or have ESOL learners who organize their persuasive essays according to a different sense of logic) in which one uses a different approach, such as an extended, circular narrative (Baldwin, Means Coleman, Gonzalez, & Shenoy-Packer, 2014).

Examples of Cultural Practices

Why do people think and act differently? Our ways of thinking and communicating have philosophical and historical roots that become deeply embedded in our psyches. Western or Eurocentric culture refers to a heritage of social norms, ethical values, traditional customs, belief systems, political systems, and specific artifacts and technologies that have some origin or association with Europe. Although regional diversity and cultural fluidity must be taken into account, Western or Eurocentric culture also applies to countries such as the United States, Canada, South America, Australia, and New Zealand. Eastern culture refers to the countries and cultures east of Europe, such as China, Japan, and Korea, as well as the African part of the Greater Middle East (except for Israel). Simply put, Western culture is steeped in ancient Greek and Roman philosophy as well as Christianity, and Eastern traditions are based on Confucian ideals and values that offer a set of pragmatic rules for daily life. Such rules include respect and reverence for parents and maintaining a hierarchical social order. The division between East and West is a product of European cultural history.

There are overt expressions of cultural traditions, such as those revealed in different types of food, holidays, and clothing. Observable features are commonly referred to as the "5 Fs": food, fashion, festivals, folklore, and flags. Overt expressions can also be seen in greetings. The way people greet or leave each other is an example of a nonverbal behavior rooted in a cultural routine. Body language communication varies from one culture to another. For example, shaking hands is a Western tradition, while bowing is commonly Eastern. Smiling in North America, especially when getting your picture taken, is a sign of happiness and competence, but in Russian society, grinning without a reason may not be common practice. Khazan (2016) writes that there is even a Russian proverb that translates, roughly, to "laughing for no reason is a sign of stupidity." In some countries, smiling can also be a sign of dishonesty, along with other negative associations.

An iceberg and an onion are two common symbols used to illustrate cultural behaviors. In these analogies, observable cultural phenomena are those above the waterline or wrapped around the outer layers of an onion, respectively. People can often recognize and adjust to these types of phenomena. American novelist Elizabeth Strout, who was raised in a homogenous small, white, Christian community in Maine, commented that it was "lovely" to see her former Jewish husband and his father kiss when they met—a gesture "incomprehensible" to her own insular, provincial family (Levy, 2017). She had never been exposed to such behavior until she moved from rural New England to New York City and married a person not of her faith. People can evaluate such practices as lovely or not; however, it is the hidden elements of behavior that prove to be most challenging to understand. These hidden elements are what most often lead to miscommunication and conflict. Deep culture (the part of the iceberg that is in the water or the bit inside the onion) includes elements such as concepts of self, child-raising beliefs, beauty, personal space, work ethic, approaches to problem solving and interpersonal relationships, moral values, world views, and personal discipline—to name a few. Misunderstandings often arise when one person uses their own meanings, values, beliefs, and assumptions to make sense of the reality of others.

High- and Low-Context Cultures

Hall, an American anthropologist whose book *The Silent Language* (1959) became a classic in the study of nonverbal aspects of communication, the social uses of space, and communication between members of different cultures, contends that culture unconsciously influences the way people think and reason. Among the many components of culture that he addresses, the notion of high- and low-context cultures is particularly relevant. Broadly speaking, a low-context culture is one in which what is said or written is fully stated and made explicit. In other words, very little is taken for granted on the part of the individuals communicating. Cultures with Western European roots, such as the United States, Canada, and Australia, are considered low-context cultures. On the other hand, a high-context culture is one in which the communicators assume a great deal of commonality of knowledge and views, the "unwritten rules," so to speak, so that less is stated explicitly. As a result, the meaning is implicit or communicated in indirect ways. Nonverbal elements such as voice tone, gestures, facial expression, and eye movement are important. Members of a high-context culture know exactly what to think and how to behave from their long history and years of interaction with each other to avoid miscommunication. Asian, African, Middle

Eastern, central European, and Latin American cultures are generally considered to be high-context cultures.

American culture tends to be low context, which reveals the following characteristics:

- Messages are thorough and direct.
- Completing tasks is more important than establishing relationships.
- Emotional reactions are more visible.
- Time is highly organized.

In comparison, Japanese culture tends to be high context, resulting in the following characteristics:

- Messages are implicit.
- Behaviors are typically reserved.
- Long-term relationships are very much valued.
- There is a strong sense of loyalty.
- Time is largely flexible and open.

Problems in communication may occur, for example, when Americans (low-context culture) find the Japanese (high-context culture) to be reluctant to provide information (which may because the Japanese assume more shared understanding than there really is) and lacking in overt expressions of feelings. The Japanese, in turn, may find Americans to be too offensively direct and loud. However, Carden (2008) argues that given that all cultures use both high- and low-context messages, it is important to understand the circumstances or context in which members of a particular culture use direct or indirect messages.

Individualism, Collectivism, and Further Dimensions

In addition to the notion of high- and low-context cultures is the concept of individualism and collectivism among cultures, which is a component of Hofstede, Hofstede, and Minkov's (2010) model of cultural dimensions. According to these researchers, who have, using scores they assigned, conducted surveys and compared countries worldwide about the values of people and written extensively about national and organizational cultures, individualism and collectivism are cultural dimensions inherent in various societies. In fact, one of the most important value orientations among Americans, and to some extent, Canadians, is individualism. People from an individualistic culture tend to demonstrate an independent view of the self with a focus on personal achievement and initiative. For example, in these cultures, people's goals and sense of independence are generally more important than their allegiance to their family or employer. This type of culture values direct, explicit communication and individual decision-making. Members of a collectivistic society, as seen in Japan, have more of a focus on the group and on the needs and goals that will benefit the group. More specifically, collectivism distinguishes between in-groups (e.g., the family, which includes parents, grandparents, aunts, uncles, cousins, and schoolmates) and out-groups, who are people outside of intimate networks. People in collectivist societies rely on and are loyal to their in-group, which is the major source of their identity, to look after them as they are "the only secure protection one has against the hardships of life" (Hofstede, Hofstede, & Minkov, 2010, p. 91). In fact, "breaking this loyalty is one of the worst things a person can do" (p. 91).

Johanne's experience on a field trip to Paris with Japanese and Canadian college students is a good illustration of these contrasting behaviors. When free time was allotted to the students to tour around by themselves, the Canadian students were more than eager to head off individually or with a couple of their classmates to explore the city on their own, while the small group of Japanese students continued to follow Johanne around, wondering what they were supposed to do now that the whole group, with whom they felt comfortable, had broken up. The other Canadian teachers, who were looking forward to having the evening to themselves, could not understand why the Japanese students were following Johanne. Finally, Johanne stopped to speak with these students and explain to them that they were to discover the city on their own now and find their way back to the hotel with the maps they had been given earlier in the day.

It is important to realize that making generalizations about cultural behaviors according to the East-West, high-low context, individualism-collectivism paradigm is problematic. Some Americans may exhibit low-context behaviors and hold collectivistic values, while some Japanese may be influenced by high-context behaviors and some individualist values. These distinctions are not cut in stone. As cultural orientations, it is best to understand East-West orientations, high and low contexts, and collectivism and individualism as spectrums, with each representation at either end.

CULTURAL DIMENSIONS

Besides collectivism and individualism, in Hofstede, Hofstede, and Minkov's (2010) model of national culture, the following dimensions are also addressed (Hofstede Insights, 2017). It is important to reflect on these dimensions given that "all cultures have their own concepts of teaching, learning and education" (Nunan, 1999, p. 4) and it is these concepts that shape the beliefs and expectations of ESOL learners as well as the pedagogical practices of their teachers.

- **Power/Distance.** This dimension is common to hierarchical cultures in which employees or students accept and expect to be treated by their employers or teachers as dependents (Hofstede, 2009). In other words, there is an unequal distribution of power. As a result, ESOL learners coming from countries such as Russia, India, Japan, and Malaysia, which are ranked high in this regard, may have utmost respect for their teachers, rarely questioning their teachers' ideas or methods, at least openly in class. Learners from these cultures are also more accustomed to classrooms that are more teacher centered (referred to as "high-structure" teaching) and will wait for their teacher to initiate communication. In addition, students may also think that teachers should be respected because of their age, ability, and experience: a respect often based on seniority (Ishizaki, 2007). Countries in which the power/distance dimension is lower tend to embrace "low-structure" teaching and provide students with more independence and opportunities for interaction (Nunan, 1999).   ➜

- **Masculinity/Femininity.** People from masculine societies (e.g., the United States, Germany) intrinsically believe that men are different from women; individuals from these countries are more competitive by nature. They have a preference for achievement, heroism, assertiveness, and material reward for success. The dominant values in feminine cultures (e.g., Norway, the Netherlands) are more consensus oriented. People draw toward cooperation, modesty, caring for others, and quality of life. ESOL learners from more feminine cultures tend to behave modestly; they are more familiar with a system that rewards their social adaption than their academic performance.

- **Uncertainty Avoidance Index (UAI).** This dimension looks at the degree to which the members of a society feel uncomfortable with the unpredictable, that is, "the dark and dangerous world that lies beyond" (Hofstede, 2009, p. 93). People from countries showing strong UAI (e.g., Korea, Russia, Iran, Singapore) have a strong emotional need for rules and structure in their life. Weak UAI societies (e.g., the United States, Denmark) maintain a more relaxed attitude in which practice counts more than principles and rules. ESOL learners from countries showing strong UAI respond to clear and precise instructions and strict timetables. They also expect their teachers to have all the answers to their questions. ESOL learners from low UAI cultures are generally rewarded for their innovation and creativity and for going above and beyond the requirements of a task. They are also more likely to smile in class (Krys et al., 2016).

- **Long-Term/Short-Term Orientation.** This dimension addresses the extent to which cultures view time and the importance of the past, present, and future. Countries such as China and Japan have a long-term orientation, placing value on persistence, perseverance, long-term commitments, and the ability to adapt to changing circumstances. Countries, such as the United States, Canada, Australia, and those in Western Europe focus more substantially on the past and present, and so these cultures tend to be opportunistic in business deals and valuing tradition, the current social hierarchy, and fulfilling social obligations. ESOL learners who come from cultures exhibiting a long-term perspective tend to view education as an obligation to parents and society; these educational systems are also steeped in rote learning, discipline, and test-taking.

- **Indulgence/Restraint.** This is the most recently added social dimension, which, according to Hofstede, Hofstede, and Minkov (2010) solves the "paradox of the poor Filipinas who are happier than the rich citizens of Hong Kong" (p. 286). Indulgence refers to people's tendency to indulge freely in gratification that allows them to have fun and enjoy their life. Alternatively, some people believe that gratification should be restrained by set rules and regulations. They tend to be more cynical and less positive about life.

Hofstede (2009) also claims, and rightly so, that cultures are holistic, and that these dimensions of culture are only guidelines that need to be examined in combination with one another. For example, China may have a high score in long-term orientation and power distance when compared to the United States. It also tends to be a collectivist-oriented society, whereas the United States is strongly individualistic. However, both countries have almost identical scores with regard to masculinity. As a cluster of values, China can be described as a culture with the following qualities: collectivist, hierarchical, long-term focus, centralization, relationships more important than contracts, holistic view, high-context communication, harmony, loyalty, and flexibility.

All in all, Hofstede's work is probably the most popular in the field of culture research. By reducing the complexity of cultural behaviors value differences into relatively easily understood dimensions, the framework can be applied effectively to everyday intercultural interactions. However, it must be noted that other frameworks continue to develop as more and more research is conducted, especially in business settings, marketing, and computer-mediated communication (Schwartz, 1994, Triandis, 2004).

PIT AND FLEXIBLE SELVES

Cambridge-based author Gish Jen has made a literary career in part from writing about the experiences of Chinese Americans. In *The Girl at the Baggage Claim: Explaining the East-West Culture Gap* (2017), she makes the case for the sociological and cultural patterns that influence and shape our identity.

She describes the Western, more specifically American, reality as "pit self" and Eastern or non-Western thought as "flexi-self," preferring to use that terminology over "individualistic" and "collectivist" or "independent" and "interdependent," which are, in her mind, too opposing and loaded in nature. With her terms, she opens the door to the idea that one is not necessarily one or the other, but can, paradoxically, be both. She says, "most importantly, these names steer the reader away from the idea that one sort of self is capable of independent action while the other is not" (Minow, 2017).

In other words, those coming from non-western backgrounds, particularly Asians, think of their identity as closely entwined with family and community while Americans strive to be independent-minded. She uses an image of a lion in the African savanna to illustrate her argument; the pit self sees the lion while the flexi-self sees the savanna in relation to the lion.

Jen goes on to say that

> just as the big pit self tends to focus narrowly and intensely on its desires and potential, and to see itself as eminently separable from its context, it also tends to view any given matter in the same way. It tends to view things in isolation, and to favor analytical modes of thought. Similarly, just as a flexi-self focuses on its role in a larger whole and does not see itself as easily separable from its context, so it tends to view any given matter in context, and to favor more holistic modes of thought—focusing, for example, on patterns and other things requiring a wide-angle focus. . . .

> The big pit self is free in the sense that it makes more choices. It expresses itself more freely. It considers other people,, [sic] but often only if reminded of them; its default assumption is that it operates by its own lights. . . . The cultural mandate to define oneself attends its every action, public or private.

> The flexi-self, on the other hand, shows signs of anxiety when making choices in the presence of others; it feels the pressure of society's gaze. But when that gaze is removed, the pressure is removed, too. It is free in a way the pit self is not; it is unselfconscious. So each model of self has a kind of freedom. (Minow, 2017) →

In Minow's (2017) article, Jen argues that there is a spectrum, and we can identify the two end points and in general say that the flexi-self dominates in the East and the pit self dominates in the West. Most people will see themselves somewhere between the two selves. Most important, whatever East-West differences there are between flexi-selves and big pit selves, they are hardly set in stone. In some form or another and to various degrees, people adapt and acculturate to their new cultural environments.

Stereotypes and Cultural Awareness

Along with the idea of spectrums, English language teachers must be acutely aware of making cultural assumptions and stereotypical comments about the way people from different cultures behave because such perceptions can taint our expectations and understanding of their behaviors. Though it is quite natural for us to generalize about people, stereotyping can be problematic in intercultural encounters because it may result in interpretations that are misinformed and overly negative.

Although ESOL learners come from a variety of backgrounds and cultures, there may be a tendency for us to "box" or slot people into broad categories to ease our own understanding of their plight. For example, Indonesia comprises people who are Javanese, Balinese, and Sudanese, depending on the island they are from, and many Indonesians have Chinese heritage as well; however, it can be common practice to label them all as Indonesian or even Asian. Countries also have national languages, such as Bahasa Indonesia in Indonesia, but students from Indonesia also communicate in different languages within their home environment. As a result, English is most likely their third or even fourth language. They may also engage in various customs and rituals based on their ethnicity and religious beliefs. What this illustrates is that even students from the same country may exhibit differences in attitudes and communication styles, both verbal (which can include tone of voice and accent) and nonverbal (which can include greetings, eye contact, and other culturally rooted mannerisms, many of which are rooted in showing signs of respect). The point is to avoid generic categorizations and instead specify exactly where students are from and/or what their heritage is (e.g., Chinese rather than Asian or Cuban rather than Latin).

We have all encountered people from the same culture or country who speak and act in different ways, yet we have the uncanny tendency to attribute predominant characteristics of a group of people to individuals without recognizing that there are individual variations within the group. As mentioned earlier, cultural traits can become stereotypical, and these perspectives can unfortunately lead to faulty assumptions and expectations of ESOL student behaviors. Students, in turn, may come to class with stereotypes of their classmates' behaviors, which can affect their interactions and the building of healthy relationships. Stereotypes are caused by one's lack of sufficient knowledge of the other culture and its people. It is true that people within a culture have a lot in common. We all exhibit shared cultural characteristics, but "who has them, to what degree as well as when, how and where they'll be expressed is what we don't know and is what we need to learn about each other as we work together" (Simons, 2013). Surely, the idea that cultures fall into high-context and low-context categories helps to reduce the complexity of a culture and in turn facilitate genuine cultural understanding. However, the concepts are still oversimplifications, and they are still stereotypes.

What we see or hear in the media probably most influences our forming of stereotypes. In other words, it is often through media representations of cultural groups that we obtain an oversimplified (and often erroneous) image of other people that can become embedded in our mind. Think about the stereotypes British comedian Sacha Baron Cohen portrayed in *Borat*, his mockumentary film targeting American culture in which he uses a variety of stereotypical accents and guises purely for comic effect. Whether he is parodying Eastern Europeans, Gypsies, or African Americans, all his jokes are at the expense of minority groups, which in the end can erroneously reinforce or even validate people's prejudices (Hemmings, 2006).

Some stereotypes are subconsciously held beliefs about a group that may convey both positive and negative messages. A common stereotype portrays all Canadians as reserved and polite, constantly saying that "they are sorry." Although this can be viewed as positive (and again for comic effect, especially when they are compared to other more assertive, less apologetic nationalities), such a stereotype is in reality an unjustified mass generalization. Jen (2017) explains further that for every overgeneralization that can lead to culture blaming and stereotyping, there are many exceptions; however, we need to realize that there is still a deeply rooted culture gap that penetrates several facets of our lives.

> It's the shortest of hops, too, from culture praise to culture blame (If they can do it, why can't you?); and it is way too easy to use culture to support stereotypes. (No, I am not a tiger mom.) Plus, what can we really say about culture when it's so hard to say what we even mean by the word "East," exactly, or, for that matter, "West"; when, whatever they are, they have intermixed from time immemorial; when all cultures are ever evolving . . . . whether or not there is an "East" or a "West," exactly, there is still an East-West culture gap. (p. xiii)

Jen (2017) goes on to say that much of the gap stems from what the East and West fail to understand about themselves and one another:

> It's a difference that underlies the way we focus and remember; it's a difference that underlies the way we talk, eat, read, and write. It underlies our ideas about testing, education, and storytelling; our ideas about architecture and space; our ideas about innovation and branding; and our ideas about law, rehabilitation, religion, freedom, and choice. It underlies our relationship to one another and to nature . . . . it underlies what we believe to be taboo and what we believe to be an obligation. (p. xiv)

Making Overgeneralizations About People

We all generalize and look for patterns in what we observe to make sense of the world around us. In fact, as Welsh (2011) explains, it is through our schooling that we are taught to look for patterns to help us understand such subjects that are composed of rules, such as mathematics, science, and the English language. English language teachers, however, also know that there are many exceptions to the rules—which drives students crazy! It is generalizing the rules and patterns that gets students into trouble. Welsh (2011) compares the overgeneralizing of grammar rules to the way we perceive and mentally process the behavior of individuals from other cultures. In observing characteristics, we are more likely to form opinions and to focus on the differences and to categorize new information into similar types of broad groupings that we already recognize, such as Asian or African, with the assumption that these are homogenous groups. What we have done in these cases, however, is stereotyped people without acknowledging individual differences. Such mental formations also become embedded, which in turn not only affect people's attitudes toward others but also intercultural understanding and communication.

English language teachers can help their students build cultural awareness by providing them with opportunities to read about other cultures, seek out cultural informants, ask questions, initiate discussions, and reflect on their own cultural upbringing. (These strategies are consistently emphasized throughout this book.) However, educators may unknowingly assert unwarranted stereotypes about other cultures and peoples or use the old stereotypes to talk about situations that have dramatically changed. For example, not all students from India live on a diet of curry, rice, and chai tea; they are more likely than in the past to eat pizza, Kentucky Fried Chicken, and hamburgers and to drink coffee given the glut of North American restaurants in India. Stereotyping can also oversimplify culture in an unrealistic manner. As Nieto (2010) points out,

> If culture is thought of in a sentimental way then it becomes little more than a yearning for a past that never existed, or an idealized, sanitized version of what really exists. The result may be an unadulterated, essentialized "culture on a pedestal" that bears little resemblance to the messy and contradictory culture of real life. (p. 9)

Any form of cultural categorization is always subjected to stereotyping and, unfortunately, embedded stereotyping can be resistant to change.

The question is, what is the connection between stereotypes and communication? Cultural stereotypes can influence intercultural interactions in different ways. They act as points of reference and help us understand what we are seeing and experiencing in social conversations, but, ultimately, they do not accurately predict our behaviors. Lehtonen (n.d.) explains that cultural stereotypes

> focus our attention on certain features, amplify them in our observation, and offer interpretations of our observations. In this way, we see what we are taught to see, and at the same time our observations also confirm the stereotype. Expectations drive our attention as observers. Having stereotypes may even lead one to see things that are not really there.

She goes on to say that when we first encounter someone from another culture, we may think about the cultural stereotype we hold of them as a source of expectation about that person and their behavior. True or not, Lehtonen (n.d.) highlights that "if the stereotype is well-grounded and justifiable, it may help to orient oneself in a certain situation, but if it is unjust and loaded with negative emotions, it will harm the interaction without question." Johanne has had students from Europe who have openly expressed their hostility toward Roma people primarily based on what they are taught to see, their observations, and harmful portrayals by the media. Yet, she has used their opinions to engage all her ESOL learners in a frank conversation about stereotypes and how these kinds of ignorant generalizations can lead to misunderstandings and affect healthy interactions among people of all cultures.

Explaining and Dealing With Stereotypes

It is important for English language teachers to talk openly about stereotypes, present realistic representations of cultural groups based on an understanding of a group's culture and heritage, and model respect for difference and diverse views. That said, teachers can face a difficult balance in having to challenge overgeneralizations, negative stereotypes, and discriminatory ideas that may be brought up in class. In class discussions, surely a range of views should be heard and valued when exploring cultural norms and behaviors. However, teachers should use their moral judgement to raise awareness of the ethical and moral values of different positions.

One of the ways teachers can deal with generalizations is to be mindful of their choice of words. For example, instead of saying, "Most Muslim women wear scarves or hijabs," say "Some Muslim women wear scarves or hijabs, depending on where they are living and the sect of Islam to which they are affiliated." Using verbs and verb phrases like *tend to*, *may*, or *likely to be*, as in "Students from China tend to have a deep respect for their parents," helps to avoid blanket stereotypes of various beliefs and behaviors as well. When comparing cultures, it can also be beneficial to first examine the students' own background culture. ESOL learners need to realize that their own culture is complex, that it cannot always be easily defined, and that it is not practiced by everyone in their native community in the same way. Addressing complexity may help students understand that another culture should not be oversimplified and that the culture of people from the English-speaking world is not uniform. Many ESOL learners may already have this understanding, as English may be their third or fourth language. Indeed, not all Americans will be watching the Super Bowl game on television, despite what the media implies.

Cultivating cultural awareness involves the ability to stand back from ourselves (as if we were looking down on the planet from outer space) and become aware of our own cultural values, beliefs, perceptions, and stereotypes. Why do we do things in a certain way? How do behaviors become normalized? For example, it has become normal behavior for North Americans to walk to work with coffee in their hands, a practice that may seem strange or even unacceptable in Italy or Morocco, where people often enjoy coffee in a bar or café. As Quappe and Cantatore (2007) point out, Italians may automatically perceive Americans as being people who always work (the rushing to work with a coffee in hand is the image propelling this notion) and talk about business over lunch. Does this mean that Italians are lazy and Americans work-obsessed? What this means, according to Quappe and Cantatore's (2007) explanation, is that what value people assign to certain activities, like having coffee or lunch, can be different according to certain cultural values inherent in the culture. In Italy, relationships are highly valued and so lunch or the simple coffee break has a specific social connotation: People get together to talk and relax and to get to know each other better. In the United States, lunches can be part of closing a deal where people discuss the outcomes and sign a contract over a sandwich.

Misinterpretations occur for several reasons. We may lack awareness of our own behavioral rules and project them onto others (e.g., assuming individuals in a group will pay individually for their coffee or meal when in some cultures, it is expected that one person will pay the bill and others will pay next time). We may also make assumptions about similarities in behaviors where there are not any. For example, young ESOL learners from different cultures often wear the same clothes (e.g., jeans, t-shirts, and running shoes) and experience comparable rituals (e.g., wearing earphones and listening to music or podcasts before coming to class) as their native-English-speaking peers, and so teachers may assume that these learners are doing just fine in their new environment. However, subtle differences do exist, and their meanings can run deep. Any of those students may be experiencing a huge culture shock; they may be lonely, anxious, and homesick, spending late hours on their computers communicating with their friends back home. And teachers may never be aware of their feelings given their outward manifestations of "global" cultural behaviors (see the section on **Cultural Adaptation** in this chapter).

It is important to step outside of our cultural boundaries to realize the impact that *our* culture has on our behavior, and to be mindful of our own assumptions. Wintergerst and McVeigh (2011) refer to the assumption of similarity as a stumbling block to cultural competence, along with language differences (sociocultural aspects), misinterpreting nonverbal communication, having preconceptions and stereotypes, and immediate evaluation of actions and assertions. These stumbling blocks apply to both English language teachers and students.

DEGREES OF CULTURAL AWARENESS

Cultural awareness involves seeing and understanding both the positive and negative aspects of cultural differences. On the positive side, diversity allows for people to learn and engage in different approaches to solving problems. On the negative side, it may be difficult for a class to make a decision when members think and act in different and unfamiliar ways. People can experience several stages of cultural awareness; it is the final stage that brings the most benefit to classrooms and organizations. The stages are as follows:

1. My way is the only way (**Parochial stage**): At the first level, people are aware of their way of doing things, but their way is the only way. They refuse to acknowledge the impact of cultural differences.

2. I know their way, but my way is better (**Ethnocentric stage**): At the second level, people are aware of other ways of doing things, but still consider their way as the best one. Cultural differences are perceived as a source of problems and people tend to ignore them or find them unimportant, and therefore reduce their significance. ➔

3. My way and their way (**Synergistic stage**): At this level, people are aware of their own way of doing things and others' ways of doing things, and they choose the best way according to the situation. People at this level realize that cultural differences can lead both to problems and benefits and are willing to use cultural diversity to create new solutions and alternatives.

4. Our Way (**Participatory Third Culture stage**): This fourth and final stage brings people from different cultural backgrounds together around a culture of shared meanings. People continually dialogue with others and create new meanings and rules to meet the needs of a particular situation.

(Quappe & Cantatore, 2007)

The primary challenge for English language teachers in the classroom is to find ways to deliver cultural information and foster intercultural understanding and competence among students in ways that do not stereotype, romanticize, or simplify cultural behaviors. Houghton (2010) makes the point that stereotypes need to be defined clearly and students need to learn to recognize their own stereotypes and stereotyping tendencies as well as those of people around them. English language teachers also need to address the advantages and disadvantages of stereotypes with particular emphasis on the problems they can pose. In short, "teachers should foster learner awareness of stereotypes to help students to monitor how categories are forming in their mind, to recognize their own over-generalizing and flexible revision of existing categories in response to new information" (Houghton, 2010, p. 186).

Most important, and for our purposes, the goals of English language instruction need to extend beyond stereotyping culture and beyond culture awareness (although it is a good place to start) that remains external to the student to the development of ICC. Developing ICC involves engaging students in developing skills to become intercultural speakers capable of exchanging meaning in communication with people across languages and cultures. Given that culture is heterogeneous and constantly changing, presenting cultural behaviors as stereotypical and oversimplified can actually inhibit students' ICC development. It is more useful for English language instructors to develop teaching materials that raise students' awareness of the sociolinguistic and sociocultural behaviors that affect the way people communicate and to provide students with language choices they can understand and utilize in interactions with native English speakers. Welsh (2015) reminds us that

> If students are to truly become global citizens and agents of transformational change for a better world, they will require an understanding of other cultures but more importantly they will also need to be able to engage constructively in intercultural spaces. (p. 241)

 See **Appendix A** for further details about cultural dimensions.

INTERCULTURAL COMMUNICATIVE COMPETENCE

Whereas cultural awareness is achieved when individuals learn about and acknowledge differences, ICC includes an understanding of and respect for those differences. However, because we were all raised in a certain culture, it is easy to be ethnocentric in our perceptions of difference. Ethnocentrism refers to the occasions when people scrutinize another culture solely by the values and standards of their own culture, which they feel is far superior to the one in question. Individuals who are ethnocentric judge other groups relative to their own ethnic group or culture, especially with regard to language, behavior, customs, and religion. The challenge is having the ability (skills) and mindset to transcend ethnocentrism, appreciate other cultures, and behave appropriately in one or more different cultures. English language teachers need to develop in themselves and their students a capacity to see cultural issues from multiple perspectives and to interact appropriately with those of other cultural backgrounds.

Before we can understand ICC, we first need to understand what we mean by intercultural communication. We know that culture has a great influence on one's identity, and more specifically, on how people act, feel, think, write, speak, and listen. *Interculturality* is when people from different cultures interact and use language appropriate to the cultural context and audience. Interculturality involves attitudes of curiosity and openness and a critical awareness of conflicting perspectives as demonstrated by a person's ability to negotiate language meaning and usage based on cultural understanding and responsiveness (Byram, 1997). Intercultural communication describes communication between individuals or groups of people who are culturally different in significant ways. For example, a conversation between a woman who was raised in Vietnam and a man who grew up in New York City would probably be an intercultural conversation because we would assume that their different sociocultural backgrounds, outside of possible linguistic barriers, would affect how they communicate with each other. In other words, they may have to overcome certain personal, social, and contextual barriers to achieve effective communication—that is, apply ICC. When people are not aware of cultural differences, an innocent exchange can lead to frustration, embarrassment, or, worse, accusations of rudeness or disrespect. ICC depends on having relevant cultural knowledge as well as appropriate attitudes, beliefs, values, and interpersonal skills. An ESOL student can learn English but not be understood because he or she does not know how to interact with a specific audience in a specific cultural context. For example, the student may not be aware of informal and formal language usage or differences in how behavior revolves around personal space in, for example, a professor's office.

What is ICC exactly? What does it mean to interact successfully with individuals from different cultures, for our purposes particularly in cultures where English is the dominant language? In simple terms, ICC is the acquisition of attitudes, knowledge, skills, and awareness that lead to intercultural understanding and to successfully interacting with persons of diverse backgrounds. It is the ability to act in linguistically and culturally complex situations, in both social and workplace contexts. More specifically, Spitzberg and Chagnon (2009) refer to ICC as the appropriate and effective management of interaction between people who, to some degree or another, represent different or divergent affective, cognitive, and behavioral orientations to the world . . . The extent to which individuals *manifest* aspects of, or are influenced by, their group or cultural affiliations and characteristics is what makes an interaction an *inter*cultural process. (p. 7)

When we find ourselves in an intercultural encounter, we also need to think about what characteristics of people's behavior are driven by their personality and which are cultural. Indeed, ICC requires sensitivity to difference and an ability to identify with others and to critically reflect on one's own cultural background.

 See **Appendix B** for Models of ICC.

The notion of *social* and *multiple* identities comes into play as well. Byram, Gribkova, and Starkey (2002) argue that ICC is the ability to establish a shared understanding by people of different social identities. The woman from Vietnam and the man from New York City will have acquired specific social identities, and they will have unconsciously acquired cultural beliefs, values, and behaviors unique to their upbringing and socialization. The woman might also be a doctor and a mother, and the man might be a musician and competitive swimmer; that is, they also portray multiple identities, earlier referred to as intersectionality, which require some consideration.

Thus, when we take into account communication and intercultural competence rooted in language education and intercultural communication studies, and concepts related to our multiple and fluid identities, ICC can also be related to the way individuals socially position themselves in interactions (e.g., according to their nationally, gender, age, social status, etc.), to their awareness of such positioning, and to their willingness and ability to recognize and negotiate the others' multiple identities as much as their own. (Borghetti, 2017, p. 2)

EFFECTIVE INTERCULTURAL COMMUNICATION

Effective intercultural communication requires

- **empathy:** an understanding of other people's behaviors and ways of thinking regardless of how different or strange they may appear
- **respect:** genuine admiration and appreciation of different ways of thinking and communication
- **tolerance:** the ability and willingness to accept and acknowledge different behaviors and ways of thinking and the existence of opinions or behavior that one does not necessarily agree with
- **sensitivity:** awareness and responsiveness to other people's behaviors and ways of thinking
- **flexibility:** willingness to adapt and openness to change and different ways of thinking

(Sun, 2014)

Many factors affect the ability of ESOL learners to develop ICC. These factors range from their level of English language proficiency and cultural awareness, willingness to take risks, and psychological preparation; the ICC development process may include the ability to "overcome shyness, enhance self esteem and improve self confidence to achieve mutual respect and mutual understanding" (Dong, Liu, Zhao, & Dong, 2014, p. 261) with individuals from the target culture. But components of ICC are not as straightforward as they appear to be when personality is taken into account. For example, is shyness a personality trait or a particular cultural behavior? Considering ESOL learners in your class who are from China, Dong et al. (2014) explain that in China, shyness is rooted in the Chinese cultural system originating primarily from Confucian philosophy. As such, shyness behavior cannot be understood at the individual level alone (as it often is in Western culture). It is also inextricably linked to group behavior and the relative status of the individual within the social hierarchy. In other words, fearful or anxious behavior due to shyness on the part of the individual also includes modest and unassuming behavior, which is often important for group activities. Shyness can directly affect a person's ICC in certain contexts, such as the workplace, where networking and participation in social activities can lead to career advancement. Looking at various models of intercultural competence can help us to more fully understand the skills and behaviors required to obtain ICC, the development process, and ICC's complexity.

INTERCULTURAL COMPETENCY: SAMPLE TRAITS

What does it mean to be an interculturally competent new immigrant or international student? How would such a student behave? The following is a sample list of traits that Jorge from Colombia exhibits while studying English at the advanced level in an English for the workplace program in the United States that comprises adult learners from different countries. His goal is to work in IT, so he is well aware that he may be working in a global context for a multinational company. In and outside of class, Jorge

- is curious to learn about U.S. cultural practices as well as the culture of the other learners in his class; he is also eager to share information about his own culture with others, pointing out commonalities and differences.

- practices his English skills as much as he can with English language speakers and continually asks them specific questions pertaining to cultural behaviors; he is willing to learn from them and have an open mind.

- accepts individuals from other cultures when interacting with them without judging their behavior, which includes clothing/dietary choices, habits, accent, and beliefs; his intent is to make them feel valued and respected and see the world from others' viewpoints, not just his own.

- tries to build relationships with people at various levels and during conversation is aware of how his responses may be interpreted by others; he adapts his responses to appropriately interact within each situation, mindful of the other person or people's expectations.

- reflects on the interactions he has with people, not just what was said, but how it was said, what went well, what was confusing or misunderstood, and how he could improve to make conversations more successful. ➔

- thinks deeply about his own cultural conditioning—his values and beliefs and how his conditioning has affected his social and professional behavior.
- reads as much as he can about other cultures, particularly the news (local and global) to help him understand the contexts in which others live; he also exposes himself to popular culture through listening to radio programs and watching films and paying attention to cultural practices.

Adapted from Deardorff (2008)

It is important to keep in mind that there are several factors affecting how people communicate with each other and interpret each other's messages in intercultural situations. First, ESOL learners are not only experiencing intercultural encounters with native English speakers in their daily lives, they are also having to function in English, which may well be their second or an additional language and one in which they may be at various levels of proficiency. The result is that communication can be difficult in itself because of the language gap. Consequently, students may be more anxious, stressed out, and exhausted than they are normally. Snow (2015) claims that those feelings may well have an impact (often subconscious) on how the participants in an encounter interpret each other's behavior. He makes the point that even the participants who are speaking English are generally also affected to some degree because it is more challenging to communicate with individuals who have limited skills in expressing themselves.

A second factor affecting feelings in intercultural encounters is violated expectations, because both parties may not be familiar with each other's cultural rules of engagement (Snow, 2015). Violated expectations can make us feel uncomfortable because they undermine our sense of predictability and control, which, in turn, causes us to have a negative and faulty interpretation of a stranger's behavior. A third factor that frequently affects feelings in intercultural encounters is culture shock (also referred to as culture fatigue or acculturative stress), as ESOL learners face the demands of adapting to an unfamiliar cultural setting.

CULTURAL ADAPTATION

Home is, for most newcomers, a complex and ever-changing process rather than a place of residence (the old country and a new country or city); it is also an inner sense of belonging to one culture while learning to live and settle in another. As such, cultural adaptation can be a challenging experience. If you have ever lived for an extended period of time in another country where you do not speak the language or practice the same cultural behaviors, you know very well what understanding and adapting to another culture can feel like not only physically, but most important, psychologically and even spiritually. Acculturation, the process of adjusting to a new linguistic and cultural environment, is ongoing for ESOL learners arriving at a new school or job in a new country. The process does not necessarily progress linearly; it can be cyclical in nature and involve positive outcomes and challenging setbacks.

Although it is commonly believed that children will acculturate to their new surroundings faster than adults, the process for some newcomers, adults and children alike, can be overwhelming. The adaptation process can also be affected by gender, age, and family dynamics, and whether a newcomer is from an urban or rural environment. An ESOL student who arrives as a preadolescent will face different challenges than one who comes as a teenager or senior. Indeed, there are challenges at many different levels—ones that go deeper than adjusting to the local climate and food. For example, gender roles and relationships, which include relationships with teachers and other authority figures, may be unfamiliar and confusing to ESOL learners who are trying to figure out the hierarchy and who is responsible for what within a new educational or workplace setting. Academic challenges and sociocultural adaptation issues can result in changes in student behaviors related to students' acculturation process.

Adults and children who arrive as immigrants, international students, or refugees will all experience the process of adjustment to a new linguistic and cultural environment. They may all experience a sense of cultural dislocation and feelings of loneliness, having left family and friends in their home countries. However, there are differences. Unlike international students who know that they are living in the new country on a temporary basis, or immigrants who have generally chosen to be in the country, refugees may experience a more tumultuous acculturation period. Children from refugee families may have been sponsored and so arrive without parents or guardians, and their education may have been interrupted as a result of conflict in the home country or spending long periods of time in a refugee camp. Students who leave a country because of war or other crises can find the transition highly emotional; they may exhibit anger and confusion resulting from trauma or posttraumatic stress. On the other hand, international students and new immigrants may embrace the opportunity to study, work, or invest in another country; they may welcome wholeheartedly the chance to explore a very new and exciting education system and cultural environment.

We must keep in mind that for acculturation to occur, newcomers and members of the English-speaking community need to have as much continuous and direct contact as possible. ICC is aided when newcomers become involved in the day-to-day life of their new community, as opposed to isolating themselves and staying in their own cultural bubble. Regarding the immigrant experience, Berry (1997) created a model and identified four modes of acculturation: assimilation, integration, separation, and marginalization. He also argued that a newcomer's level of acculturation depends on the degree to which the newcomer approaches or avoids interaction with the new culture and the degree to which the newcomer maintains or relinquishes their native culture's attributes. Such models further our understanding of the process, yet we need to realize that conceptualizations of acculturation strategies have become increasingly more complex because of our understanding of multiple identities, advances in technology, and globalization (Berry & Sam, 2016). More recent research regarding intercultural competence and acculturation to the United States among the Hispanic population reveals that effective cultural adaptation involves a delicate balance between competencies that emerge from both American and Hispanic cultural contexts. Not only are competencies (e.g., taking initiative and contributing to one's surroundings) important, but also important are the abilities to maintain connections with family and to cultivate smooth, interpersonal friendships; relationship building; and networking within the Latino community (Torres, 2009).

We can correctly assume that the goal for most ESOL learners is to acculturate to their new surroundings as smoothly and quickly as possible (unless they know they will be returning to their home countries). This cultural transition largely depends on a number of factors, including a student's ability to adapt based on his or her age, gender, family responsibilities, past experiences adapting to new living situations, and other sociocultural qualities, as well as access to settlement support services (Cushner & Karim, 2004). If a student is experiencing some form of culture shock, and is expressing it through feelings of, for example, homesickness, sadness, an overdependence on other students from the same cultural background, withdrawal from class participation, and absenteeism, it is definitely a good idea to reach out to that student and offer strategies to help them get through this particular stage of acculturation. Students may also become negative toward their adaptive country. For example, in their observations of an adult ESOL classroom in Montreal, Dytynyshyn and Collins (2012) observed a teacher helping students put together a booklet for other newcomers to the country. One of the tasks was to

> prepare a list of things they wish they had known (which was also the language focus of that particular task) about Canada before they arrived. In the teacher-fronted wrap-up, the groups reported to the class. However, what happened was that a group of three men dominated many turns as the discussion opened. They wished they had known about all the bureaucracy in Canada, how money was god, how little hospitality there was, how long hospital wait times were, and how artificial relationships were. (p. 59)

The teacher knew that these men were particularly unhappy and indeed might have been experiencing culture shock; she decided to acknowledge the points and not to pass judgment but "maintain a harmonious class atmosphere" (p. 60) by deferring the issue.

Culture shock can instill a variety of stress-filled reactions, both physically and psychologically. Such reactions are completely natural. It would be more surprising to hear from a student that are not or have never experienced any signs or symptoms. According to Landis, Bennett, and Bennett (2004) and Mizzi (2008), individuals who are experiencing culture shock tend to feel the following:

- **Cultural fatigue:** Students feel that they do not want to participate, observe, or enjoy a classroom activity or certain event (e.g., a festival, performance, film, or guest speaker) that expresses the English-oriented traditions, beliefs, or rituals because they can't "take in" anymore and are tired of learning.

- **Language shock:** Students realize that they need to learn English to survive and function. However, they also realize that acquiring the language is more difficult than they imagined, even though they may be fluent in several other languages.

- **Role shock:** Students might experience anxiety when they further understand that their power and position in the new country and culture has been radically diminished or altered. For example, the social status of *teacher* might be one of a lesser degree than in their home culture. School-age students who excelled and took leadership positions at their school in their home country might feel less capable and confident.

- **Education shock:** Students know they have to adjust to life in an academic environment that is very different from their own, but such an adjustment can be challenging and disorienting as they are confronted with different teaching styles and ways of assessing their learning.

Culture shock can also be a positive experience, at least as far as the results are concerned. Although stressful and disorientating, Ting-Toomey (1999) asserts that if culture shock is managed effectively, several positive outcomes can emerge, such as a greater sense of well-being and self-esteem, open-mindedness, flexibility, a greater appreciation for difference and ambiguity, enhanced self-confidence, and the ability to communicate in culturally appropriate ways (i.e., the acquisition of ICC).

CULTURE SHOCK

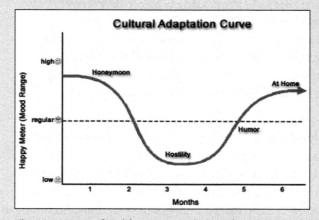

The "U curve" is often used to describe the process of adapting to a new culture and to overcome culture shock. Honeymoon > Crisis > Recovery > Adjustment

The University of California at Berkeley identifies the following on a list of culture shock symptoms experienced by international students who are going through the crisis stage:

- Changes in eating and sleeping habits
- Acute homesickness; students making more calls home than usual
- Being hostile/complaining frequently about the host culture/country
- Irritability, sadness, depression
- Frequent frustration, feeling easily angered
- Sense of failure
- Frequent illnesses

Wittencamp (2014)

To conclude this chapter about culture, ICC, and cultural adaption, it is appropriate to also include an adult learning theory that fits in nicely with lifelong learning and the change required to develop ICC. Jarvis (2012) states that we are fundamentally exposed to two states of being in our lives: harmony and disjuncture. When there is harmony, we can take our world for granted. When there is disjuncture (or degrees of it), we cannot take our world for granted, and so we are forced to ask ourselves questions: "Why? How? What does it mean? and so forth . . . we have to find new explanations, new knowledge, new ways of doing things—in other words, we must learn" (Jarvis, 2012, p. 2).

What does this mean for ESOL learners who are learning to communicate in English and to survive in new cultural surroundings? Well, when they were speaking their native language and living in their native country, life was for the most part harmonious. However, they experience disjuncture when they have to adjust to a new linguistic and culture environment, which requires learning—a response to the differences they experience in their new life. Jarvis (2012) goes on to say that in formal classroom situations, the disjuncture is created by the instruction, whereas in everyday life it occurs naturally in social interactions, which is one of the reasons English language proficiency is so important to ICC development. The more opportunities ESOL learners have as their language skills progress to engage with native English speakers, the more likely they are to develop ICC, overcome culture shock, and settle into a more harmonious world.

CLASSROOM BEST PRACTICES

Teaching Strategies for Accommodating the Transition Process

As English language teachers, it is best to watch out for signals of culture stress, for example, when ESOL learners show signs of aggressive and noncompliant behaviors, apathy, withdrawal, and disinterest in classroom activities. During the difficult times, it is important for you to be sensitive to and understanding of how your students are feeling, particularly during the first 2–6 months of their arrival. Providing them with special attention and support once you notice specific signs and symptoms can help them adapt to their new surroundings and make a positive adjustment.

- *Take a lesson in class to identify the stages and symptoms of culture shock.* You can write "culture shock" on the board with its various symptoms (boredom, homesickness, fatigue, sleeping a lot or little, etc.) and use a graph visual to explain the process. Students can access the meaning of words or use gestures and mime to enhance understanding, depending on their language proficiency. As a class, ask the students to brainstorm at least two possible ways to deal with the stress of culture shock. Form small groups and ask each group to suggest other coping strategies for cultural adjustment. Make a list on the board. Revisit the symptoms later in the course to see how students are feeling and if they were able to cope with the effects of culture shock and make a positive transition.

- *Include student narratives.* Specifically, include student narratives that encourage self-reflection and discovery of cultural identity through journaling/sharing with others using social media and other formats. Raising the issue of student engagement in language and cultural learning is also about exploring the meaning of culture as students' own lived experiences, which shape awareness and influence their thinking and decision-making in the transition.

- *Provide and/or invite students to make comparisons of cultural practices from their home countries and those they've observed in their new environment.* Addressing differences through text or pictures, depending on the students' English language proficiency, helps to acknowledge and affirm their feelings of difference, which they can share with their classmates. Ask students what it is like to straddle two or more cultures. Allow them to explore what remains difficult or has become easy for them and their strategies to handle cross-generational and/or cross-cultural differences (Alberta Teachers of English as a Second Language, 2009).

- *Use case studies in which a student is experiencing culture shock.* Pose a set of questions or prompts whereby students analyze the case and outline coping strategies.

- *Invite a local resident or newcomer who has been in the country for a while to the class.* Have students make a list of questions based on situations that they have felt particularly uneasy about. The guests may have been in the same situation and could share what they have learned about culturally appropriate ways to deal with the situation. They could be former ESOL learners of the program and/or other individuals from the community.

- *Set up a peer-pairing/mentoring program or friendship network.* Students can feel a sense of comfort knowing that they have the social and psychological support of their peers, who may have experienced the same feelings as them when they first arrived.

- *Use humor to address the adjustment process.* Laughter in the class can do wonders to mediate symptoms of culture shock.

Activity: Draw a Model to Talk About Culture and Various Layers

First, ask your students to brainstorm what comes to mind when they think about aspects of culture. Write the words randomly on the board. You can introduce and explain new vocabulary with visuals, if need be. The iceberg and onion models are commonly used to illustrate the different layers of culture. After the brainstorming session, draw an iceberg coming out of the water or an onion with its various layers and have your students name things that appear at the tip of the iceberg or outer layers of the onion, such as styles of dress, music preferences, rituals, and religious customs. Then, gradually get to the hidden or unobservable dimensions of culture illustrated below the water line or in the inner layers of the onion, such as values, beliefs about raising children and education, and concepts of personal space and fairness. You can divide the class into small groups representing each of their respective countries to do this activity and then bring everyone together to compare and discuss those invisible layers. Highlight that understanding culture is a lifelong journey and that we should avoid making broad generalizations and judgments about others.

Another model you can use is the apple tree analogy, which was introduced to Johanne by Melissa Toupin Laforge, who designed this activity as part of a predeparture training program for volunteers preparing for international assignments (Toupin Laforge, 2017). The analogy focuses on the intercultural classroom and encourages people to look as various aspects of culture. In this case, each part of the apple tree (roots, trunk, and leaves) represents a component of culture. The roots represent political structures and ideologies, beliefs about education, and child rearing. The trunk represents gender roles, use of technology, and other numerous and distinct social structures that bind groups of people together. Each leaf on the tree represents that every individual is unique. Physical, cognitive, spiritual, and other factors shape who we are and impact the way see and understand the world around us. The apple tree itself is a metaphor for humanity. Our social and cultural constructions may differ, but we all share characteristics in common, such as our need for food, safety, love, and belonging. Draw an apple tree on the board and ask your students the following questions:

- **Roots (institutions and systems):** What kind of political structures are in place in your country? Where do some of the traditional customs stem from? Is there a free press or censorship? Has there been a history of war? If so, how has that impacted the country? Are there many immigrants? How do institutions and systems affect our behavior?

- **Trunk (social structures):** Can everyone go to school? Are there different types of schools for different groups of people? Are there support groups for women who suffer spousal abuse and others for people with disabilities? Are there sports teams? Can everyone take part in team sports if they want? How does religion impact one's daily life? How can people gain social status? Are immigrants welcomed?

- **Leaves (individuals):** Can women decide who they want to marry or are arranged marriages more common? If a man is gay, can he disclose his sexual preference? If a young adult wants to move to the city or to another country, will their family accept the decision? Do people express their political and/or religious ideologies openly?

Following this activity, you can facilitate a discussion about cultural identity; the various visible and invisible components that make up one's identity; how our cultural identities affect our behavior; and how we describe, interpret, and evaluate the behavior of people different from ourselves. The following questions are adapted from Apedaile and Schill (2008).

Activity: Create Cultural Profiles

After exploring key concepts about culture, cultural identity, and adaptation, develop a bank of elements in a cultural profile that focuses on key aspects of culture to which students can refer. Write the following headings on the board with question prompts:

- **Family:** What does family mean to you? Who is included in your family? How important is your family to you? How do you communicate with your family members?

- **Education:** How do you like to learn? What style of teaching are you most familiar with? Do you prefer to be corrected by your teacher or to discover the mistakes you make on your own? How do you like your school/classroom to be structured? How do you wish to be assessed?

- **Community:** What does community mean to you? Who is included in your community?

- **Work:** What kind of work did you do in your home country and how did you choose it? What do you value at work (e.g., making friends with coworkers, money, room for advancement)? How do you view authority? Do you prefer to work independently or with coworkers in a team? How are you expected to dress for work?

- **Customs:** What traditions do you celebrate and how important are they to you? What is a custom that you cherish and want to pass on to your own children? Does your culture of origin have special forms of address or titles for people who are older, have higher social status, or special professions?

- **Sense of space:** How do you like to be greeted? Is there a difference when being greeted by a man or woman or child? How close do you like to be to people when you are in conversation with them? How comfortable are you with eye contact and silence? What do you consider to be private information and public information?

- **Sense of time:** What does time mean to you? Is it important for people to be punctual? How do you feel when people are late or keep you waiting for a long time? If a party starts at 7 pm, what time would you arrive and why?

- **Nonverbal communication and gestures:** How do you show agreement or disagreement through gestures? How do you show affection and friendship? Are you comfortable with direct eye contact? What is acceptable nonverbal behavior and what is unacceptable from your cultural perspective?

Activity: Use Critical Incidents to Explore Intercultural Communicative Competence

Critical incidents are designed to increase our awareness of intercultural issues by stimulating meaningful discussion about common situations to which there are no right or wrong answers. Each incident or story poses an area of conflict through a misunderstanding or problem resulting from cultural differences. After reading the story, students are required to answer questions focused on the possible cause of the misunderstanding and what might remedy the situation.

In presenting critical incidents, it is important to keep in mind the three ethnocentric and ethnorelative states of intercultural sensitivity development as outlined in Bennett's (2004, 2014) developmental model of intercultural sensitivity (see **Appendix B**): The ethnocentric stages range from denial that there are any differences or distinctions to defense, which refers to a polarized "us" and "them" position, followed by minimization, a stage in which students recognize differences but believe that people are all the same. Snow (2015) explains that our interpretations are ethnocentric when we judge quickly (or subconsciously) and go for the interpretation that seems most obvious based on the norms of our personal experiences, which generally take place within our own culture. The three ethnorelative stages of cultural sensitivity are (1) acceptance, in which students understand that their culture is one of many valid cultures; (2) adaptation, in which students can behave in situations where other cultural norms and values are needed; and (3) integration, in which students can easily identify and move in multiple cultures (i.e., the bicultural/multicultural person).

Through analysis and discussion of critical incidents, ESOL learners begin to change and let go of habits and static and absolute notions of culture; they move from the ethnocentric stage to an ethnorelative one. They soon begin to recognize that cultures must be understood in relation to one another and in the context in which those cultures have developed. Snow (2015) advises that critical incidents, sometimes referred to as cultural encounters, are more likely to be effective in language courses if both teachers and students have a clear understanding of what aspects of ICC they intend to build upon and how they propose to do it.

After establishing a cultural profile in which students have addressed their own culture and their respective thoughts and behaviors, present them with model critical incident cards (modified to their level of English language proficiency so that the focus is not on vocabulary) to discuss in pairs, in small groups, or with the whole class. After students have reviewed and discussed the model cards, provide them with the opportunity to write their own incidents based on experiences they have had living in their new culture. Students can brainstorm and list experiences or questions they have regarding communicative, intercultural, or general social situations. Examples of culture shock or miscommunication leading to misunderstandings work well. Students should write down their own interpretations, which can be shared and discussed.

For each incident, present the following question prompts:

- What is happening and what is the problem?

- Is this problem familiar to you? Can you relate to it?

- What are the different expectations of the people in the story?

- Why do you think the people are acting the way they do?

- Is the behavior influenced by culture or personality or both?

- How can the problem be overcome?

Ongoing practice with critical incidents whereby students come up with their own explanations for the misunderstanding

> make students more alert to intercultural problem situations in which they need to think more thoroughly and carefully, rather than responding naturally and automatically . . . [students are able to] create a mental category, the intercultural encounter, which makes them more aware of a particular kind of situation that calls for particular strategies. (Snow, 2015, p. 292)

Remember, it is always best to create your own scenarios based on your learners' experiences or on any experiences you might have had living and working in an unfamiliar culture yourself. It is also important to keep in mind that you really do not want to facilitate a negatively charged discussion of stereotypical behaviors. Be mindful that there are considerable individual differences between members of the same culture, so it is best for learners to think in dominant cultural patterns or generalizations as opposed to particulars. Dominant patterns and cultural generalizations are statements of likelihood and potential—not statements of certainty.

At the School of English where Johanne and Tuula taught English for academic purposes for several years, students would commonly go to extreme measures to change their initial classroom placement levels. The following critical incident has been adapted from Apedaile and Schill (2008).

> **SAMPLE CRITICAL INCIDENT: SCHOOL AND STUDENT PLACEMENTS**
>
> Chin-Sun, a student from Korea, was not happy with the class she was placed in at the School of English. She felt that her English skills were better than the rest of the class and she would be bored at the intermediate level. First, she asked her teacher if she could move to the advanced level, but he said that students were not allowed to move levels at this time. Also, the results of the placement testing showed that she should be at the intermediate level. Chin-Sun was still unsatisfied, so she decided to talk to the school counselor, who also told her that she was at the right level and that it was best that she stay at the level she was placed in. Next, she made an appointment to see the director of the language school, who told her that if she was allowed to move levels, then other students would be asking to do the same, which would create a lot of chaos and confusion. She was told that the placements were set and that was the policy of the school. However, she was still upset, so she decided to talk to the dean of the Faculty of Arts and Science, under which the School of English was placed. Meanwhile, the teacher couldn't understand why Chin-Sun did not just accept that policies were in place so that no matter how high up she went in the college hierarchy, the decision to place her at the intermediate level could not be changed.

An offshoot of the critical incident is the cultural assimilator, or intercultural sensitizer, activity. These incidents are written as short scenarios or vignettes with multiple-choice questions that include a list of possible explanations for or interpretations of the situation and an answer key that discusses the merits of each possible explanation (Snow, 2015). With the added questions, you would require more time to prepare the activity. Learners first read or listen to the situation, then discuss the merits of the possible answers, and finally check to see which answer is likely the most appropriate response. The primary task is for them to guess which explanation of a given situation members of the target culture are most likely to choose. This way, learners not only learn about cultural behaviors, but they also improve their ability to see situations from the perspective of others and their culture. Because these scenarios tend to be short and use multiple-choice questions, they are more easily adapted to low-level ESOL classes than the critical incidents, which require more advanced English language skills. Advanced students can be asked to provide their own interpretations, which allows them to give more thought to the situation and discuss and compare their responses among classmates and ideally a cultural informant or resource person (Wright, 1995).

Activity: Promote Cultural Understanding Through Banks's Stages of Ethnicity or Bennett's Developmental Model of Intercultural Sensitivity

Richard-Amato (2010) offers an activity for increasing awareness among ESOL learners using Banks's (2004) typology of ethnic identity development, which applies to situations in which majority (dominant) and minority (nondominant) cultural groups live together in society (Bennett's [2004, 2014] developmental model of intercultural sensitivity and the Degrees of Cultural Awareness outlined in this chapter would work just as well).

She suggests hypothetical role-playing based on the various stages to afford participants the experience of going through three of the stages and the feelings such an experience may evoke.

- **Prepare students:** First, ask students which minority ethnic or cultural group they want to represent (e.g., Latino, Korean, Vietnamese, Chinese, Somalian). They then decide which group they want to join.

- **Stage 1:** Ethnic Psychological Captivity, which is when members of the minority group feel rejected and shameful about their cultural heritage. They feel strongly about the stereotypes the majority group may have about their culture. When the students are in their groups, they bring examples of materials that illustrate how this group is experiencing oppression at the hands of the majority group (e.g., songs, pictures, stories, film clips). Members of this group may be speaking poor or very accented English and exhibit socially inept behaviors. For example, a disgruntled, cartoonish and obnoxious Chinese man as depicted by Mickey Rooney in the film *Breakfast at Tiffany's* or the Latino hotel maid played by Jennifer Lopez in *Maid in Manhattan*). Students in this group can also list negative feelings about the self and the ethnic group created by this experience and discuss why they might have these feelings.

- **Stage 2:** Ethnic Encapsulation, which is when members of the minority group resent how they are being treated by the majority and so they may feel defensive and participate primarily with members of their own group. Students discuss the negative feelings they have developed based on their chosen culture and, once they have communicated those feelings, they may become more positive about their own and other cultural groups. They may also share cultural items that cause them to feel proud of their own cultures.

- **Stage 3:** Ethnic Identity Clarification is when members of the minority group accept themselves and respond more positively to other groups. Students continue to reflect on the positive attributes and achievement of other cultural groups by sharing their songs, literature, artifacts, and so on. They begin to develop a realistic view of their own ethnic group in relation to others.

You will find that just going through these three stages will precipitate discussions related to cultural diversity and inclusiveness and other issues that concern the class. In Banks's (2004) typology there are three additional stages: Stage 4, Bioethnicity; Stage 5, Multiculturalism and Reflective Nationalism; and Stage 6, Globalism and Global Competency. In these latter stages, individuals move from having a strong sense of their own and other cultures to showing a commitment to the new culture and an ability to function effectively in different ethnic groups. Finally, they demonstrate the knowledge, skills, and attitude required to function successfully in a global world. Banks (2004) reinforces the notion that we must nurture, support, and affirm the identities of students from marginalized cultural, ethnic, and language groups if we expect them to endorse national values, become cosmopolitans, and work to make their local communities, the nation, and the world more just and humane. (p. 297)

Games and Simulations

There are a wealth of cultural simulation games that effectively introduce ESOL learners to issues of cultural awareness and intercultural communication. Films and videos can also be used as prompts for classroom discussions. In choosing these items, it is important to recognize that they should be easily understood by your ESOL learners, so they don't get bogged down with unknown vocabulary and complicated language. Following is a selection of games and simulations, but there are plenty more you can retrieve from the Center for Advanced Research on Language Acquisition (http://carla.umn.edu/culture/resources/exercises.html) and Wilderdom (www.wilderdom.com/games/MulticulturalExperiential Activities).

Activity: Barnga

Barnga is a card game that Johanne used several times in her advanced English for academic purposes class. It was developed to explore factors related to communication challenges and the assumptions people make in intercultural situations. The game reveals that subtle cultural differences create greater problems in communication than the obvious ones. Every team receives a distinct set of rules, without being aware of it. In other words, each team thinks that everyone has received the same set of rules, which is not the case. When they play, students may not communicate verbally—they are only allowed to use nonverbal cues. As the game goes on, participants rotate tables and enter groups where the rules are different from the ones they learned in their own groups. As a result, they begin to feel uneasy and frustrated, wondering if there is something missing. This can lead to discussions about hidden (implied or tacit) rules in societies, how culturally competent people respond when other people behave differently from their expectations, nonverbal expression across cultures, and how the game applies to intercultural communication in the real world (Thiagarajan, 2006).

Activity: BaFa' BaFa' Simulation Game

BaFa' BaFa' is often used to introduce the notion of cultures, followed up with a discussion and analysis of specific cultures and the way they are formed. It is most often used in diversity training. The intention is for students to understand basic cultural issues and how they affect individual and organizational behaviors. You can also use BaFa' BaFa' to help students understand how stereotypes of other cultures are formed and perpetuated and why it is important for them to acquire good observational skills.

Students in the classroom are divided into two fictional cultures and are asked to travel back and forth between them. The Alpha culture is hierarchical, family oriented, and cooperative. Alphans are comfortable with close personal space. The Beta culture is competitive, task oriented, and nonhierarchical. Betans are uncomfortable with close personal contact. Players try to understand the other culture through their visits with each other while they maintain their own cultural role. (As an option, depending on students' English language skills, you could give the groups a specific reason for visiting each other or task, such as trying to convince the other group to purchase a product.) Betans also speak a "foreign" language made up of a combination of vowels and consonants. It is easy to learn and use but difficult to understand if one doesn't know the rules governing its use. When Alphans come to the Beta culture and hear the language, they are often intimidated by it and withdraw from the culture, creating an impossible communications barrier. Others are able to make themselves understood very easily with gestures, sign language, and facial expressions. "They're cold, greedy, all they do is work" are some of the words Alphans use to describe Betans. The Betans come to believe the Alphans are "lazy, unfriendly to outsiders, and don't like females." The simulation gives students an opportunity to analyze and discuss how such stereotypes are formed as well as methods for overcoming their negative effects. Rafa' Rafa' is a simplified version, a real-time, face-to-face, noncomputer based, cross-cultural simulation for students in the fifth through eighth grade (Simulation Training Systems, n.d.; Intercultural Learning, n.d.)

Activity: *The nature walk*

In this game, you conceive a list of statements of your choice on sensitive topics (things that you think participants may relate to, e.g., feelings of incompetence or alienation in their new cultural environment). Place a line of tape down the center of the room and have all participants stand on one side of the line. Then, as you read the first statement (e.g., "At a restaurant, we all ask for individual bills"), all students who feel uncomfortable with it cross over the line to the other side of the room. They are then asked: "What would you wish others would know about you?," "What annoys you most about this scenario?," and "How could we best help you?"

Afterward, everyone returns behind the starting line again and the game continues with other statements that follow in the same manner.

CASE IN POINT: CULTURE DOES MATTER

The following case study is about an international student who is having difficulty adjusting to her college program.

CASE STUDY: AMINA

Amina is an international student from Cameroon who has lived in the United States for 2 years and is enrolled in a full-time intensive career bridging program at a community college. The program prepares students for the North American workplace and will help her find a job in her field of social science as a researcher. ➔

She has two postgraduate degrees, one in biology, and the other in international relations. Amina lives alone in the United States without close family and is not having a good experience in the college program. She is frequently absent from classes because of colds and stomach problems, and she is falling behind in meeting the academic requirements. The college counseling staff has scheduled appointments with her at the request of her professors. Amina responds negatively with increasing hostility toward people at the college; she is also isolating herself more from classmates and blames the college for not understanding her situation and circumstances. She is often angry and shows hostility in interactions with others.

1. What stage of culture shock is Amina experiencing?
2. What can be done on the part of the college administration, counseling services, and her professors to help her adjust to her new surroundings?

Though the outward behaviors of people experiencing culture shock are naturally of immediate concern to those who provide help to individuals in adjusting to a new culture, it is not common for those helping to focus on asking the *why* questions about cultural differences. Why is the student behaving the way Amina is in the case study? Why is she not receptive to the counseling that is provided to her? What really is "wrong" with her?

Asking, however, more culturally specific questions would involve having to look more closely at the norms and values of cultures, both the host culture and the other, to explore more deeply the reasons why students or newcomers from other cultures experience the discomfort and stress they do.

Raising these questions will inevitably also highlight the need to train counselors and advisors to acquire cultural competencies and the ability to identify culture shock symptoms. Understanding this complex emotional process is the first step in learning how to teach strategies and coping mechanisms that produce positive results.

References

Alberta Teachers of English as a Second Language. (2009). *Adult ESL curriculum framework: Intercultural communicative competence.* Retrieved from https://www.atesl.ca /documents/1455/Intercultural_Communicative_Competence.pdf

Apedaile, S., & Schill, L. (2008). *Critical incidents for intercultural communication: An interactive tool for developing awareness, knowledge and skills.* Edmonton, Alberta, Canada: Norquest College Intercultural Education Programs. Retrieved from https://www.norquest.ca/NorquestCollege/media/pdf/centres/intercultural /CriticalIncidentsBooklet.pdf

Baldwin, J., Means Coleman, R., Gonzalez, A., & Shenoy-Packer, S. (2014). *Intercultural communication for everyday life.* Chichester, England: Wiley Blackwell.

Banks, J. A. (2004). Teaching for social justice, diversity, and citizenship in a global world. *The Educational Forum, 68,* 289–298. Retrieved from http://depts.washington.edu /centerme/Fs04banks.pdf

Bennett, M. J. (2004). Developing intercultural sensitivity: An integrative approach to global and domestic diversity. In D. Landis, J. Bennett, & M. Bennett (Eds.), *Handbook of intercultural training* (pp. 147–165). Thousand Oaks, CA: Sage.

Bennett, M. J. (2014). *The development model of intercultural sensitivity.* Retrieved from http://www.idrinstitute.org/page.asp?menu1=15

Berry, J. (1997). Immigration, acculturation and adaptation. *Applied Psychology: An International Review, 46,* 5–68.

Berry, J., & Sam, D. (2016). Theoretical perspectives. In D. Sam & J. Berry (Eds.), *The Cambridge handbook of acculturation psychology* (pp. 11–29). Cambridge, England: Cambridge University Press.

Bhabha, H. (2011). Cultural diversity and cultural differences. Retrieved from http://monumenttotransformation.org/atlas-of-transformation/html/c/cultural-diversity/cultural-diversity-and-cultural-differences-homi-k-bhabha.html

Borghetti, C. (2017). Is there really a need for assessing intercultural competence? *Journal of Intercultural Communication, 44.* Retrieved from https://immi.se/intercultural/nr44/borghetti.html

Byram, M. (1997). *Teaching and assessing intercultural communicative competence.* Clevedon, England: Multilingual Matters.

Byram, M., Gribkova, B., & Starkey, H. (2002). *Developing the intercultural dimension in language teaching.* Strasbourg, France: Council of Europe. Retrieved from https://www.coe.int/t/dg4/linguistic/Source/Guide_dimintercult_EN.pdf

Carden, P. (2008). A critique of Hall's contexting model. *Journal of Business and Technical Communication, 22*(4), 399–428.

Cushner, K., & Karim, A. (2004). Study abroad at the university level. In D. Landis, J. M. Bennett, & M. J. Bennett (Eds.), *Handbook of intercultural training* (3rd ed., pp. 289–308). Thousand Oaks, CA: Sage.

Deardorff, D. (2008). Intercultural competence: A definition, model and implications for education abroad. In V. Savicki (Ed.), *Developing intercultural competence and transformation* (pp. 32–52). Sterling, VA: Stylus.

Dong, Q., Liu, Y., Zhao, P., & Dong, D. (2014). Shyness, self-esteem and intercultural communication competence. In X. Dai & G. Chen (Eds.), *Intercultural communication competence: Conceptualization and its development in cultural contexts and interactions* (pp. 261–274) Newcastle upon Tyne, England: Cambridge Scholars.

Dytynyshyn, N., & Collins, L. (2012). Culture and interculturality in the adult ESL context in urban Quebec: A case study. *TESL Canada, 30*(1), 45–68.

Hall, E. (1959). *The silent language.* New York, NY: Doubleday.

Harklau, L. (2007). The adolescent English language learner: Identities lost and found. *International Handbook of English Language Teaching, 15,* 639–653.

Haupt, J. (2013). Interview with Gish Jen: Tiger writer. *Psychology Today.* Retrieved from https://www.psychologytoday.com/us/blog/one-true-thing/201312/interview-gish-jen-tiger-writer

Hemmings, C. (2006, October 26). Is Borat offensive? *The Guardian*. Retrieved from https://www.theguardian.com/film/2006/oct/26/features.features11

Hofstede, G. (2009). The moral circle in intercultural competence. In D. Deardoff (Ed.), *The Sage handbook of intercultural competence* (pp. 85–99). Thousand Oaks, CA: Sage.

Hofstede, G., Hofstede, G. J., & Minkov, M. (2010). *Cultures and organizations: Software of the mind*. New York, NY: McGraw-Hill.

Hofstede Insights. (2017). *Compare countries*. Retrieved from https://www.hofstede-insights.com/product/compare-countries/

Houghton, S. (2010). Managing stereotypes through experiential learning. *Intercultural Communication Studies, XIX*(1), 182–198. Retrieved from http://web.uri.edu/iaics/files/14StephanieHoughton.pdf

Intercultural Learning (n.d.). Bafa Bafa. Retrieved from http://intercultural-learning.eu/Portfolio-Item/bafa-bafa/

Ishizaki, A. M. S. (2007). *Power distance in the EFL/ESL classroom*. Retrieved from http://www.birmingham.ac.uk/Documents/college-artslaw/cels/essays/languageteaching/SIshizakiPowerDistanceessayMod1LT0607.pdf

Iyer, P. (2013, June). *Pico Iyer: TEDGlobal 2013: Where is home?* [Video file]. Retrieved from http://www.ted.com/talks/pico_iyer_where_is_home?language=en

Jarvis, P. (2012). Learning from everyday life. *Human & Social Studies Research and Practice 1*(1), 1–20.

Jen, G. (2017). *The girl at the baggage claim: Explaining the east-west culture gap*. New York, NY: Alfred A. Knopf.

Khazan, O. (2016, May 27). Why some cultures frown on smiling. *The Atlantic*. Retrieved from https://www.theatlantic.com/science/archive/2016/05/culture-and-smiling/483827/

Kramsch, C. (2009). Third culture and language education. In V. Cook & L. Wei (Eds.), *Contemporary applied linguistics* (pp. 233–254). London, England: Continuum. Retrieved from http://lrc.cornell.edu/events/past/2008-2009/papers08/third.pdf

Krys, K., Vauclair, C.-M., Capaldi, C. A., Lun, V. M.-C., Bond, M. H., Domínguez-Espinosa, A., ... Arriola Yu, A. (2016). Be careful where you smile: Culture shapes judgments of intelligence and honesty of smiling individuals. *Journal of Nonverbal Behavior 40*(2), 101–116.

Landis, D., Bennett, J., & Bennett, M. (Eds.). (2004). *Handbook of intercultural training*. (3rd ed.). Thousand Oaks, CA: Sage.

Laroche, L., & Yang, C. (2014). *Danger and opportunity: Building cultural diversity for competitive advantage*. New York, NY: Routledge.

Lehtonen, J. (n.d.). Views to Finnish culture: Cultural stereotypes. Retrieved from https://www.jyu.fi/viesti/verkkotuotanto/kp/vf/jaakko.shtml

Levy, A. (2017, May 1). A long homecoming: The novelist Elizabeth Strout left Maine, but it didn't leave her. *The New Yorker*, 22–26.

Minow, N. (2017, June 3). Gish Jen on her new book about east and west, the girl at the baggage claim. *Huffington Post*. Retrieved from http://www.huffingtonpost.com/entry/gish-jen-on-her-new-book-about-east-and-west-the-girl_us_58bd85fde4b0fa65b844b61a

Mizzi, R. (Ed.). (2008). *Learning with adults in an intercultural setting: A course reader*. Kingston, Ontario: Queen's University.

Nieto, S. (2010). *Language, culture, and teaching: Critical perspectives*. New York, NY: Routledge.

Nunan, D. (1999). *Second language teaching and learning*. Boston, MA: Heinle and Heinle.

Núñez, M. (2014). Employing multilevel intersectionality in educational research: Latino identities, contexts, and college access. *Educational Researcher, 43*(2), 85–92.

Quappe, S., & Cantatore, G. (2007). *What is cultural awareness, anyway? How do I build it?* Retrieved from http://www.culturosity.com/articles/whatisculturalawareness.htm

Richard-Amato, P. (2010). *Making it happen: From interactive to participatory language teaching*. White Plains, NY: Pearson Longman.

Schwartz, S. H. (1994). Beyond individualism/collectivism: New cultural dimensions of values. In U. Kim, H. Triandis, C. Kagitcibasi, S. Choi, & G. Yoon (Eds.), *Individualism and collectivism: Theory, method, and applications* (pp. 85–119). Thousand Oaks, CA: Sage.

Simons, G. (2013, January 18). Re: Intercultural work—stuck in its own past? [Blog comment]. Retrieved from http://ning.interculturalnewmedia.com/profiles/blogs/intercultural-work-stuck-in-its-own-past

Simulation Training Systems. (n.d.). Bafa' bafa'. Retrieved from https://www.simulationtrainingsystems.com/schools-and-charities/products/bafa-bafa/

Snow, D. (2015). Language teaching, intercultural competence and critical incident exercises. *Language and Intercultural Communication, 15*(2), 285–299.

Spitzberg, B., & Chagnon, G. (2009). Conceptualizing intercultural competence. In D. Deardoff (Ed.) *The Sage handbook of intercultural competence* (pp. 2–52). Thousand Oaks, CA: Sage.

Sun, Y. (2014, December 15). *What is intercultural communicative competence?* Retrieved from http://blog.tesol.org/what-is-intercultural-communicative-competence/

Thiagarajan, S. (2006). *Barnga: A simulation game on cultural clashes*. Boston, MA: Intercultural Press.

Ting-Toomey, S. (1999). *Communicating across cultures*. New York, NY: Guilford Press.

Toupin Laforge, M. (2017). *Apple tree metaphor*. Scope Global Facilitator Guide—Australian Volunteers for International Development (AVID) Pre-departure Training. Adelaide, Australia: Australian Volunteers for International Development.

Torres, L. (2009). Latino definitions of success: A cultural model of intercultural competence. *Hispanic Journal of Behavioral Science, 31*(4), 576–593.

Triandis, H. (2004). The many dimensions of culture. *The Academy of Management Executive, 18*(1), 88–93.

Welsh, A. (2011). Avoiding stereotyping and enhancing intercultural understanding, *TEFLIN Journal, 22*(1), 34–44.

Welsh, A. (2015). Promoting a respect for difference through language teaching. *TEFLIN Journal, 15*(2), 233–242.

Wintergerst, A., & McVeigh, J. (2011). *Tips for teaching culture: Practical approaches to intercultural communication.* White Plains, NY: Pearson Longman.

Wittencamp, C. (2014). *Building bridges across cultural differences: Why don't I follow your norms?* Retrieved from https://bookboon.com/en/building-bridges-across-cultural-differences-ebook

Wright, A. (1995). The critical incident as a training tool. In S. Fowler & M. Mumford (Eds)., *Intercultural sourcebook: Cross-cultural training methods* (pp. 127–140). Yarmouth, ME: Intercultural Press.

Yep, G. A. (2015). Intersectionality. *Key Concepts in Intercultural Dialogue, 49.* Retrieved from https://centerforinterculturaldialogue.files.wordpress.com/2015/02/key-concept-intersectionality.pdf

THE ROLE OF INTERCULTURAL COMMUNICATIVE COMPETENCE IN LANGUAGE TEACHING AND LEARNING

CHAPTER 2

OVERVIEW

In linking the fields of second language acquisition and intercultural communicative competence (ICC), for the purposes of this book it is noteworthy to acknowledge that language skills alone do not guarantee one's competency in the culture. Indeed, English language acquisition for new immigrants and international students affects the quality and quantity of their interactions with first-language speakers of English. In language teaching, the concept of communicative competence emphasizes that English to speakers of other languages (ESOL) learners need to acquire not just grammatical competence but also the knowledge of what is appropriate language to behave and communicate effectively and appropriately in a new cultural context. Yang and Fleming (2013) explain that "the goal of English language teaching has gradually changed from a narrow focus on linguistic competence . . . to communicative competence [to] intercultural communicative competence" (p. 297). More specifically, the term *linguaculture* is also used to recognize the relevance of both language proficiency and culture as an integral whole (Fantini, 1997; Shaules, 2016).

In this chapter, we discuss the connection between language and culture and introduce the notion of intercultural pragmatics. We also discuss ways to connect ICC with English second language teaching and learning curricula.

THINKING ABOUT THE TOPIC

ICC training is part and parcel of ESOL instruction, whether or not instructors are aware of it. The following questions will help you think more deeply about the field and its connection to second language acquisition.

- How do I go about understanding ICC in relation to the language curriculum I am following?
- How does pragmatics complement my attention to ICC development?

- What are the components of ICC and can they be effectively measured?

- Is it a good idea to be prescriptive in my approach to teaching cultural strategies?

- How can I effectively foster intercultural sensitivity in my teaching and classroom activities?

- How can I know that students are applying the strategies I am teaching in class?

THEORETICAL PERSPECTIVES

Language and Culture

All ESOL learners bring different cultural and social contexts to the classroom. Although some of the challenges students have are linguistically based, others may stem from social or cultural attitudes and beliefs acquired in their home countries. They may evaluate situations and come to conclusions about what they observe and experience based on misinformation, misperceptions, and faulty assumptions. Such perceptions can reinforce stereotypes, impede the acculturation process, and prevent the development of ICC, as mentioned in Chapter 1. Although a large percentage of newcomers are well educated and learn to speak English fluently, there can still be misinterpretations that continue to cause misunderstandings. However, as ESOL learners become more fluent in English, they are also more able to participate in various intercultural experiences. No doubt, language skills provide acculturating individuals with the means and confidence to establish the interpersonal relationships and social support that have been shown to facilitate culture learning, sociocultural adaptation, and ICC (Ward & Wilson, 2014). ESOL teachers work with diverse populations and serve as cultural brokers, bringing together different ways of thinking and practices and promoting understanding across cultures. It is ESOL teachers' task to assist their learners in adapting to their new language and cultural environment. The ultimate goal is for students to become confident and competent members of society.

Learning a new language and embracing a new culture entail transforming the self: taking on or forging, to some extent, a new cultural identity or orientation. In fact, acculturation research reveals that immigrants and other minority members often develop complex identities as they "mix, blend and combine" (Liebkind, Mahonen, Varjonen, & Jasinskaja-Lahti, 2016, p. 34) various cultural and ethnic identities in the transition process. Such change, successful or not, can be emotionally unsettling. The safety of belonging may not come to them automatically as they start to speak their new language and live with people in their new culture. Some ESOL learners even voluntarily take on a new English name. If we ask immigrants and international students about how they feel communicating in English, they may tell us that they find it not only exhausting, but also challenging and frustrating. They find it hard not to be able to express their deep feelings. They can also become despondent when what they say isn't exactly what they mean, especially when the feedback they receive is unexpected, even hostile. They may also tell us how difficult it is to turn acquaintances—both other ESOL learners and native English speakers alike—into friends because of the uncertainty of the proper ways to approach others. Communication problems can take place when the implicit messages conveyed in interactions are misinterpreted. For school-age children, learners may constantly wonder if they have been or if they will ever be accepted as a member of a peer group not affiliated with their own cultural and linguistic milieu. Adults may fret over acceptance by other employees in a workplace setting (Li, Myles, & Robinson, 2011).

Language and intercultural dynamics go hand in hand. In fact, language and culture are increasingly considered to be two sides of the same coin—with linguistic meaning reflecting the cultural perspective of linguaculture communities (Shaules, 2016). Indeed, communication is rarely culture-free, and given the increasingly global and multicultural world we live in, developing students' intercultural communication skills is a vital component of ESOL instruction. Such competence informs the language choices students make in communication. Kramsch (2006) summarizes the relationship between language and culture as follows:

- Language expresses cultural reality because when people speak or write, their words express their beliefs, views, and attitudes, as well those of others.

- Language embodies cultural reality in that people give meaning to their experience through choosing spoken, written, or visual media (e.g., phone calls, letters, gestures or drawings) that they perceive as proper and understandable to their social group (e.g., family, workplace, school).

- Language symbolizes cultural reality for the reason that people identify themselves in society through the use of language or the inability to use a language.

Given the importance of language and culture in communication, we also need to recognize that language is limited in many ways. It cannot always accurately describe one's true feelings, especially after a traumatic or surprising event. We all have the experience of being at a loss for words, frantically searching for words that just won't come or, when they do, do not actually reflect how we are feeling. Those who communicate and have been socialized in the same language will no doubt understand implicitly signals referring to requests or contradictions, and psychological stances of certainty and uncertainty, emotional intensity, and politeness. These functions also have corresponding forms cross-linguistically, which can be helpful to ESOL learners. Communication breakdown can occur, however,

> when an action or stance is not expected by one or another interlocutor or went on too long or too briefly or at the wrong time and place in the particular activity underway or for a particular social role, status, or relationship. (Ochs, 2002, p. 114)

Think about the tacit knowledge (knowledge that cannot be explained in concrete terms) and implicit messages that cannot be conveyed through language but, instead, have to be acquired and shared through common life experiences. For example, in a social gathering of a group of friends or colleagues where someone starts explaining details about a medical procedure he went through that the others do not want to hear about because it makes them feel uncomfortable, someone might say to the speaker, "too much information." The expression refers to tacit cultural knowledge that the information the speaker is sharing is inappropriate to talk about in a social gathering. If the same group of people are eating in a restaurant, each member would be expected to pay for their own meal unless one person says, "This will be my treat." Paying your way is tacit knowledge in some cultures, as opposed to everyone knowing that there will be one person who will get the bill, which can be common practice in other cultures.

LANGUAGE AND INTERCULTURAL COMMUNICATION

According to the Center for Intercultural Dialogue,

> Language is a core element in intercultural communication. As language is closely tied to one's identity, worldview, and positioning, it influences how people from different cultural backgrounds interact and perceive one another. Language and cultural misunderstandings and identity misalignments can hamper intercultural relations. Language barriers may be mistaken for cultural barriers if one does not have an adequate understanding of linguistic elements and the communication process. To enhance intercultural dialogue, it is vital to have a solid grasp of the linguistic dimension of intercultural communication. (Jackson, 2016, para. 3)

Language does not always serve people effectively in their attempt to express feelings and thoughts; it may not record history truthfully as it has happened, and it may fail people in their communication if the speaker does not possess enough cultural knowledge or linguistic skills for accurate interpretation of messages. Therefore, when we discuss the importance of language, we should also bear in mind its limitations. If we understand the constraints of our first language, think about how frustrating it can be for ESOL learners to express their true feelings, aspirations, and desires. Furthermore, that language transmits knowledge and preserves culture should not be accepted without scrutiny. Language is a system for organizing and releasing information and thoughts. Nevertheless, we cannot impose our thoughts on others; we can only assist them to understand our thoughts through ways of thinking and doing. In reality, regardless of where an ESOL learner is speaking with someone in English, that student will develop skills independently through negotiating understanding, asking for clarification, and reformulating sentences. Clearly, given that "words are merely pointers, and what they point to may or may not be what they appear to mean" (Codrescu, 1995, p. 12), learning how to communicate in a second language or culture is enhanced through "misunderstanding, mishearing, and mistranslating," for these "are often more powerful hearing tools than accuracy" (Codrescu, 1995, p. 13). This is where intercultural pragmatics comes into play.

Pragmatics and Intercultural Pragmatics

Pragmatics refers to ESOL students' ability to use appropriate language skills in a variety of communicative contexts, such as in community, work, and study settings. The term is commonly used by teachers and researchers in the field of linguistics and second language acquisition. For example, in their book for second language teachers entitled *Teaching and Learning Pragmatics: Where Language and Culture Meet*, Ishihara and Cohen (2010) highlight that pragmatics has become commonplace in the teaching and learning of second and foreign languages. It is not only a "cognitive process, but also a social phenomenon, looking into how second language speakers construct and negotiate their identities as they become socialized into the community" (p. x). That said, pragmatics certainly has an important role to play in ICC development for ESOL learners. According to research by Arasaratnam-Smith (2016), learning a second (or third) language in and of itself is advantageous for developing ICC.

PRAGMATICS

Pragmatics consists of (but is not limited to) the following elements:

- politeness/impoliteness
- speech acts, which are actions performed through utterances such as greetings, thanks, requests, compliments, apologies, complaints, and invitations (affected by familiarity, social status, age, gender, etc.)
- conversational style (level of formality and directness)
- humor, teasing, and sarcasm (tone of voice)
- conversational implicature, which is what is meant by a speaker's utterance that is not what is explicitly said. Such an utterance can be challenging for ESOL learners to comprehend because the meaning is not literal—it is implied. For example: a husband and wife are preparing to go out for dinner and the husband asks his wife, "How much longer are you going to be?" The wife answers, "Have another coffee." The implied message is that she doesn't know how long she will be and that he might as well keep waiting (Nordquist, 2017).
- deixis, which are words and phrases that cannot be fully understood without additional contextual information (e.g., personal pronouns like *she* and demonstrative pronouns like *this, that, those*) that refer to the time, place, or situation in which the person is speaking.

(Center for Advanced Research on Second Language Acquisition, 2016)

Pragmatics as it is applied to ESOL programs and curricula complements ICC nicely, because teachers acknowledge that pragmatic use of language is essential to effective communication. In *intercultural* pragmatic performance, ESOL learners need to interpret "intercultural meanings appropriately—which implies that as listeners or readers, learners are able to interpret the intended meanings of what is said or written, the assumptions, purposes or goals, and the kinds of actions that are being performed" (Cohen & Sykes, 2013, pp. 89–90). What does intercultural pragmatic ability mean for oral communication in English? ESOL learners need to make culturally informed choices about which language to use and how to express themselves. They need to be aware of the norms for politeness, directness, and formality in different situations. For example, they need to know when and how to compliment a teacher compared to complimenting another student or close friend. They also need to know what to say and what not to say, and when communicating nonverbally is more appropriate to the conversation. In writing, ESOL learners need to be aware of how native English speakers write their messages and, again, choosing language that addresses the appropriate level of politeness, directness, formality, genre, and rhetorical structure, whether it is an email message to a landlord complaining about a plumbing issue or a Facebook post to a friend.

 See Chapter 6, **Technology and Computer-Mediated Intercultural Communication**.

Essentially, ESOL learners "must be able to balance their own beliefs about culture with those of target-language speakers in each given situation—an endeavor that if performed appropriately, contributes to the quality of intercultural communication" (Cohen & Sykes, 2013, p. 90). Lenchuk and Ahmed (2013) emphasize the importance of including open discussions about the sociolinguistic and sociocultural variables that inform the choices native English speakers make so that ESOL learners develop a solid understanding of why native speakers choose one expression over another (when, e.g., they are asking to borrow a book or even some money). Think about the way we deliver and receive compliments. In American English, compliments are given for a variety of reasons: to express admiration or approval of someone's work/appearance/taste; to establish/confirm/ maintain solidarity; to replace greetings/gratitude/apologies/congratulations; to soften face-threatening acts such as apologies, requests, and criticism; to open and sustain conversation; and to reinforce desired behavior. The majority of compliments are also addressed to people of similar age and status to the compliment giver. Interestingly, people also rarely accept compliments or praise when they are given them (Center for Advanced Research on Language Acquisition, 2016). Americans may tend to give compliments more frequently than in some other cultures and finding this out would require extensive research in applied linguistics. Nevertheless, unless giving and responding to compliments is specifically addressed in the classroom, ESOL learners may not to be aware of the importance of compliments and the way they are used in cultural contexts for specific purposes.

In addition to incorporating language knowledge and pragmatics into classwork, it is important for ESOL teachers to also consider symbolic competence. The first chapter discussed issues related to identity and the "third place"; Kramsch (2006) also refers to "symbolic competence," emphasizing that "language learners are not just communicators and problem-solvers, but whole persons with hearts, bodies, and minds, with memories, fantasies, loyalties, identities. . . . Symbolic forms are not just items of vocabulary or communication strategies, but embodied experiences, emotional resonances, and moral imaginings" (p. 251). For example, when we enter a room of people, let's say, at a cocktail party, we have to quickly figure out how we are going to fit in, become part of the group, and be listened to. For this to happen, it is important to know who has power in the group and how we are going to enter into a conversation that is socially acceptable and legitimate. Learning how to behave in a culturally appropriate way in social contexts requires looking critically at the big picture and deeply reflecting on the kinds of words being spoken, whose interests are being served, and who is saying what to whom and for what reason.

A word of caution: As in intercultural training and the possible stereotyping of cultural behaviors that can take place, we also warn ESOL teachers against imposing native-English-speaker norms on students when focusing on intercultural pragmatics and language use. Ishihara and Cohen (2012) explain that teaching commonly accepted norms of behavior in a given context is valuable for students, and students should be given plenty of opportunity to produce and practice common expressions in the classroom. However, once they are proficient, they then have a choice to rely on those norms or diverge from them as a means of asserting their own identity. In other words, the native-speaker baseline is intended to serve as a potential reference for students, not as their sole model.

ESOL teachers may have the assumption that learning English both in and outside of the classroom will automatically result in ICC. However, this is not necessarily the case. Clearly, attending class (without instruction explicitly focusing on cultural competence) or shopping for food in a supermarket (where automatic checkouts may prevent communication) does not guarantee that students understand the sociocultural and pragmatic uses of language. Indeed, many ESOL learners have limited opportunities to use English in real life. Along with and complementary to ESOL training, teachers need to prepare students by providing them with the knowledge and skills to develop an understanding of underlying cultural values, communication styles, and worldviews so that they can become culturally conscious, interculturally competent, and, hence, successful in their new sociocultural environment. Adequate preparation, substantive intercultural interactions, and relationship building "through observing, listening, and asking those who are from different backgrounds to teach, share, to enter into dialogue together about relevant needs and issues" (Bok, 2009, p. xiii) are key components to the development of ICC.

COMMUNICATIVE COMPETENCE VS INTERCULTURAL COMMUNICATIVE COMPETENCE

Communicative competence refers to a learner's ability to communicate effectively using language that is both formally accurate and contextually appropriate, for example, in "its degree of formality, politeness, and directness," the focus is on "how language is used to . . . achieve strategic goals" (Corbett, 2014, para. 1). ESOL teachers use role playing activities, writing prompts, and reading and listening comprehension tests to assess their learners' communicative competence in English.

Intercultural communicative competence is an extension of communicative competence related to "knowledge of what to do when cultural norms of appropriate linguistic behavior may not be shared, but strategic communicative goals still need to be achieved. Such knowledge requires that ESOL learners are mindful and sensitive to "the possibility of different culturally conditioned interactional styles" (Corbett, 2014, para. 3.).

An intercultural approach to language teaching supports ESOL learners in acquiring cultural skills as they develop proficiency in the traditional four language skills of reading, writing, listening, and speaking (Corbett, 2003).

If intercultural pragmatics is recognized as essential to communicative competence, how can ESOL teachers provide students with opportunities to acquire such competence? Is using evidence-based second language acquisition methods in their lessons effective? Scarino and Crichton (2007) argue that current approaches in languages education, such as communicative language teaching or task-based language teaching, do not adequately address the importance of ICC. True, ESOL learners need to recognize that English has a structural, grammatical system of its own and that such a system foregrounds language in use; however, English, like any other language, is always subject to the interpretations of the participants in interaction. Scarino and Crichton (2007) further explain that

> in communicating interculturally students come to know that the forms of a language and knowledge of facts about culture are only part of what is involved when people interact to exchange meanings in the particular target language. They are important only as socially shared communicative resources that people draw upon in different ways in different contexts. The variable sociocultural contexts of use which students experience as participants in communication across cultures cannot be reduced to an inventory of items to be mastered. They are too rich and variable. For students, managing the variability is part of the process of learning to be intercultural. (p. 4)

THE ISSUE OF TRANSLATION

At the beginning or even intermediate stages of second language acquisition, ESOL learners tend to think in their first language; they will continually translate back and forth between languages. Sometimes, after a particularly exhausting day, advanced students will also resort to translation as well. There are many situations, however, in which translation can backfire and there is serious miscommunication; such miscommunication can be interpreted as a lack of respect and even cost people their jobs.

Laroche and Yang (2014) give the example of a Russian information technology (IT) specialist working at the help desk of a large American corporation's head office. An employee needed some help with her computer and, when he arrived to provide support, he started the conversation by saying, "What's wrong with you?," a translation from Russian, when he meant, "What problem are you experiencing?" The employee felt insulted, thinking that the specialist was telling her she was incapable of doing her job. She complained to the manager and human resources about the IT specialist treating her rudely. Apparently, he had been given similar feedback on several other occasions, and the company was getting increasingly frustrated with his inappropriate manner. As a result, his contract was terminated.

Communication is complicated because there are so many factors influencing the way we interact with people; it is an interplay of verbal and nonverbal behaviors that are both direct and indirect. The Russian IT specialist's choice of words in the previous example was much too direct and inappropriate as a result of the way he translated what he wanted to say from his first language. He could have said, in a more cheerful manner, "What can I do for you?" A person's tone of voice, pronunciation, and mannerisms also impact the message, which can be interpreted as disrespectful—too blunt. Silence or long pauses can also be interpreted as a person's being disinterested or disengaged in the discussion, or even incompetent. Whether in the classroom or workplace, misunderstandings due to intercultural behaviors (in combination with language proficiency) can lead to poor relationships and frustration among all parties. In other words, although a new immigrant or international student may have outstanding technical skills, they may unintentionally exhibit poor interpersonal (or soft) skills because their communication style is culturally embedded. Laroche and Yang (2014) mention that in North America and other English-speaking countries, soft skills matter more than they do in countries that are more hierarchical and authoritarian in their cultural orientation. For adults, cultural behaviors are difficult to change but not impossible; acquiring ICC through training that is attentive to both cultural and emotional intelligence can help newcomers navigate and communicate effectively and appropriately in their new setting. Certainly, straddling two or more cultures is a precarious position to be in but one that offers the individual personal growth and opportunity.

 See Chapter 5, **Employment Preparation Programs and Cultural Integration**.

INTEGRATING INTERCULTURAL COMMUNICATIVE COMPETENCE INTO ESOL CURRICULA

There is no question about it: The development of ICC needs to be taken seriously in ESOL classes. ESOL pedagogy is traditionally thought about in terms of concrete knowledge and skills, such as vocabulary development or grammar structures, and cultural goals are thought of in abstract terms, such as global mindset or intercultural awareness (Shaules, 2016). In practice, a change in mindset is required of ESOL teachers because integrating culture into language education involves a complete reconceptualization of the nature of language teaching and learning. In other words, teachers cannot simply add culture to language learning; they must rethink their approach to pedagogy (Shaules, 2016, p. 4). There are no two identical groups of students or courses, which makes reconceptualizing adult education and ESOL course content an art in itself.

The question is, what role do English language teachers play in fostering intercultural sensitivity and development and in helping students acquire higher levels of cultural intelligence? An intercultural orientation to ESOL teaching is attentive to the transformation of students' identities in the act of learning. According to Scarino (2010), this transformation requires students' ability to continually navigate between the English language and their own language. In such a practice, they

> decenter from their linguistic and cultural world to consider their own situatedness from the perspective of another. They learn to constantly move between their linguistic and cultural world and that of the users of the

target language. In this process, they come to understand culture not only as information about diverse people and their practices but also, and most importantly, as the contextual framework that people use to exchange meaning in communication with others and through which they understand their social world. (Scarino, 2010, p. 324)

Scarino (2010) goes on to argue that students use the first language as a constant reference point for understanding the world of meanings made available to them in English. In the process of learning, they are both in the world of the first language(s) and the world of English, constantly moving backward and forward across the space between the two languages and their respective worlds of cultural meanings. A friend told a story she had heard from a Colombian-born woman who was not feeling well and went to the doctor for tests. There was a worry that she might have cancer. The test results came back as "negative." However, she became upset because she thought that a "negative" result was bad. She had been hoping that the test would be "positive." Thankfully, those around her were able to clarify the situation. How easy it is for misunderstandings to occur!

Multiethnic and linguistic adult ESOL classes offer learners from diverse cultural backgrounds the opportunity to learn not only English for use in their adoptive community, but also ICC in a safe and supportive context. As teachers in these classes, we know that learners from widely varied ethnic, national, and religious backgrounds commonly develop relationships with each other that involve active engagement through, for example, exchanging phone numbers and email addresses, becoming friends (in real life and on social media), and sharing personal feelings and experiences over coffee on a classroom break. Such relationships with those normally seen as "different" may be an indication of increasing ICC. In fact, openness to people of other cultures and the ability to suspend judgment have been consistently identified as attitudes that are part of the complex construct of ICC (Deardorff, 2006, 2011). Dytynyshyn and Collins (2012) mention that

> forming relationships of trust with those normally seen as other is not part of the definition of interculturality. . . . We argue that developing intercultural relationships of trust may represent acts of looking beyond otherness or of transcending ethnocentrism. Intercultural friendships are not equivalent to intercultural competence, but they reflect attitudes that are aspects of it. (p. 63)

Clearly, without ESOL teachers' ability to take advantage of the natural contact between varying cultures in the classroom and explore and include ICC as part of the language curriculum, changes in cultural awareness and understanding may not necessarily take place.

No doubt, discussions about culture in ESOL teaching and learning have been going on for a long time now. Much has changed since Atkinson's 1999 article, "TESOL and Culture," in which he begins the conversation by posing six general principles for analyzing culture, with, interestingly, no reference made to ideas stemming from the field of intercultural communication (see **Appendix C**). In response to his article, Sparrow (2000) suggests that all practicing teachers need to

a. be aware of underlying cultural concepts about language and learning in the curriculum of instruction;

b. keep in mind their students' needs and goals, which are culturally based; and

c. be mindful of their own assumptions and values, which arise naturally from their backgrounds and previous intercultural and teaching experiences.

We know that culture cannot be separated from language, and so it seems most appropriate to view intercultural communicative language teaching as more of a stance than a body of content to be covered or a teaching method. Integrating ICC into curriculum and instruction is about intentionally highlighting this component "within existing program goals, language learning outcomes, tasks, materials, and assessments" (Alberta Teachers of English as a Second Language, 2009, S7-8). Following, four frameworks that present ICC as a goal in one form or another are presented.

The Canadian Language Benchmarks

The Canadian Language Benchmarks is an example of a framework that incorporates ICC in its mandate, although the terms it uses are more linguistic oriented than intercultural. The Canadian Language Benchmarks is a 12-stage reference model for learning, teaching, programming, and assessing adult ESOL learners in Canada (Citizenship and Immigration Canada, 2012). Curriculum is framed around a description of communicative competencies and performance tasks through which students demonstrate application of language knowledge and skills. English language ability is defined as the ability to communicate, that is, "to interact, to express, to interpret and to negotiate meaning, and to create discourse in a variety of social contexts and situations" (Citizenship and Immigration Canada, 2012, p. VI). According to the framework, there are two major components: language knowledge, which comprises organizational knowledge (grammatical and textual) and pragmatic knowledge (functional and sociolinguistic), and strategic competence, which is necessary for effective communication. Strategic competence is students' ability to "manage the integration and application of all other components of language ability to the specific context and situation of language use." As such, it "involves planning and assessing communication, avoiding or repairing difficulties in communication, coping with communication breakdown and using affective devices" (Citizenship and Immigration Canada, 2012, p. VIII). For example, at the initial stages of listening (CLB 1–4), a learner may ask for help, request repetition, seek clarification and confirmation, and show interest in what is being spoken. Intercultural capabilities have commonly been described as strategic competence and considered to be an intrinsic part of communicative competence. Sociolinguistic knowledge is particularly relevant as well because it comprises

> rules of politeness; sensitivity to register, dialect or variety; norms of stylistic appropriateness; sensitivity to "naturalness"; knowledge of idioms and

figurative language; knowledge of culture, customs and institutions; knowledge of cultural references; and uses of language through interactional skills to establish and maintain social relationships. (Citizenship and Immigration Canada, 2012, p.VIII)

THE CANADIAN LANGUAGE BENCHMARKS (CLBS)

Each CLB includes a Profile of Ability, Competency Statements, and Sample Indicators of Ability.

Profile of Ability

The Profile of Ability gives an overall picture of a person's language ability in one skill at one benchmark level. It includes an overall statement of ability, features of the communication, and characteristics (strengths and limitations) that are typically demonstrated at that benchmark in that language skill. For example, at CLB 6 (Developing Intermediate Ability)—Speaking, the ESOL learner can ask for and give information in some detail and can express opinions, feelings, obligation, ability, and certainty one-on-one and in small group discussions or meetings.

Competency Area

For each language skill, there are four broad representative competency areas, each reflecting different purposes or functions of language use.

- Interacting With Others (All Skills): communication to maintain or change interpersonal relationships and to foster social cohesion.
- Comprehending Instructions (Reading and Listening): communication to understand instructions and directions.
- Giving Instructions (Speaking): communication to convey instructions and directions.
- Getting Things Done (All Skills): communication to get things done, obtain services, inform decisions, persuade, or learn what others want done.
- Comprehending Information (Reading and Listening): communication to learn and understand information and ideas.
- Sharing Information (Speaking and Writing): communication to inform others and to share or present information and ideas.
- Reproducing Information (Writing): communication to reduce or reproduce information to summarize, learn, record, or remember information.

Sample Indicators of Ability

Sample Indicators of Ability appear under Competency Statements to provide a general indication of what a person might need to do when attempting authentic language tasks related to a particular competency. For example, at CLB 6 (Developing Intermediate Ability)—Speaking, the ESOL learner can provide necessary information, ask relevant questions, summarize information and ideas to confirm understanding, agree and disagree appropriately, thank others for their contributions and information, and participate effectively in interactions with some degree of support from others.

(Citizenship and Immigration Canada, 2012)

For ESOL learners to acquire both language knowledge and strategic competence at the advanced level, they need to display ICC; they should be able to "communicate effectively, appropriately, accurately, and fluently about most topics in a range of [social, educational, and work-related] contexts and situations, from predictable to unfamiliar, from general to professionally complex and from specific to nuanced, in communicatively demanding contexts" (Citizenship and Immigration Canada, 2012, p. X). Along with accessible CLB Can-Do statements, which help facilitate discussions between ESOL teachers and their learners about learner progress and what they need to develop, what we see in this model is the perfect intersection of ICC and English language ability.

The Massachusetts Framework

The *Massachusetts Adult Basic Education Curriculum Framework for ESOL* was developed as part of a comprehensive set of standards for monitoring and assessing adult ESOL learners attending classes in the United States (Massachusetts Department of Education, Adult and Community Learning Services, 2005). It has also been adapted by the Alberta Teachers of English as a Second Language Adult ESL Curriculum Framework (2009), who built on the Massachusetts framework's Intercultural Knowledge and Skills strand (Alberta Teachers of English as a Second Language Adult ESL Curriculum Framework, 2009, p. 9). This strand focuses on the need for ESOL learners to become familiar with the concept of culture and cultural differences with the understanding that people exhibit culturally defined behaviors, which are influenced by race, ethnicity, age, gender, social class, and religion. The framework outlines seven standards or ways of demonstrating awareness of cultural differences, as well as the knowledge, skills, and attitudes needed to successfully function in a multicultural society. Standards are similar to learning outcomes and can be used as such for curriculum planning. They are meant to describe what ESOL learners should know (knowledge) and be able to do (skills) to develop ICC.

THE MASSACHUSETTS FRAMEWORK

According to the intercultural knowledge and skills strand of the Massachusetts framework, ESOL learners will

- identify and describe the significance of cultural images and symbols—U.S. cultures and their own. Refer to symbols (e.g., maple leaf) and statues (e.g., Statue of Liberty) and the emotions they evoke.

- analyze everyday behaviors in U.S. cultures and compare and contrast these with their own. Examples of behavior include daily routines, dress, food, food preparation, table manners, or personal hygiene.

- identify culturally determined behavior patterns, such as small talk, nonverbal communication, taboo topics, telephone protocol, degrees of familiarity, eye contact, and use of time and space.

- analyze and describe diversity in the United States in terms of ethnicity, race, class, gender, and age by looking at pop culture, songs, communication styles, and subcultures (e.g., hip-hop). →

- compare and contrast the differences and similarities in the values and beliefs in their own culture and in U.S. cultures through examining attitudes about male/female roles, work ethic, aging, independence, competition, individualism, materialism, time, and money.

- recognize cultural stereotypes—favorable and discriminatory—and describe how they impact their own and others' behavior.

- examine their own cultural adjustment process and the personal balance that must be struck between acculturation and preserving their own culture. Examples include parental rights and limitations, bilingual homes, home remedies, religious and social practices, values, and attitudes about male and female roles.

(Massachusetts Department of Education, Adult and Community Learning Services, 2005, pp. 18–20)

The Common European Framework

The Common European Framework of Reference for Languages (CEFR), developed by the Council of Europe (2001), is yet another example taken from the language arena that provides a common ground and specific guidelines for the development of language syllabi, curricula, resources, and assessment tools across Europe. With regards to learning, the framework focuses on the development of two types of competence: communicative language competencies (linguistic, sociolinguistic, and pragmatic components), which reflect the language knowledge component of the Canadian Language Benchmarks, and general competencies of the individual: declarative knowledge (knowledge of the world, e.g., sociocultural knowledge and intercultural awareness), skills and know-how, and existential competence (attitudes, motivation, and the ability to learn and integrate new knowledge and language awareness). Using the CEFR as a guide, ICC, which includes the learning of culture and interculturality in a logical sequence, has been addressed in, for example, Canadian educational institutions at every level (Council of Ministers of Education Canada, 2010). Again, we see connections here with language-oriented knowledge and skills that lead to ICC.

In his critique of the CEFR, Byram (2009) stresses that foreign language (and we would add ESOL) instructors need to explicitly include ICC in their pedagogical goals so that students become intercultural speakers (briefly referred to in Chapter 1). The term *intercultural speaker* was coined by Byram and Zarate (1996) to move away from the notion of native-speaker competencies. The intercultural speaker is "someone who has the ability to interact with 'others,' to accept other perspectives and perceptions of the world, to mediate between different perspectives, to be conscious of their evaluations of difference" (Byram, 2001, p. 5). The intercultural speaker or mediator is viewed as a social actor who interacts on equal terms with other individuals in multilingual or unilingual settings, such as in an English-speaking workplace to which the speaker is a newcomer. Byram (2001) claims that knowing how to communicate with people who have different ways of thinking, believing, and behaving more or less parallels the aims of communicative language teaching, which is the most common approach to ESOL instruction. The result is communication that posits respect for individuals who are seen as having multiple identities to avoid the stereotyping that can take place when a person is viewed as having one identity, often based solely on their ethnicity or nationality (e.g., She is Russian). With specific reference to the "subjectively" successful new immigrant, House (2007) argues that despite culture shock, identity crisis and issues pertaining to maladjustments, the intercultural speaker is a person

> who has managed to settle for the In-between, who knows and can perform in both his and her native culture and in another one acquired at some later date . . . he or she is a person who has managed to develop his or her own third way, in between the other cultures he or she is familiar with. (p. 19)

Byram (2009) also asserts that the term *intercultural speaker* should be introduced into language and culture teaching as an attempt to overcome the power hierarchy that takes place between native-English speakers and nonnative English speakers or students aspiring to be as proficient and fluent in the language as native speakers. The label has implications not only for ICC goals but also for linguistic competence as students develop confidence, feel better about themselves, and become more motivated to improve their skills. He also adds the dimension of *critical cultural awareness*, "the ability to evaluate critically and, on the basis of explicit criteria, perspectives, practices and products in one's own and other cultures and countries" (Byram, 2009, p. 323)—a dimension that fits in well with critical language awareness, in which students are encouraged to examine how language shapes and reproduces power relations hidden in society. For example, ESOL instructors can help students become more critically aware of English language and culture by deconstructing (examining the language used, assumptions made, and implied meanings) newspaper articles or television news broadcasts to investigate whose interests they serve and what messages are both explicitly and implicitly conveyed.

The goal of incorporating (and hence *ensuring*) ICC development into curricula is not to change students' values, but to make them explicit and to encourage students to be conscious of their values when they interact with individuals outside their native language cultural milieu. The role of the ESOL teacher is therefore to not only provide learning activities that facilitate the learning of the target culture and country, but also to help students develop skills, strategies, attitudes, and awareness of their own and others' values to develop ICC (Byram, Gribkova, & Starkey, 2002). Cultural activities and awareness strategies should be part and parcel of the curriculum right from the start and for all age groups. Reid (2015) outlines the most fundamental components necessary for the development of ICC in ESOL classes:

- Sociocultural knowledge (e.g., everyday living, living conditions, interpersonal relations, history, values, beliefs, taboos, social conventions, ritual behavior)
- Sociolinguistic competences (e.g., greetings, addressing, dialect, accent, register, positive and negative politeness, idioms),
- Pragmatic competences (e.g., advising, persuading, urging, socializing, interaction patterns) and
- Nonverbal communication (e.g., body language, gestures, eye contact, proxemics)

How Can We Successfully Incorporate Intercultural Communicative Competence Into the Curriculum?

In integrated language learning, ESOL curriculum usually comprises a variety of components designed to foster language competence in four skill areas. A package may be divided into units with themes and topics that include grammatical structures, vocabulary, language functions, and possible contexts with related cultural components and tips. With communicative and task-based approaches, groups of integrated tasks (e.g., ordering food in a restaurant or asking a bus driver for information) are outlined and ordered within topics or themes. Such tasks are considered to be acts of communication or items of learning within a unit or lesson and covered and assessed within a structured time frame. In adult classes, teachers are also encouraged to be aware of students' needs, interests, and goals so that the curriculum can take these items into account. Scarino (2007) claims that doing a needs analysis as a precursor to programming leads to two problems: (1) The needs are normally understood according to the categories or themes and topics already outlined in the program, and (2) students' needs are often changing, so a static curriculum refutes the benefits of conducting a needs analysis in the first place. She also argues that best practices are too often showcased without attention to the big picture—the relationship a method, approach, or program may have within a particular context, which includes the school and its community, teachers, students, and learning process.

Integrating an ICC orientation into the curriculum requires work and time. For students to acquire ICC, the content of language and culture (as expressed in traditional unit and lesson plan formats) and the needs analysis are only a part of the picture. Teachers need to be attentive to the way students are interpreting and exchanging meanings in classroom interactions. More specifically, students act or

> participate simultaneously as performers and audience, contributing their own meanings and seeking to understand those of others, and considering how their contribution influences others and how others' contributions influence them. As a consequence, they learn to decenter from their own social, linguistic, and cultural world and thereby come to a different understanding of themselves in relationship to others. The focus on the reciprocal interpretation and making of meaning across languages and cultures captures the lived reality and experience of communication in general. (Scarino, 2010, p. 326)

Where, though, do these processes that view students as interpreters and meaning-makers fit into a tightly sequenced set of knowledge and skills? How can a curriculum address what really takes place in an interaction whereby the individuals must dig deep into their cultural repertoire, interpret what is going on, and respond accordingly? More than documenting the thematic content or tasks, a program that takes ICC into account needs to capture the opportunities and scenarios for interaction and the process of interpreting interaction.

Promoting open dialogue, discussion, and reflection is key to engaging ESOL learners in stimulating their thinking about ICC. Menard-Warwick (2009) claims that cultural discursive fault lines (areas of cultural difference or misunderstanding) can be used as prompts for helping students address, analyze, and problematize their own cultural views and interact with those expressed by others. Using fault lines are a good start, but the challenge is to move from superficial views to a deeper engagement with the issues given the students' language constraints, among other factors. Her qualitative research focused on ways that both the teachers and students "represented cultural issues in particular classroom discussions" (Menard-Warwick, 2009, p. 31), for example, in a discussion where the values of students differ from the prevailing values held by political figures in the country. With that in mind, she noticed that none of the teachers in her California classroom made much effort to ask the immigrant students in-depth questions about their countries, although they had a chance to differentiate U.S. media images from their own experiences. She also observed that dialogue addressing cultural conflict took place in these classes, but it was not a top priority. She went on to say that after discussion activities, students were too often left in their native cultural mindsets,

> more concerned with convincing others of the correctness of their own evaluations than with listening to their classmates. Moreover, the teachers' desires for a collaborative atmosphere often led them to "paper over" differences before going on to the next activity. (Menard-Warwick, 2009, p. 43)

She argues that every lesson, from a discussion about a controversial topic in an advanced class to a grammar point for beginners, should contain representations of culture and attention to interculturality. More than opportunities for oral practice, it is important that discussions around cultural representations provide opportunities for dialogue: listening and comprehending other perspectives and points of view.

COMMITTING CULTURAL FAUX PAS

As our students become more acculturated and familiar with the new cultural norms and customs, they are bound to make mistakes. Learning that results from committing faux pas is not only inevitable but also perhaps a more direct way to learn about the differences in cultural practices that so often remain unspoken until tested. Customs that surround various holiday celebrations in local and home contexts are an excellent example of how important it is for both English language instructors and students to share cultural information.

An incident that took place in the community college where Tuula teaches shows an example of how easily these errors can happen. A campus coordinator, himself a new immigrant to Canada, in a learning program set up for internationally educated professionals, innocently sent the students, instructors, and administrative personnel his greetings for the Christmas season by email. He assumed that it would be fine to send an explicitly Christian greeting with the picture of Maria, Joseph, and baby Jesus to everyone. It is not surprising that he thought this was fine; many Christmas cards in stores display pictures of the birth of Christ.   ➔

The instructors and college staff were stunned as they realized that the sender was not aware that in Canadian workplaces the staff simply do not send religious group email messages to people of many diverse religious, ethnic, and cultural backgrounds. The students, however, were not confused. Most of them assumed this was a Canadian custom because the mail came from a college staff member. The incident provided a great opportunity to talk with the students about the customs that are followed and respected in the holiday season in a multicultural society like Canada. They learned that in a multidenominational context, it is best not to make assumptions about anyone's observances of faith unless the sender of the greeting knows well the recipients as individuals. He may not have assumed that everyone on his list was Christian, but the religious message in itself was inappropriate in his new context. Many students found it puzzling that in Canada people may share being Christians but that only those who more actively observe their faith are likely to exchange specifically religious Christmas greetings with each other.

Developmental Model of Intercultural Sensitivity

Bennett's (2014) development model of intercultural sensitivity (as described in **Appendix B**) can be applied to curriculum development in the ESOL classroom. Teachers can use this model, which focuses on five stages (denial, polarization, minimalization, acceptance, and adaption) as a tool to develop curriculum that includes learning outcomes, tasks, activities, and assignments attentive to both intercultural pragmatics and ICC development (Waugh, 2013). For example, in an online course for ESOL learners and the workplace, Waugh (2013) included two components in each unit:

- pragmatic forms of language that focused on a particular speech act by introducing common conversational gambits, such as "I was wondering if you could . . ." for making a request

- intercultural communication that focused on culture-general frameworks (e.g., individualism and collectivism, high- and low-power distance) as well as cultural differences in nonverbal communication and cultures of learning

Each unit also contained an assessment component (usually a recorded response to a discourse completion task), a reflection on cultural differences and similarities at work or in the community, and questions for discussion with a workplace coach. Waugh (2013) used case studies that illustrated relevant cultural themes, for example, showing how various cultures value time, which included issues revolving around punctuality and turn-taking. He based homework assignments on analyzing cultural differences using the development model of intercultural sensitivity as a guide, and he assessed ICC using a pre- and post-Intercultural Development Inventory (see the **Assessment** section in this chapter), in which students responded to scenarios that contain pragmatic errors that could possibly cause communication breakdowns, misunderstandings, and conflict.

Developmental Model of Linguaculture Learning

And finally, the developmental model of linguaculture learning attempts to address theories of second language acquisition and the field of ICC learning in classroom practice. It is designed to help English as a foreign language teachers understand language and culture learning as an integrated process. In other words, the framework intends

> to go beyond the "skill vs. awareness" dichotomy found in language and intercultural education. It proposes a roadmap of cognitive development—one that describes how language and cultural knowledge become more sophisticated over time . . . .This evolution results not only in increased linguistic ability or cultural understanding, but also in an expanded sense of self. (Shaules, 2016, p. 8)

The framework comprises four levels:

- **Encountering:** The first step in learning is an encounter with "difference"—something that was new and previously unknown (e.g., memorizing phrases, practicing sounds, learning new vocabulary). Students learn the facts about their new culture and surroundings (e.g., geography, politics, places).

- **Experimenting:** The second step happens when students start to make connections through a process referred to as cognitive mapping. They combine their knowledge in new ways by stringing words together in sentences and by thinking about the culture in terms of its rules and why people might behave the way they do (e.g., dos and don'ts, proper etiquette, social expectations). Cultural behavior is viewed in superficial terms.

- **Integrating:** When students begin to internalize and integrate language patterns, they also focus on both form *and* meaning. They can express themselves more fluently, actually "losing themselves in the act of communication" (Shaules, 2016, p. 11) and feeling more like an English speaker. They are also able to understand cultural patterns as a system (as opposed to rules and facts), which "represents a paradigm shift in cultural understanding," and they understand that "other worldviews have an internal logic that is all their own" (Shaules, 2016, p. 11). They are able to suspend judgment and adapt their behavior to better coincide with a new mindset and way of looking at their cultural surroundings. They see their own cultural perspective as one of many, which may lead to a cultural identity issue as they feel caught between different and contrasting worldviews.

- **Bridging:** Students become comfortable easily switching between languages and between cultural perspectives. They extend their learning beyond the patterns (e.g., collectivism vs. individualism) found in a particular community. Knowledge is often intuitive and difficult to articulate. For example, Shaules (2016) claims that experienced interculturalists "may not have a ready definition for the concept of culture, yet they may be highly competent interculturally" (p. 12). In other words, the complexity of their knowledge is shown by their ability to manage complex patterns creatively and without a need to consciously think about it.

The developmental model of linguaculture learning focuses on learning goals related to acquiring both language and cultural awareness. When ESOL teachers focus on both language and culture equally, learners can alternate their attention to both elements in a way that reinforces ICC development, cultural exploration, and personal growth. Shaules (2016) outlines elements of a linguaculture classroom approach to pedagogy, which includes the following:

- **Reflection:** Teachers raise student awareness of the learning process as they are encouraged to reflect on their relationship to and understanding of the new culture (Where am I now?)

- **Vision:** Students think about their inner qualities and changes they would like to make with regard to the learning process and their new cultural self (Where am I going?)

- **Roadmap:** Students gain awareness of the learning process with regard to the four levels of the framework (How did I get here?)

- **Community:** Students create and take responsibility for maintaining a linguaculture learning community (How can we go together?)

We seem to have come to a crossroads here. There are models and guidelines for instruction that are rooted in the language teaching and linguistic areas (Cohen & Sykes, 2013; Kramsch, 2006; Byram, 2001) and those that are more common to the field of intercultural communication and training (Bennett, 2014; Deardorff, 2009). We also notice that whatever model or guideline one is using, all of them seem to have the same outcome in mind: for students to develop language and cultural skills to be able to communicate effectively and appropriately in various cultural contexts and situations. Whichever model is applied to instruction, the main point to be emphasized is that English language proficiency is absolutely central to the development of ICC in English-speaking countries. Fantini (2009) reminds us that "grappling with a second language causes us to confront how we perceive, conceptualize, express, behave, and interact. It promotes alternative communication strategies—and on someone else's terms. And it helps expand and transform our habitual view of the world" (p. 459). As ESOL learners develop their English language skills, they are more able to move from being ethnocentric observers to functioning as ethnorelative participants and experienced interculturalists.

ESOL LEARNERS AND ORGANIZATION OF IDEAS

When ESOL learners answer questions and participate in whole-class or small-group discussions, some may organize their ideas orally and in writing differently from those who are more familiar with the dominant and normalized Western cultural style, one in which students respond in a way that is linear, concise, and direct, characteristic of a topic-centered style of communication. In oral interaction, it is expected that students maintain eye contact, limit enthusiastic gesturing, avoid digression, and keep their feelings to themselves. In contrast, some ESOL learners may be more accustomed to communicating by waving their hands around and speaking loudly. For example, although there are variations (and gender is a consideration), ESOL learners from Hispanic and North African cultures tend to use large, illustrative gestures when expressing themselves. In contrast, students from East Asian cultures are often discouraged from using such gestures at a young age, especially in public (Jackson, 2014). The latter may practically whisper their answers in class to avoid calling attention to themselves.

In addition, some ESOL learners may communicate in a style that uses topic association or topic chaining—a circular, rather indirect communication style that may seem as though the speaker is rambling, disjointed, and unfocused because they go on to a new thought before finishing a previous one. They may be thought of as not responding to questions directly and, hence, be encouraged by their teacher and English speakers with whom they are communicating to "get to the point," and stop "beating around the bush." It is important for ESOL teachers to be mindful of these different culturally based styles of expression and not jump to conclusions too quickly. Teachers can also address these styles of communication in class as they may affect behaviors in, for example, interviews and various jobs in the service industry that require effective communication with the public.

Classroom Talk and Intercultural Communicative Competence

Classroom talk is an important component of both second language acquisition and content. Dooley (2009) maintains that having oral competence and confidence depends on the ESOL student's participation in a learning community where there is meaningful talk and repeated use of key language. Yet, we need to recognize that talk is a two-way, interactive process, which means that students need to have the chance to converse with native English speakers or advanced-level learners in the class as much as possible to practice their English language skills and gain ICC. They need to connect and engage with their classmates in a natural way, with "interest and enthusiasm" (Dooley, 2009, p. 498) and in a manner that inspires learning despite differences in linguistic abilities and cultural orientations. That said, research shows that White, monolingual English speakers are more likely to judge "what counts as 'good English,' reject speakers of so-called 'accented' English as conversation partners, and not carry a fair share of the burden to achieve understanding in conversation" (Dooley, 2009, p. 498). To address the needs of both ESOL learners and fluent English speakers, teachers can teach strategies to help both groups share the communicative burden equally and thus "critique their exercise of social power in conversation, develop an ethics of care for others, and understand the difficulties of learning and using a second language" (Dooley, 2009, p. 499). Understanding is obtained when students actively engage with each other cooperatively across linguistic and cultural differences. They do this by building an intercultural bridge, and, with that bridge, both parties can ask each other for explanations and clarifications when they are confused or misunderstood.

Although student engagement is ideal, it cannot be taken for granted. One reason is that conversation across difference can be face threatening, which, in Dooley's (2009) research was a significant theme in the accounts of schooling provided to her by African students from Sudan, Burundi, and Rwanda. These students praised teachers who were relatively easy to understand and who understood them well. However, some of the students said that they did not feel comfortable answering or asking questions in class for fear of being ridiculed. Instead, they preferred to ask their friends for help or consult with their teachers after class—tactics both authors of this book have witnessed while observing mixed classes. Students are likely to apply themselves most to the face-threatening work of negotiating understanding across linguistic and cultural difference if the risk is minimal, if the learning environment feels safe, and if the classroom is a place where students feel they belong.

OPPORTUNITIES FOR MEANINGFUL INTERACTION

There should be opportunities to bring English-speaking individuals together with ESOL learners in meaningful interactions to facilitate relationship building. Whether they are new immigrants or international students, such opportunities could involve volunteer community service, mentoring, language partnering, book or film club discussions, and even sports.

When Johanne was teaching in an advanced college English for academic purposes program, she set up weekly discussion sessions with English-speaking domestic students who volunteered to participate in the program. The students were interspersed into small groups in which they discussed such topics as intermarriage, roles of women in society, and capital punishment. The ESOL learners chose the topics and each week there was a leader to facilitate the discussion with prepared commentary and question prompts. During the wrap-up period, in addition to new vocabulary, language use, and grammar points, Johanne asked specific questions about cultural differences and similarities. Focus was also placed on the discussion process itself, which included turn-taking, use of gestures, eye contact, and issues pertaining to inclusiveness. When the session was over, Johanne encouraged the ESOL learners to reflect in their journals about any other intercultural issues arising from the experience and how they might change their behavior using an intercultural perspective to engage more fully in the discussions.

Reflection is the key word here. One of the key elements in fostering ICC among ESOL learners in your class is to design purposeful language tasks that stimulate and allow opportunities for reflection. Although many cultures, including American culture, place a high value on doing activities and accomplishing tasks that leave little time or space for reflection, it must be emphasized that reflection is an essential component of ICC development. Certainly, teachers can present tasks that involve information gap activities, competitive quizzes, oral presentations, and discussions to aid language acquisition. However, most important, time should be allotted for reflection on the intercultural, which can include incidental comparisons in the form of question prompts and journal entries or whole-class discussions that address cultural behaviors. When time is at a premium, teachers can administer an exit card or ticket, which is a half sheet of paper collected at the end of a lesson commonly used to assess student learning, monitor questions, and receive feedback on teaching; however, teachers can utilize exit tickets to write a prompt that also addresses an intercultural aspect of the lesson, such as, "Would people in your culture address appreciation in the same way?," "In your culture, how would this lesson be taught?," or "What challenges do you have, besides language, that affect your participation in class?" Student answers can be addressed at the beginning of the next lesson to call attention to ICC components.

ASSESSMENT OF INTERCULTURAL COMMUNICATIVE COMPETENCE

The fundamental question is, how linguistically and culturally prepared are ESOL learners for living and working in their new cultural environment? How do teachers know that they are developing ICC? According to Moloney (2008), students demonstrate their competence when they

- see themselves as purposeful language users in a meaningful context,
- display metalinguistic connections and reflective critical thinking (noticing, describing, analyzing),
- develop an independent cultural identity and are aware of a relationship between their first language and culture and the English language and culture, and
- understand intercultural development in themselves and feel pride in their roles as nonnative-English-language users

Assessing ICC in the ESOL classroom can be challenging because acquiring such competence is very much a learning process over time. Because it is very likely that your students come to class from different cultural backgrounds and with differing worldviews and mindsets, it becomes almost impossible to expect them to learn and grow interculturally at the same rate. This is the reason it is useful and realistic to describe the development of ICC as a process, one that takes place in and out of the classroom. Deardorff (2006) reminds us that for ESOL learners, the journey is never-ending as they continue to learn, change, evolve, and become transformed over time.

With this process in mind, when it comes to assessing ICC with your ESOL learners, you must know exactly what you are assessing. For that, you have to be clear you understand the definition of ICC, or what it means in practice for ESOL learners to engage in effective and appropriate behavior and communication when they are interacting with native and advanced ESOL speakers of English in particular contexts. Because ICC development is an ongoing process, students should be given plenty of opportunities to reflect on and assess their learning and development on a regular basis. Furthermore, any assessment of culture-specific knowledge needs to go beyond the conventional surface-level knowledge of foods, greetings, customs, and so on. Clearly, assessing ICC development is complicated.

As ESOL teachers, we know that it is easier to assess knowledge and understanding in the classroom through oral and written tests and other alternative forms of assessment. One such method is the oral dialogue journal in which ESOL learners have the opportunity to explore intercultural issues related to their new cultural surroundings through recorded oral communication with their teacher (Makarchuk, 2010). Students can also embark on written dialogue journals with their teachers or, if possible, English-speaking peers who have the experience and understanding of the acculturation process. These peers may also have had interactions that have led to misunderstandings. Written work can bring some less visible aspects of ICC to light, particularly when ESOL learners are asked to reflect on certain issues and to report their reactions to a specific intercultural exchange. For beginning-level students, it may be advantageous to allow students to communicate in their native language so that they can express their feelings and concerns more deeply and share them with a cultural informant from their home country. In fact, it is important to keep in mind that limited English language proficiency does not prevent ESOL learners from internalizing cultural perspectives; it only hinders them from expressing their thoughts and feelings in English.

In summary, assessment tools can include a combination of the following:

- observations and analyses of interactions in real or simulated social settings

  — If students are living with host families, the family could be asked to answer questions that focus on their guest's changes in behavior during this time.

- role-playing (with native or advanced-level English speakers)

- individual progress conferences that explore student strategies in intercultural encounters

- administration of survey instruments and questionnaires, such as the Intercultural Development Inventory, an assessment tool which English language teachers can use to assess and reflect on stages of cultural sensitivity, as conceptualized by Bennett's (2014) developmental model of intercultural sensitivity

- written work (e.g., self-reports, portfolios, reflective journals, and learning logs)

  — Students can create individual learning contracts in which they discuss with their teacher what they want to learn, how they will learn it, a timeline, evidence of learning, and action taken as a result of the learning.

  — Students keep hard copy or electronic portfolios that contain, among other language learning material, reflections on their intercultural learning based on written prompts, such as "I learned that . . . ," "This is important because . . . ," and "As a result of this learning I will. . . ." Through reflections, they examine their personal opinions, attitudes, feelings, concerns, and changes they would like to make as a result of their newly acquired culture knowledge and experiences. The portfolio with samples of work in differing stages of reflective thinking works very well in ascertaining student progress.

The combination of individual progress conferences and journal writing works well to track student behavior and feelings. For example, students can reflect on their own language and culture learning in their journals and share their reflections with their peers and teacher. It can be beneficial to include a random group of advanced or native English speakers who have lived in Western cultures for a significant period of time in the assessment process. However, knowledge and understanding are only two components of ICC. ESOL instructors also need to assess their students' ability to apply their knowledge, to "step outside their taken for granted perspectives and to act on the basis of new perspectives" (Byram, Gribkova, & Starkey, 2002). A traditional assessment outlook is not sufficient to capture this understanding of language, culture, and learning within an intercultural orientation because the focus is primarily on testing content through objective and sometimes standardized methods. The challenge is to find out whether students have changed their attitudes—their ability to be more respectful, open, and curious about their new cultural surroundings. Are they acting appropriately in their present cultural context? And finally, ICC development also includes the students' ability to see from others' perspectives, to understand other worldviews and mindsets. Such assessment involves attention to how ESOL learners interpret and negotiate meaning, make informed judgments, and express themselves using culturally appropriate language.

According to Scarino (2010), assessing ICC involves several dimensions:

- Communicating (in speaking and writing) in English whereby students have the opportunity to negotiate meaning through interpreting and using language in diverse contexts while interacting with people with diverse social, linguistic, and cultural life-worlds. Criteria for assessment should be on the accuracy, fluency, appropriateness, and complexity of language used in the exchange as well as on how students negotiate meaning in interaction and how they manage the variability demanded by the particular context of communication (e.g., workplace, restaurant, classroom).

- Eliciting responses that illustrate how students perceive and interpret the world and interact and communicate, how the first language(s) and culture(s) come into play in exchanging meaning, and how they themselves and those with whom they communicate are already situated in their own language(s) and culture(s)

- Eliciting students' meta-awareness of the connection between language and culture in communicative interactions and their ability to analyze, explain, and elaborate on their awareness

- Positioning students as both English language users and students who are able to reflect on the growth that has taken place with regard to their knowledge, skills, and attitude

It is also important for ESOL learners to become responsible for their own learning. Given that intentional goal-setting, self-reflection, and self-assessment of knowledge, skills, and attitudinal changes toward one's own and other cultures are major factors in the development of ICC, can-do statements work well in this regard. With these statements, ESOL learners have a concrete way of monitoring their progress and tracking their intercultural skill learning in a variety of contexts. In lesson planning, teachers can create their own can-do statements that reflect their curriculum, or they can use published can-do statements in which ICC is listed as an outcome (Byram & Wagner, 2018).

Although the NCSSFL-ACTFL (National Council of State Supervisors for Languages-American Council on the Teaching of Foreign Languages) Can-Do Statements for Intercultural Communication and the Intercultural Reflection Tool for Learners are primarily aimed at foreign language learning, they can be effectively applied to ESOL instruction as well. They are designed to "provide a set of examples and scenarios that show how learners use the target language and knowledge of culture to demonstrate their Intercultural Communicative Competence" (American Council on the Teaching of Foreign Languages, 2017). Under Intercultural Communication, Can-Do statements involve both "Investigation of Cultural Practices and Interaction with Others in and from Another Culture" in particular situations. For example, "In my own and other cultures I can compare how and why houses, buildings, and towns affect lifestyles; I can use learned behaviors when visiting someone's home or business and notice when I make a cultural mistake," are statements that reflect learners' knowledge, skills, and attitude at the Intermediate Proficiency Benchmark. In addition to the Can-Do Statements, the Reflection Tool provides sample questions teachers can use as prompts for journal writing and discussions following classroom activities (American Council on the Teaching of Foreign Languages, 2017).

Instruments for Measuring Intercultural Communicative Competence

Ideally, assessment of ICC should be formative and ongoing. Several tools have been developed to measure ICC among a diverse group of participants, including English-speaking exchange, study abroad, and ESOL international students. Such instruments, such as the aforementioned Intercultural Development Inventory, have generally involved students answering a set of standardized questions or responding to statements based on cognitive, affective, and behavioral dimensions. Sample statements include, "I enjoy starting conversations with people from cultures," to assess motivation; "I do not trust people who are different," to assess ethnocentrism; and "I often change the way I communicate depending on who I am speaking to," to assess ICC. Nevertheless, as Scarino (2007) points out, the difficulty with any instrument is that it inevitably involves some form of categorization or breaking down of concepts (such as motivation, ethnocentrism and ICC), into component parts. Despite their popularity, especially among large groups of participants, such instruments can undermine a student's holistic understanding of ICC and ability to apply their knowledge and skills in real contexts.

An alternative to asking participants to complete standardized questions regarding their ICC development is using what Holmes and O'Neill (2012) refer to as the PEER model, which is designed to assess ICC over time. In their research, university students, many of them ESOL and from a variety of countries and cultures, were asked to choose a partner (a Cultural Other) whom they did not know and meet with them weekly for an hour or more over a 6-week period. The objective was for them to find out more about their partner's culture and evaluate their own ICC. The model "embodies a process for continued relationship building" (Holmes and O'Neill, 2012, p. 711) and incorporates four phases:

1. Prepare: Before meeting their partner, students identify any assumptions, prejudices, and stereotypes they have about their Cultural Other.

2. Engage: Students meet with their partners and are given guiding topics to use as prompts for conversation and suggestions for social activities that they could do together, such as sharing a meal.

3. Evaluation: Students are asked to think about previously taught concepts related to culture and ICC to help them interpret their experiences. They also document their activities and thoughts after each session by writing field notes and a journal.

4. Reflection: Students access their notes and journal to reflect critically on their sessions. They document any challenges to the preconceptions they may have had or difficulties communicating that may have led to changes in their behavior—in other words, any renegotiating of "taken-for-granted ways of thinking, behaving and communicating" (Holmes and O'Neill, 2012, p. 711).

According to Holmes and O'Neill (2012), the PEER (prepare/engage/evaluate/reflect) model "encourages individuals to self-reflect through questioning, emotional involvement and self-discovery, thus leading to self-evaluation of intercultural competence in the intercultural encounter" (p. 711). Most important is that students realize within themselves that they have moved from, for example, feeling fearful and reluctant before an encounter to becoming more respectful, sensitive to, and curious about the Other's culture. Partaking in the experience and reflecting on that experience through guided journal writing both during and after the sessions, students have the opportunity to become more knowledgeable about themselves and the Other, even when they are confused and communication is difficult. All in all, ESOL teachers can use a combination of questionnaires and experiences that involve self-reflection over time to assess their learners' ICC development.

CLASSROOM BEST PRACTICES

True, intercultural communication awareness and training are generally incorporated at least implicitly in ESOL classes; however, to be effective, intercultural pragmatics (attention to linguistic differences *and* culture) should be front and center of every lesson. Classroom activities should be designed to encourage learners to discover the impact of their own cultural assumptions on their own expectations, behaviors, choices, values, and communication styles. Activities should facilitate an understanding of the way those cultural assumptions affect the people with whom they are communicating. It is also important to realize that pedagogical practices must take into account differences in ESOL learners' needs and goals as well as other relevant contextual factors that may be affecting their lives.

See **Appendix D** for activities related to observing and analyzing cultural behaviors, nonverbal communication, people-watching, and language use in context.

The Culture Learning Approach

The culture learning approach focuses on social skills and social interaction. It is a form of instruction that emphasizes behavioral change as the basis for intercultural competence and sociocultural adaptation (Ward, 2004, Masgoret & Ward, 2006). Culture learning can begin with the identification of cross-cultural differences in verbal and nonverbal communication rules, conventions, norms and practices that contribute to intercultural misunderstandings. Culture-specific knowledge includes not only language and facts about the culture (e.g., information about cultural signs, symbols, and artifacts), but also subtle aspects of social interaction (e.g., eye contact, gestures, proxemics, and interpreting silence). Instructors then provide students with skills and strategies (e.g., through role-plays, modeling, case studies, simulations, and feedback) to help them minimize or even eradicate confusing, culturally infused encounters and develop more confidence in their abilities. Having the opportunity to participate in community service or volunteer work-place placements exposes students to contexts in which they can make observations and apply their culture learning and skills.

It is important that English language instructors develop classroom activities that encourage students to discuss and come to their own conclusions based on their observations and experience of their new cultural surroundings. For example, providing information about historical sites or how to rent an apartment or tip for service rendered (if that is common practice) is very useful, or even essential; however, teachers should also provide students with opportunities to make comparisons with their own cultural behaviors in order to bring differences to the forefront of their consciousness. It is important for students to develop noticing skills—in this case, the ability to identify common culturally embedded communicative behaviors in different contexts, understand how they are realized in these contexts, and predict how people will behave in future interactions (Hinkel, 2013). Starting the class with questions like, "What did you notice about culture on your way to school this morning?" and "What was similar to the experience you had in your native country compared to the experience you are having now?" can help students develop noticing skills.

ESOL learners learn about cultural behaviors by observing and discussing their observations of cultural acts for themselves. After observations, they should use a framework (or at least guidelines) for analyzing what occurred, making comparisons, and discussing what their observations meant to them and their learning. For example, Ilieva (2001) created a process with the following steps for students:

1. Naming, which refers to describing the situation (What do you see? What is happening?)

2. Summarizing and interpreting the observations from their own perspective

3. Relating, which refers to their feelings, thoughts, and personal experiences (How does this behavior relate to your lives?)

4. Determining the meaning of various observed behaviors (What is your reaction? Is this a problem for you? Why do you think you react this way?). Students discuss their own verbal and nonverbal behavior in these kinds of situations; compare experiences with each other; and think about possible reasons for these differences, which could be based on gender, social class, or other identity markers.

5. Dealing with situations like this (How do you plan to deal with situations like this?)

Ilieva (2001) also advocates that students learn to live with the "ambiguity that accompanies them in their everyday dealings with a new culture . . . to make them aware of the impossibility of providing ESOL learners with a body of 'knowledge' to act on in any situation" (p. 4). She goes on to say that

> once students have experienced the ambiguity and inconsistency of inter-preting events, activities, or relationships through the culture exploration classroom discussions, they will be more willing to probe and not assume that their perceptions and understandings of a situation necessarily coincide with or are in sharp contrast with those of other participants in the situation. (Ilieva, 2001, p. 12)

Predicting the expectations of what certain cultural values are and what behaviors might manifest before the observation takes place could be added to the observation guidelines (Walsh-Marr, 2011). Such predictions could facilitate further discussion and the opportunity for more critical reflection of cultural behaviors before students go out into the community to observe interactions.

FOCUS ON INTERCULTURAL DIMENSIONS

Learning activities that include the intercultural dimensions focus on helping students to understand how intercultural interactions take place and what strategies to use in those interactions. Students need to know

- how social identities (values, beliefs, worldviews, expectations) are part of all interaction,
- how their perceptions of other people and other people's perceptions of them influence the success of communication, and
- how they can find out more about the people with whom they are communicating.

(Adapted from Byram, Gribkova, & Starkey, 2002)

The following is a sample of approaches and activities instructors can use in their classes to promote both English language acquisition and ICC. The first focus is on iden-tity; activities center around stereotypes, cultural symbols, and general cultural behaviors.

Cultural Conversation: Storytelling About Culture and Identity

In ESOL pedagogy, storytelling has often been used as a tool to develop speaking and writing, sometimes through journaling and keeping a diary. Using narratives is also a very powerful way for our students to explore intercultural dilemmas and questions, not to mention sharing their stories about moving from one side of the world to the other or growing up in a multicultural society. As American author Toni Morrison once said, "If there is a book that you want to read, but it hasn't been written yet, you must be the one to write it" (Brainy Quote, 2018).

Drawing pictures and telling stories in pictures and text are some of the more creative ways to do storytelling. Lynda Barry, who calls herself the "accidental professor," introduces in her wonderful book *Syllabus* (2014) the art of creating course content, tasks, and activities that use teacher and learner drawings. Learners, especially those who learn best visually, prefer a more hands-on approach and appreciate having the opportunity to be creative. Doing drawings can also provide learners of diverse cultural backgrounds an added chance to "draw-tell" their stories, which may not be as easily explained in words.

Activity: Drawing jam

1. Everyone folds one 8.5" × 11" sheet of paper into 16 chambers or squares.
2. Students draw lines along the creases and edges to make quick borders and another set of lines to make a narrow (heading) space.
3. Decide on a category (e.g., personality traits, occupations) and have each student write one example of this category in the first heading space (e.g., *plumber* for occupation or *talkative* for personality trait). Then, students pass their paper to the person beside them and write another example in the next heading space. Repeat until all the heading spaces are filled with examples, giving students only 10 seconds for each space:

Personality Traits

Stylistic	Shy	Serious	Artistic
Flamboyant	Talkative	Quiet	Risk-taker

Occupations

Plumber	Nurse	Writer	Veterinarian
Doctor	Chef	Teacher	Engineer

4. When all the header rows are filled, give students 1 minute to draw into one of the boxes (on the piece of paper they've ended up with) the type of person described in the heading. No stick people! Then, have them switch papers. Repeat until all the drawing boxes are full.

5. Post on the wall as in an art gallery and take a walk to look at each other's artwork.

6. Discuss the various images, encouraging learners to share information and exchange views on what their drawings tell/show about the occupations and personality descriptions in different cultures, which could be their home culture or the culture in which they are presently living.

Who am I? Identities as cultural narratives

Where is Home? This is a great question to explore with all learners, especially in ESOL classrooms, using draw-tell and other tools to represent the different worlds people come from and live in. Storytelling is one approach that has been used successfully in various instructional contexts to represent complex biographies and cultural identities. In our ESOL classrooms, it is worthwhile to explore themes such as home to allow learners to express the process of change that many newcomers share with each other. Expressions that students often use, such as "back home" or "going home" illustrate in language the many meanings of cultural identity and the sense of belonging and attachment that are also shifting over time. Engaging learners in storytelling will also give them the welcome opportunity to understand their own settling in a new culture as an ongoing process of change and transformation.

Activity: What is in a name?

Names are a common topic in an ESOL course because they allow learners to share intercultural perspectives and personal information. Names are both culturally and linguistically specific and lend themselves perfectly to storytelling and sharing of information about cultures and countries of origin.

As an instructor, Tuula often shares a story about her first name to demonstrate what she has learned through lived experiences having a "different" name, one that prompts people to inquire about the country and culture of her origins. Our names are not only about identity but also embedded in intercultural knowledge and understanding of the world and often of the more complex perceptions we have of our place in it. Because her name sounds the same as the Greek name *Toula*, she is often asked if she is Greek or if she has seen the film *Big Fat Greek Wedding*. In the film, the main character, Toula, is engaged in a personal transformation from a young waitress in her dad's Greek restaurant into a successful college graduate and later a manager and owner of a travel agency. Her success story resonates with immigrant learners who can identify with Toula's personal journey to find her own voice and a new identity, in her case in the Greek ethnic community and in the larger North American society.

Have your learners share information about the meaning of their names; it personalizes learning and goes a long way to help bridge the intercultural communication and information gaps between people who do not share the same cultural origins. Names are also about families and inform us about the social and cultural histories of people over periods of time and in vastly different places.

Focus on Cultural Knowledge and Make Comparisons

Activities: Cultural stereotypes

Recognize cultural stereotypes—favorable and problematic—and describe how they impact students' own and others' behaviors.

- For more advanced-level classes, encourage a discussion of factors that influence cultural stereotypes with a focus on race, gender, ethnicity, class, sexual orientation, age, etc.

- Explore and discuss the validity of cultural profiles. For example, stereotypes of Americans on the Wikipedia site state that positive stereotypes portray Americans as generous, optimistic, and hardworking; negative stereotypes say they are obese, gun-obsessed, arrogant, and materialistic, and that they lack curiosity and cultural awareness. You can brainstorm a list of traits and behaviors beforehand from which students can choose and ask them the following questions (Humphrey, 2002):

  — Can you think of some stereotypical images people have of your cultural or ethnic group? Write a list.

  — Are they generally positive or negative images?

  — Which cultural group has this image of your cultural group?

  — Do you feel that some of the images are true for everyone in your cultural group? If they are not, which group would be exempt from these stereotypes?

  Share proverbs from different countries and discuss how they represent or misrepresent cultural behaviors (e.g., time is money—United States; Accusation always follows the cat—Iraq; Shrimp that fall asleep get carried away by the current—Colombia). Discuss the values and behaviors embedded in the English proverbs and how differences might highlight historical and cultural backgrounds.

 See **ELT Teacher's Corner**, "15 Proverbs From Around the World to Teach Values and Refresh Vocabulary," at www.teachers-corner.co.uk/15-proverbs -from-around-the-world-to-teach-values-and-refresh-vocabulary.

- So that students see how they have changed with regard to their initial observations of cultural behaviors, near the beginning of the course or program or unit of study, gather the whole class together around a large piece of paper and ask them to brainstorm and share words and ideas that pertain to what they have observed about their new cultural surroundings in a particular environment, such as a shopping mall, parking lot, or even a bus stop. As they come up with vocabulary describing their observations and views, record their initial perceptions on paper to use as a reference guide throughout the duration of the class. In the meantime, you will have covered some basic cultural information about verbal and nonverbal behaviors, and students will have learned and practiced their English language skills. At the end of the unit or class, reconvene around the original piece of paper, which documented their preconceived ideas, and discuss the changes that have taken place (if any) in their attitudes and beliefs. This activity provides time for students to record and reconsider their preconceived attitudes toward citizens of their new cultural environment (Moeller & Nugent, 2014).

Activities: Cultural symbols

Identify and describe the significance of cultural images and symbols in Western cultures and the students' native culture.

- Look at historical symbols, such as the maple leaf in Canada, stars and stripes and the bald eagle in the United States, popular culture images from mass media, folk culture images, and holiday images and rituals.

- Present students with objects or images (e.g., figurines, tools, jewelry, art) from a particular culture and ask them to find information about these object(s), either by doing research or investigating clues provided. Students might discuss the cultural relevance of the objects in pairs or small groups or make a presentation. You can provide open-ended questions about the artefact, such as

  — Who would use it?

  — What is its purpose?

  — Why is it used?

  — Is there a connection between this artifact and one from your native culture?

- For example, at an Iranian wedding, there is a tablecloth or *Sofré*, which is laden with various symbolic objects, such as a mirror, symbolizing eternity, and candlesticks, with light and fire represent the brightness of the future and eternal passion.

- Design tasks and projects that require students to describe images and/or symbols in Western culture, express the feelings they have about them, and compare them with national images and symbols from their own cultural background. You can use the following question prompts:

  — What is this symbol and where is it from?

  — Why is it important?

  — How does it represent a dimension of a culture?

  — How does this symbol compare with those in other cultures?

- Students can go into the community to collect information about English and Western cultures. For example, students may conduct and record interviews with their English-speaking neighbors, obtain and present an oral family history, or interview a professional about his workplace culture. Classroom preparation would be needed to review vocabulary, create questions, and role-play interactions before students do the interviews.

Activity: Values and belief systems

Compare and contrast differences and similarities in values and beliefs in students' own cultures and in Western cultures. Topics can include attitudes about male/female roles, raising children, work ethic, capital punishment, aging, independence, materialism, time, money, and cross-generational communication and expectations. Advanced classes may address controversial topics that focus on, for example, sexual harassment in the workplace, the "glass ceiling," coverings such as the hijab, human rights, and the LGBT community.

Practice Ongoing Self-Reflection About Cultural Behaviors

In the process of ongoing self-reflection, we identify our thoughts, values, and behaviors about our own culture in relationship to the cultures represented by the ESOL learners in our class. Such reflection allows us to gain deeper levels of self-knowledge and recognize how our values and personal worldviews can influence our instructional practices and expectations about students and their performance. The process involves documenting and analyzing such topics as male and female relationships, forms of discipline and classroom behaviors, and social play from multiple perspectives. Teachers can then develop teaching strategies that reflect this analysis.

Some teachers may believe that they do not actually *have* a culture because their opinions, values, and expectations about education and behavior are the norm—they are part of the dominant cultural perspective, and they cannot see outside of it (The IRIS Center, 2009). However, engaging in self-reflection and even sharing observations and thoughts with colleagues can foster better understanding of what we perceive as the norm and other cultural attributes that define our behaviors.

DEVELOPING CULTURALLY RESPONSIVE TEACHING PRACTICES

ESOL teachers can recognize their implicit cultural bias in action by following the mindful reflection protocol, which is based on the work of teacher educators Dray and Wisneski (see Hammond, 2015). Although the protocol is intended for kindergarten through secondary school teachers, it can be applied equally well to adult educators.

Originally developed by intercultural trainers Bennett and Bennett in the 1970s, the protocol asks teachers to look at an incident through three stages: **description, interpretation, and evaluation** (DIE; Pusch, 2004). Their main goal has been to teach participants in intercultural workshops how to suspend judgment and evaluation while interacting with individuals across cultures. Since the 1970s, the DIE model has become one of the most widely used intercultural activities worldwide and can be nicely adapted to ESOL learners and teachers alike. ➜

DIE is grounded in the notion that we often respond to unfamiliar people or situations with subjective evaluations, projecting our judgments onto what we think we see (or hear or feel or otherwise perceive). This kind of projection is especially problematic when people from a similar cultural background, such as a group of ESOL teachers, share their reactions and find confirmation in their agreement. The DIE exercise encourages reversing the usual order of response by making observations and withholding one's initial reactions (with words such as *weird*, *exotic*, or *unacceptable*), which may be culturally based and emotionally laden, and in the process become more aware of how easily and unconsciously one immediately judges and evaluates a situation according to one's own cultural background and mindset.

Description: Teachers observe and describe what is going on literally, with no value judgments or guesses. What did the learner say or do? How did the event unfold? For example, if a learner is looking out the window, some teachers may think they see a learner who is daydreaming, others may think the learner is deeply thinking about the task, and others may think the learner is rude or lazy because they are not paying attention. These are all subjective notions; a literal description of the action would be "a learner is looking out the window." It can be difficult to think objectively about an observation without coming to conclusions.

Interpretation: Teachers focus on nonjudgmental interpreting, giving meaning to or making informed guesses about the action. What does it mean to you when a learner behaves in a particular way? For example, if a male learner is reluctant to shake the hand of a female learner during a mock interview role-play, a teacher may interpret that the learner is transferring his native cultural behavior or the learner has a cold and doesn't want to spread his germs.

Evaluation: Teachers reflect on how they judge the action or behavior—what value do they give to their interpretation? What is the positive or negative significance of the action based on their interpretation? For example, if the male learner, as in the aforementioned example, does not want to shake hands with women, a teacher who thinks the learner is transferring his behavior may evaluate that he is not adapting to his new cultural environment. If the action is interpreted as the learner has a cold, then the teacher may evaluate that the learner is being considerate of his classmates. It is important for teachers to be aware that their evaluations can lead to overgeneralizations and prejudice, which is not the intention. Follow-up involves helping learners to consciously select culturally different ways of interacting based on what is acceptable and appropriate to the situation.

In 2008, a new version of DIE was introduced, because making the distinction between interpretation and evaluation can be problematic (as is the acronym itself, for obvious reasons). The new version is called DAE.

Describe: What is going on?

Analyze: Why is this happening?

Evaluate: How do I feel about it? How do I think he or she feels?

Nam and Condon (2010) explain that the protocol goes beyond one that emphasizes careful observation, critical thinking, and suspension of judgment; in this protocol, the learning connects the objective with feelings, which in turn may also lead to increased respect and understanding among both teachers and learners. Teachers can use both versions equally well. The primary requirement is that learners understand and distinguish among the three stages.   →

Other variations of the DIE/DAE protocol have been developed and, depending on the English language proficiency of ESOL learners, they can be used as well. For example, the ODIS method refers to mindful observation (verbal and nonverbal signals), description (of behavior, e.g., she is not maintaining eye contact with me while I am talking to her), interpretation (e.g., maybe from her cultural orientation, not making eye contact is a sign of respect, as compared to my culture in which eye contact avoidance is considered rude), and suspending ethnocentric evaluations (e.g., respect the differences but also engage in a mental dialogue to monitor feelings and thoughts (Ting-Toomey, 1999). The intention is to engage in what Ting-Toomey (1999) refers to as "mindful reflexivity," which "requires us to tune in to our own cultural and personal habitual assumptions in viewing an interaction scene" (p. 267) so that we are less likely to make quick, unconscious judgments and evaluations about unfamiliar behaviors.

CASE IN POINT: CULTURE DOES MATTER

In this case study, the context is one-on-one online teaching Tuula did with a professional newcomer, a Chinese medical doctor whose speaking and listening skills in English were assessed at the elementary level. At the time, Yan Li could read and write at the intermediate level of proficiency.[1] She had asked to be enrolled in the Language Instruction for Newcomers to Canada Home Study program that combines self-study with a weekly call with a teacher online.

The student in the Home Study program has 24-7 access to a web-based portal with a full curriculum organized into themes of community, workplace, and education with multiple modules and additional web-based language focused resources, including videos and audio links. The content is both culturally and linguistically rich as well as organized by language proficiency levels around the four skills of reading, writing, listening, and speaking. All students are encouraged to use the portal for self-study in addition to instructor-led weekly lessons and homework.

CASE STUDY: YAN LI

Yan Li and her daughter had lived in Canada for a year in a small city, Fredericton, New Brunswick. Her husband still worked in Shanghai in the IT industry and traveled to Canada every 3 months to see the family for a short holiday. The daughter was in Grade 7 in a Canadian school, leaving the mother isolated at home for most of the weekdays.

Yan Li's only regular exposure to English was a weekly online study call with Tuula as her Language Instruction for Newcomers to Canada Home Study teacher. Occasionally, she met some of her neighbors while she was shoveling snow or did yard work in front of her house. Even though Tuula tried to joke about the snowstorms, she could tell that Yan Li was having trouble even talking about her daily chores in   ➔

[1] Student name is a pseudonym.

English. She used Mandarin on the phone with her husband and in conversations with her daughter. She was struggling to understand Tuula on Skype, and they often used Instant Messaging to clarify meaning by writing notes to each other. If Tuula found it frustrating to teach, Yan Li felt exhausted by the effort of keeping up.

Tuula became Yan Li's cultural informant in a hurry. She quickly realized that Yan Li was in culture shock and had a hard time adjusting to the weather and the new city she and her family had settled in. To make her situation even more complicated, she was now living as a housewife and cut off from her profession as the practitioner of traditional Chinese medicine.

This example shows how difficult settlement is in a smaller city that does not have a sizeable community representing a learner's home culture. Some of the more long-standing and larger immigrant populations in big cities have developed internally cohesive communities with places of worship, community networks, a newspaper, and other own-language media and services in which their native language survives. As a health care professional and caregiver by occupation, Yan Li was also more likely to expect herself to be able to deal with the adjustment better than she did. She lived "in Mandarin" but in a city that is culturally and linguistically predominantly English Canadian.

What could the teacher recommend? Given the difficulties they had communicating via Skype, Tuula advised her to consider enrolling in a face-to-face classroom ESOL course in her community. This option, she explained, was more beneficial at the time because Yan Li needed to become more integrated in her local English-speaking community and meet other students and residents. She needed to listen to English and speak the language in interaction with others to give her the much-needed intercultural practice. Going outside the home to a class would also help her become less isolated and more integrated into the new culture.

What could a teacher do as a classroom strategist with only one student?

There were two approaches that Tuula considered as she got to know Yan Li better and started to understand her situation. First, she suggested that Yan Li start a daily diary and use her writing skills, which were stronger than her speaking skills, to express her ideas and thoughts in English. Yan Li soon learned to love writing about what she felt and how she and her family's lives were changing. This way, she maintained her self-confidence in her ability to continue learning by using her writing skills while working on her weaker listening and speaking.

Second, even though she could not yet practice her profession in Canada, Yan Li could learn from other traditional Chinese medicine practitioners and start to establish contacts in the network of health care professionals in her field. Even if she was not yet able to join in on their discussions in English, she could watch and listen to YouTube videos with closed captions to follow the trends and start finding out more information. She soon found out about the expectations and regulatory practices of her field in Canada and could start developing her short- and long-term plans to return to her profession.

INTERCULTURAL ADJUSTMENT AND CHALLENGES

All ESOL teachers are most likely familiar with the culture shock Yan Li is experiencing in this scenario. Tuula found it immensely helpful as Yan Li's instructor to recall her own experiences as a new immigrant to Canada decades earlier. Her lived experiences left her with indelible changes. She still recalls clearly how difficult it was to adjust to the many differences while, on the one hand, she often felt homesick and, on the other hand, excited about a new life in a new country. Expatriates also share these feelings of simultaneous discomfort and excitement. These often conflicting and contradictory emotions and feelings about home are significant cultural knowledge to share with your learners. If you have never experienced this kind of disconnect, you can begin by familiarizing yourself with the research on acculturation and the changes that take place physically and psychologically when someone ventures into a new and uncertain cultural domain.

References

Alberta Teachers of English as a Second Language. (2009). *Adult ESL curriculum framework: Intercultural communicative competence*. Retrieved from https://www.atesl.ca/resources/atesl-adult-esl-curriculum-framework/

American Council on the Teaching of Foreign Languages. (2017). NCSSFL-ACTFL Can-do statements. Retrieved from https://www.actfl.org/publications/guidelines-and-manuals/ncssfl-actfl-can-do-statements

Arasaratnam, L. A. (2009, May). The development of a new instrument of intercultural communication competence. *Journal of Intercultural Communication, 20*.

Arasaratnam, L. A., & Doerfel, M. L. (2005). Intercultural communication competence: Identifying key components from multicultural perspectives. *International Journal of Intercultural Relations, 29*(2), 137–163.

Arasaratnam-Smith, L. A. (2016) An exploration of the relationship between intercultural communication competence and bilingualism. *Communication Research Reports, 33*(3), 231–238.

Atkinson, D. (1999). TESOL and culture. *TESOL Quarterly, 33*(4), 625–654.

Barry, L. (2014). *Syllabus: Notes from an accidental professor*. Montreal, Quebec, Canada: Drawn and Quarterly.

Bennett, M. J. (2014). *The development model of intercultural sensitivity*. Retrieved from http://www.idrinstitute.org/page.asp?menu1=15

Bok, D. (2009). Foreword. In D. Deardorff (Ed.), *The Sage handbook of intercultural competence* (pp. ix–xiv). Thousand Oaks, CA: Sage.

Brainy Quote. (2018). Toni Morrison quotes. Retrieved from https://www.brainyquote.com/authors/toni_morrison

Byram, M. (2001). Introduction. In M. Byram, A. Nichols, & D. Stevens (Eds.), *Developing intercultural competence in practice* (pp. 1–8). Bristol, England: Multilingual Matters.

Byram, M. (2009). The intercultural speaker and the pedagogy of foreign language education. In D. Deardorff (Ed.), *The Sage handbook of intercultural competence* (pp. 321–332). Thousand Oaks, CA: Sage.

Byram, M., Gribkova, B., & Starkey, H. (2002). *Developing the intercultural dimension in language teaching: A practical introduction for teachers.* Strasbourg, France: Council of Europe. Retrieved from https://www.coe.int/t/dg4/linguistic/Source/Guide _dimintercult_EN.pdf

Byram, M., & Wagner, M. (2018). Making a difference: Language teaching for intercultural and international dialogue. *Foreign Language Annals, 51,* 140–151. Retrieved from https://onlinelibrary.wiley.com/doi/full/10.1111/flan.12319

Byram, M., & Zarate, G. (1996). Defining and assessing intercultural competence: Some principles and proposals for the European context. *Language Teaching, 29,* 239–243.

Center for Advanced Research on Language Acquisition. (2016). Pragmatics and speech acts. Retrieved from http://carla.umn.edu/speechacts/index.html

Citizenship and Immigration Canada. (2012). *Canadian language benchmarks: English as a second language for adults.* Retrieved from http://www.cic.gc.ca/english/pdf/pub /language-benchmarks.pdf

Codrescu, A. (1995, Fall). Navigating among cultures: Why we should revive the oral tradition. *International Educator,* 11–14.

Cohen, A., & Sykes, J. (2013). Strategy-based learning of pragmatics for intercultural education. In F. Dervin & A. Liddicoat (Eds.), *Linguistics for intercultural education* (pp. 87–111). Amsterdam, the Netherlands: John Benjamins.

Corbett, J. (2003). *An intercultural approach to English language teaching.* Clevedon, England: Multilingual Matters.

Corbett, J. (2014). Communicative competence. *Key Concepts in Intercultural Dialogue, 9.* Retrieved from https://centerforinterculturaldialogue.files.wordpress.com/2014/04 /key-concept-communicative-competence.pdf

Council of Europe. (2001). *Common European framework of reference for languages: Learning, teaching, assessment.* Cambridge, England: Cambridge University Press.

Council of Ministers of Education Canada. (2010). *Working with the Common European Framework of Reference for Languages (CEFR) in the Canadian context: Guide for policy-makers and curriculum designers.* Retrieved from http://www.cmec.ca/docs /assessment/CEFR-canadian-context.pdf

Deardorff, D. (2006). Identification and assessment of intercultural competence as a student outcome of internationalization. *Journal of Studies in International Education, 10*(3), 241–266.

Deardorff, D. (Ed.). (2009). *The Sage handbook of intercultural competence.* Thousand Oaks, CA: Sage.

Deardorff, D. (2011). Assessing intercultural competence. *New Directions for Institutional Research, 149,* 65–79.

Dooley, K. (2009). Intercultural conversation: Building understanding together. *Journal of Adolescent and Adult Literacy, 52*(6), 497–506.

Dytynyshyn, N., & Collins, L. (2012). Culture and interculturality in the adult ESL context in urban Quebec: A case study. *TESL Canada, 30*(1), 45–68.

Fantini, A. (Ed.). (1997). *New ways of teaching culture.* Alexandria, VA: TESOL International Association.

Fantini, A. (2009). Assessing intercultural competence: Issues and tools. In D. Deardorff (Ed.), *The Sage handbook of intercultural competence* (pp. 456–476). Thousand Oaks, CA: Sage.

Hammond, Z. (2015). *Culturally responsive teaching and the brain: Promoting authentic engagement and rigor among culturally and linguistically diverse students.* Thousand Oaks, CA: Corwin.

Hinkel, E. (2013). Culture and pragmatics in language teaching and learning. In M. Celce-Murcia, D. Brinton, & M. Snow (Eds.), *Teaching English as a second or foreign language* (4th ed., pp. 394–408). Boston, MA: National Geographic Learning.

Holmes, P., & O'Neill, G. (2012). Developing and evaluating intercultural competence: Ethnographies of intercultural encounters. *International Journal of Intercultural Relations, 36*, 707–718.

House, J. (2007). What is an 'intercultural speaker'? In E. Soler & M. Jordà (Eds.), *Intercultural language use and language learning* (pp. 7–22). Dordrecht, the Netherlands: Springer.

Humphrey, D. (2002). Intercultural communication: A teaching and learning framework. Center for Languages, Linguistics & Area Studies. Retrieved from https://www.llas.ac.uk/resources/paper/1303

Ilieva, R. (2001). Living with ambiguity: Toward culture exploration in adult second-language classrooms. *TESL Canada Journal, 19*, 1–16.

The IRIS Center. (2009). Cultural and linguistic differences: What teachers should know. Retrieved from https://iris.peabody.vanderbilt.edu/module/clde/

Ishihara, N., & Cohen, A. (2010). *Teaching and learning pragmatics: Where language and culture meet.* London, England: Routledge.

Ishihara, N., & Cohen, A. (2012). Teaching and learning pragmatics: Response to Peter Grundy. *ELT Journal, 66*(3), 377–379.

Iyer, P. (2013, June). *Pico Iyer: TEDGlobal 2013: Where is home?* [Video file]. Retrieved from https://www.ted.com/talks/pico_iyer_where_is_home

Jackson, J. (2016). Language and intercultural communication. *Key Concepts in Intercultural Dialogue, 78*. Retrieved from https://centerforinterculturaldialogue.files.wordpress.com/2016/06/kc78-lg-icc.pdf

Kramsch, C. (2006). From communicative competence to symbolic competence. *Modern Language Journal, 90*, 249–252.

Laroche, L., & Yang, C. (2014). *Danger and opportunity: Building cultural diversity for competitive advantage.* New York, NY: Routledge.

Lenchuk, I., & Ahmed, A. (2013). Teaching pragmatic competence: A journey from teaching cultural facts to teaching cultural awareness. *TESL Canada Journal, 30*(7), 82–97.

Li, X., Myles, J., & Robinson, P. (2011). *Teaching ESL in Canada.* Don Mills, Ontario, Canada: Oxford University Press.

Liebkind, K., Mahonen, T., Varjonen, S., & Jasinskaja-Lahti, I. (2016). Acculturation and identity. In D. Sam & J. Berry (Eds.), *The Cambridge handbook of acculturation psychology* (pp. 30–49). Cambridge, England: Cambridge University Press.

Makarchuk, D. (2010). Oral dialogue journals: Theory and implementation in the classroom. *English Teaching, 65*(1), 189–219.

Masgoret, A., & Ward, C. (2006). Culture learning approach to acculturation. In D. Sam & J. Berry (Eds.), *The Cambridge handbook of acculturation psychology* (pp. 58–77). New York, NY: Cambridge University Press.

Massachusetts Department of Education, Adult and Community Learning Services. (2005). *Massachusetts adult education curriculum framework for English for speakers of other languages (ESOL).* Retrieved from http://www.doe.mass.edu/acls/frameworks /esol.pdf

Menard-Warwick, J. (2009). Co-constructing representations of culture in ESL and EFL classrooms: Discursive faultlines in Chile and California. *The Modern Language Journal, 93*(1), 30–45.

Moeller, A. K., & Nugent, K. (2014). Building intercultural competence in the language classroom. In S. Dhonau (Ed.), *Unlock the gateway to communication* (pp. 1–18). Retrieved from http://digitalcommons.unl.edu/cgi/viewcontent.cgi?article=1160 &context=teachlearnfacpub

Moloney, R. (2008). You just want to be like that teacher: Modelling and intercultural competence in young language learners. *Babel, 42*(3). 10–16.

Nam, K., & Condon, J. (2010). The DIE is cast: The continuing evolution of intercultural communication's favorite classroom exercise. *International Journal of Intercultural Relations, 34*(1), 81–87.

Nordquist, R. (2017). Conversational implicature definition and examples. Retrieved from https://www.thoughtco.com/conversational-implicature-speech-acts-1689922

Ochs, E. (2002). Becoming a speaker of culture. In C. Kramsch (Ed.), *Ecological perspectives on language acquisition and language socialization* (pp. 99–120). London, England: Continuum.

Pusch, M. (2004). Intercultural training in historical perspective. In D. Landis, J. Bennett, & M. Bennett (Eds.), *Handbook of intercultural training* (pp. 13–36). Thousand Oaks, CA: Sage.

Reid, E. (2015). Techniques developing intercultural communicative competences in English language lessons. *Procedia-Social and Behavioral Sciences, 86*, 939–943.

Scarino, A. (2007). *Discussion paper 6: Assessing intercultural language learning.* Retrieved from http://www.iltlp.unisa.edu.au/papers.html#paper6

Scarino, A. (2010). Assessing intercultural capability in learning languages: A renewed understanding of language, culture, learning, and the nature of assessment. *The Modern Language Journal, 94*(2), 324–329.

Scarino, A., & Crichton, J. (2007). *Discussion paper 1: Why the intercultural matters to languages teaching and learning: An orientation to the ILTLP programme.* Retrieved from http://www.iltlp.unisa.edu.au/papers.html#paper1

Shaules, J. (2016). The developmental model of linguaculture learning: An integrated approach to language and culture pedagogy. *Juntendo Journal of Global Studies, 1,* 2–17. Retrieved from https://www.researchgate.net/publication/307013176_The _Developmental_Model_of_Linguaculture_Learning_An_integrated_approach _to_language_and_culture_pedagogy

Sparrow, L. (2000). Comments on Dwight Atkinson's TESOL and culture: Another reader reacts. *TESOL Quarterly, 34,* 747–752.

Ting-Toomey, S. (1999). *Communicating across cultures.* New York, NY: The Guilford Press.

Walsh-Marr, J. (2011). Keeping up the conversation on culture: A response to Robert Courchêne and others. *TESL Canada Journal, 29*(1), 115–120.

Ward, C., & Wilson, J. (2014). Conceptualizing, measuring and predicting intercultural competence. In X. Dai & G. Chen (Eds.), *Intercultural communication competence* (pp. 41–68). Newcastle upon Tyne, England: Cambridge Scholars.

Waugh, E. (2013). Teaching pragmatics and intercultural communication online. *TESL Canada Journal, 30*(7), 82–97.

Yang, L., & Fleming, M. (2013). How Chinese college students make sense of foreign films and TV series: Implications for the development intercultural communicative competence in ELT. *The Language Learning Journal, 41*(3), 297–310.

TEACHER AS A CULTURAL INFORMANT AND CLASSROOM STRATEGIST

OVERVIEW

The culturally diverse English to speakers of other languages (ESOL) classroom is challenging, complicated, and extremely rewarding as teachers face an array of students from different cultures and backgrounds. It is the teacher to whom students refer for not only modeling English language and culture, but also advice on every life situation. In this respect, the teacher acts as a cultural informant and role model. It is also the teacher, in the role of mediator, who may realize that some students are not getting along well with others and that the reason may be misunderstandings because of differences in cultural perceptions. Instructors (and/or settlement workers) are often the first contacts that newcomers have in an English-speaking community, and they impact the way students view their physical surroundings; their new place of residence; their understandings of unfamiliar belief systems, values, and practices; and how they enter into new social and professional relationships (Hawkins & Norton, 2009).

In this chapter, we discuss teacher cultural beliefs and biases, the role of the teacher as a cultural informant and strategist, English language teachers from countries in which English is not the dominant language, and managing cultural conflicts should they arise.

THINKING ABOUT THE TOPIC

Here are a few questions for further reflection on how to teach ESOL learners in cultural transition, what might be required to more effectively integrate cultural knowledge into the curriculum, and how to teach communicative competence.

- How do I become more informed on intercultural/global issues and how can I understand them from other perspectives?

- How do I develop a better understanding of my students' perspectives and backgrounds?

- How can I come to terms with my own cultural biases?

- How can I become better at being a cultural informant, especially if I am from another cultural and language background than my students?

- How am I already working as a classroom strategist? How can I improve?

- How can I resolve cultural conflicts in the classroom? What makes the conflict specifically cultural?

- Which conflict resolution strategies are most effective in the ESOL classroom?

THEORETICAL PERSPECTIVES

A Teacher's Culture, Beliefs, and Biases

To be effective in our role as cultural informant and classroom strategist, it is paramount that teachers identify their own needs in culture learning. In other words, it is important to explore how our own socioculturally determined beliefs, assumptions, biases, and expectations affect our classroom behaviors and views on education. In a multicultural, multilingual ESOL classroom, teachers' attitudes toward other cultures and cultural differences, as well as their professional knowledge and teaching strategies and methods, all play an important role in learning outcomes. What teachers know and believe provides the underlying framework that guides our instructional judgments and classroom actions at every level of educational practice. Sharing personal stories is a good way to start. For example, if an American native-English-speaking teacher (NEST) has at one time been the primary caregiver for his children, he can share his experiences with his ESOL class to perhaps counter cultural stereotypes about Western male roles held by his students and to enhance multidirectional learning through thought-provoking discussions (Li, Myles, & Robinson, 2012).

As teachers, our beliefs about education stem from our own learning and teaching experiences and from common practices in the social context that has nurtured us. When Johanne was teaching English for academic purposes in Indonesia, she wondered why her students were having so much difficulty writing essays and critically discussing academic topics. At the time, she was told by other Australian and British teachers that she, unlike her students, was able to write and critique the way she did because of her unique enculturation into a sociocultural and educational environment that promoted a strong individualism and a utilitarian or Eurocentric way of thinking steeped in Judeo-Christian values. Scollon, Scollon, and Jones (2012) outline the ideological principles of utilitarian thinking. They also remind us that these principles could easily be taken as the governing principles of public schools in European-based societies.

1. Good is defined as what will give the greatest happiness for the largest number of people.

2. Progress (aimed at happiness, wealth, and individuality) is the goal of society.

3. The free and equal individual is the basis of society.

4. Humans are seen to be rational and economic.

5. Technology and invention are the sources of societal wealth.

6. Creative, inventive individuals are the most valuable in society.

7. Statistics (e.g., using public opinion polls and market surveys) are the best means of determining values.

The expectations that English language teachers and ESOL learners have for one another may not always align because their beliefs about language learning and teaching are shaped by their respective cultural bearings. Johanne had never thought of herself as having a distinct Judeo-Christian, individualistic, utilitarian cultural background. However, upon reflection, she realized that the culture in which she had grown up was very different from that of her ESOL learners, many of whom were raised in a more collective-oriented culture. Differences, such as adherence to authority, which in a collectivistic culture are often exhibited in teacher-centered forms of instruction with few opportunities to under-stand issues from multiple perspectives, affect ways of thinking and forms of expression in a major way (Widi Nugroho, 2008).

Besides Johanne's family orientation and more learner-centered schooling, her daily exposure to Western media (particularly television shows that debate current affairs and newspapers with editorials that critique the government) have had an impact on her thoughts and actions. For example, the focus on inquiry, group activities, and project-based learning would likely lead to different ways of learning than in a culture with a focus on understanding and acquiring knowledge that can be systematically tested. In this regard, students may not be totally comfortable with what material a teacher presents to the class, or how they present it (Li, Myles, & Robinson, 2012). Such variations in the perceptions and practices in language learning raise the following questions:

- Should English language teachers try to modify their learners' cultural perceptions and learning styles or should they affirm them, by recognizing those perceptions and styles as different ways of learning, and try to make accommodations?

- How do teachers know what their learners expect from them? And is it teachers' duty to comply with student expectations?

Teachers' attitudes toward learners' home cultures and their cultural practices can greatly affect the classroom dynamic and learning. When teachers acknowledge, appreciate, and show curiosity about cultural practices different from their own, learners gain affirmation and confidence in themselves. As was mentioned in previous chapters, affirming cultural orientations is not just about "show and tell"; it involves the day-to-day, moment-to-moment interactions students have with their teachers and classmates. For example, knowing that it is a learner's birthday can bring forth a discussion about differ-ent ways people celebrate birthdays around the world. What kind of gifts are given, if any?

Who supplies the cake, if there is one? Is it the individual whose birthday it is or a family member or friend? And why might the cake be provided by the person whose birthday it is in some cultures and not in others? On a deeper level, however, students may decide to discuss or present topics that are perfectly fine to raise in their home culture but not usually mentioned in a public forum, such as those concerning personal hygiene or economic status. When these cases occur, it is important that teachers do not mock, judge, or depreciate such choices but address the situation diplomatically and turn the lesson into a cultural learning experience for everyone.

Hofstede (1986) emphasizes that teacher training courses need to encourage candidates to learn about their own culture and come to terms with the reality, both intellectually and emotionally, that in other societies, people learn in different ways. Such an exercise involves taking a step back from one's values and personal beliefs and looking at the big teaching picture, which is far from easy. Indeed, there may be occasions that require teachers to adopt pedagogy considered to be out of date and ineffective. But Hofstede (1986) also gives an example of how teachers can be creative in accommodating learners who may feel threatened. He mentions the case of a teacher who was having difficulty getting her mostly Asian students to speak up in class. In this particular situation, they were expected to give an evaluation of what they had learned. To encourage participation, the teacher decided to pass a pencil around, and whoever had the pencil was expected to speak. Passing the pencil was a nice, symbolic way of institutionalizing the "speaking up" process.

English language teachers' beliefs and practices are not static; they may evolve over time when teachers receive more professional (in this case) intercultural training and are exposed to a variety of cultures, through their classes, travel, or teaching and living abroad. Attitudes, teacher beliefs, and reflective practice that focus on culture learning all play a role in shaping the ESOL classroom as teachers engage with their students, who are also meeting classmates from different cultures. In short, English language teachers need to develop an informed awareness of their own culture. For example, reflecting on her personal experiences, women's studies professor Peggy McIntosh wrote an article in 1989, which has since become a classic, entitled "White Privilege: Unpacking the Invisible Knapsack." In the article, she reflects on the power and privilege she has as a White person living in a culture that systematically advantages White people in all walks of life. Teachers also need to understand how the power dynamic, cultural values, and culture as forms of knowledge and skills play out in the classroom.

ASKING CULTURAL QUESTIONS

English language teachers can ask themselves the following questions:

- **Attitudes:** Do I prejudge my students? Am I eager to learn from them? How do I react when I don't understand something my students are doing or saying?
- **Knowledge:** Am I aware of my own and my students' cultural behaviors and why we think and act the way we do?   ➔

- **Skills:** How much do I really listen to my students? Do I evaluate first before understanding their behaviors?
- **Internal Outcome:** Am I aware of how my students wish to be treated? Do I meet students where they are at or do I have other expectations of their behavior based on feelings I have about my own culture? How adaptable am I? How flexible?
- **External Outcome:** How culturally appropriate have I been with my students when I interact with them? What can I do differently in the future?

Based on Deardorff's (2006) model of intercultural competence.

 See **A Step-by-Step Guide to Understanding One's Cultural Identity** in the Classroom Best Practices section of this chapter.

Cultural Informants

In some languages, only one word is used for both *teach* and *learn*, as in Czech, *učit*. Teaching and learning, in other words, are expressed as two sides of the same process. With regard to teaching and learning the many sociopragmatic aspects of language, teachers also have a great deal to learn from our learners by making inquiries related to indigenous cultural practices. The role of being a cultural informant and a classroom strategist is a two-way relationship that to be successful requires sharing of cultural perspectives in the classroom. The teacher as a cultural informant and a strategist not only integrates cultural knowledge into teaching but is also willing to engage students in developing more critical intercultural awareness. No doubt as cultural informants, English language teachers have a valuable role to play in the classroom and a lot of self-exploration to do in recognizing their own behaviors.

The term *cultural informant* is used widely in anthropology, particularly ethnographic fieldwork, whereby anthropologists spend a great deal of time with their cultural informants to find out more about the communities they are studying (McCurdy, Spradley, & Shandy, 2005). Cultural informants are also mentioned in literature that focuses on intercultural training and study-abroad for college and university students (Kinginger, 2013). However, English language teachers, by the very nature of their work, are cultural informants in every sense of the word. They are able to shed light on aspects of the target culture through their behavior and explicit instruction and guidance; they answer questions and act as role models.

As cultural informants, English language teachers explain, break down, and illustrate some of the differences between the culture in which students are immersed and that of their home countries. As Hinkel (2013) claims, teachers need to understand how students' first cultures work and how it impacts their behaviors and ability to learn. She gives the example of some students rarely speaking or asking questions in class even though they do not understand instructions or a point in the lesson. However, other students may dominate most classroom interactions, eagerly waving their hands and interrupting the flow. Why might this be the case?

LANGUAGES AND CULTURE

When Tuula lived and worked in southern India for a few years as a Canadian learning professional, she wanted to greet local people and neighbors in the morning with *Namaste*, a common Hindi word to say hello. She soon discovered though that it was *not* to be used with a Muslim person, who should be greeted with *As-salaam alaikum* instead.

Because as an outsider she clearly lacked the ability the locals have to tell an Indian Muslim from a Hindu, she mostly ended up using English to avoid a potentially embarrassing situation. In fact, she quickly realized that despite her best intentions of learning some Hindi and Telugu used in the southern state she lived in, she ended up using English as her default language of communication. It was simply a whole lot easier. The locals inevitably saw her as a non-Indian outsider to begin with and felt most comfortable when she *sounded* like a foreigner, too.

Later, as Tuula became more familiar hearing Hindi spoken around her, she was told that because India is such a large subcontinent with hundreds of local languages, many Indians also use local varieties of Hindi. Again, as an outsider she would have gotten lost testing her "bookish" Hindi on Indians who mixed English with theirs to make sure they also were understood by others who didn't use the same particular Hindi variety. In short, the intricate skill of mixing these languages to produce *Hinglish* in speaking is a fine-tuned skill acquired through a lifetime of use in the specific sociocultural context of India.

Another aspect to consider is that of power relationships and how hierarchies are created and sustained in the classroom. Teachers of ESOL adults form relationships with students; they also share experiences and information related to course content. For students to be treated fairly and feel respected and valued, teachers need to be aware of their own power as English speakers with a broad understanding of target culture structures and behaviors. They also need to be cognizant of how the power dynamic based on cultural differences unfolds among students in the classroom. It is important to ask yourself questions, such as:

- Are all learners being included in whole class discussions and taking leadership roles when working in groups?

- Are all learners encouraged to ask questions and are their questions answered appropriately?

- Are you paying more attention to learners who come from cultures more aligned to your own?

- Are you making accommodations for learners who have dietary restrictions and traditions based on their cultural orientation?

- How are you adjusting your teaching practices to take into account power dynamics in the classroom?

- Are you as a teacher also sharing anecdotes and stories of your own cross-cultural experiences and challenges with learners?

Classroom Strategists

How do teachers act as classroom strategists? What do we mean by *strategist*? The teacher as strategist involves two components: the strategies teachers use in class instruction and the strategies they teach their learners to better prepare them for the culture in which they are immersed. Teachers use a range of strategies for planning and implementing lessons, facilitating classroom discussions and activities, and assessing learning, among other instructional practices. Teachers also make decisions, and some of them are made on the spot, such as determining if a particular grammatical structure requires a teaching moment.

In adult ESOL classrooms, cultural issues come up all the time. Some of these issues may be general, such as what to bring a host whose house you've been invited to for dinner, while others may be of a more sensitive nature, such as how to communicate with a family doctor about a personal health concern. As a strategist, English language teachers need to determine what kind of cultural issues are of importance to the whole class and what may best be addressed in private, or among a small group of students. They need to be aware of gender relations and their cultural orientations that may differ from those of the target culture. Topics related to global politics, religion, and sociocultural attitudes also need to be handled diplomatically.

The logical extension of an English language teacher's role is to inform learners of the cultural practices and strategies they need to know. Sociolinguistic elements of language are closely tied to teaching pragmatics and the discourses that go with context-specific learning. Studies of other cultures (e.g., how politeness is expressed socially in different parts of the world) provide the broader context for English language teachers to appreciate just how challenging it can be to adjust to and negotiate new linguistic and cultural norms. ESOL learners also need to learn and apply strategies in their daily lives. For example, when an English language teacher advises and guides immigrant parents in how to use language in a meeting with the teacher of their children at school, the teacher is acting as a cultural informant and a strategist. The situation requires knowledge and understanding of what to say and how to speak to the teacher as well as the strategies that work best, including active listening, responding constructively to feedback, and asking appropriate questions. Another example is the myriad ways people greet each other across cultures. A verbal greeting is only a small, although significant, part of a more complex show of appropriate body language, tone of voice, and demeanor. What to say, how, and in which situations are all part of the complex cultural knowledge our learners expect their teacher to share with them.

Teaching an ESOL learner job search strategies and how to handle a North American job interview process are other examples of how knowing more about the sociocultural expectations help make a student's experience successful. Knowing not only what to say but also *how* to behave in a job interview is as important as having fluency and accuracy of language. Here, understanding cultures and intercultural communication goes beyond teaching the linguistic elements of language. The sociopragmatic knowledge—the situation-specific discourses that are required to know what and how to say something—

are as important as learners knowing English grammar, pronunciation, and mastering the art of writing effectively.

 See **Preparing for a Job Interview** in Chapter 5 for a few suggestions on how you might want to prepare and offer concrete strategies to your learners for job interviews in a North American cultural context.

However diverse the curricula and the ESOL learners we have in our classrooms, the teacher is still the one person who can act as the best cultural informant and strategist because our learners—newcomers and international students alike—do not as a rule "live in English." They are in cultural transition and live in their own communities. They generally communicate in their first language and surround themselves with familiar cultural rituals and values. The ESOL classroom is often a place in which learners are introduced to other practices that are not only intercultural but also individually new and challenging, such as finding a place to live or obtaining a driver's license. Acting as a trusted adviser by providing advice and suggestions for dealing with unfamiliar situations is also part of being an ESOL teacher and classroom strategist. The term *trusted advisor* stems from the business community but applies equally well to the English language teacher. Again, as teachers they are on the front lines; they build relationships between learners, and students trust their judgment and expertise to the degree that they will be the first, if not only, people their students approach on matters related to everyday family or work situations. For example, if a landlord communicates in a way that a student interprets as "he refused us the apartment because he doesn't want to rent to a family with small children," the teacher can explain the student's rights and legislation involved with regards to housing practices, human rights, and landlord behavior.

Tuula has found that adult ESOL learners may at times ask for advice about issues that are more personal than she would expect. For example, during a coffee break in her college writing course, an Iranian student whose daughter had just started in the college's law enforcement training program asked Tuula if she could recommend how to talk to her daughter about the anxiety her daughter felt being one of the very few young women in the male-dominated study program. Though Tuula realized she had to be careful in how to respond appropriately to her student in this situation, she also realized that the student had approached her because she would probably have talked to her teacher in her home country. Teachers in general are held in high regard in many cultures and countries as trusted advisors.

STUDENTS AS CULTURAL INFORMANTS

Teaching online without face-to-face contact or pictures can have its own set of cultural challenges. In Johanne's online additional qualifications course in ESL, teachers post an introduction to themselves on the discussion board at the beginning of the course. She puts together a summary of their introductions, so they are available to the students in one document. After posting the document, she received an email from Rupinder Kaur, one of the teachers who trained in the Montessori Method, as follows:

> Thanks for creating the personal profiles . . . It was hilarious though to see my profile with He/his. I forgot to mention in my profile about my gender as my name may not indicate it. I would like to add here an additional information on last names from our community (Sikhs). Most last names are either Kaur or Singh which means all Kaurs are women and all Singhs are men.

Rather embarrassed, if not mortified because she should have known better, Johanne replied in the following way:

> Ah! Thank you so much for informing me about your gender. I am so sorry for this mishap, you know I should have checked your name before making assumptions that Rupinder Kaur was a male. Even though you have Montessori and early childhood education training, I didn't assume you were a female considering that probably 95% of those teachers are female! Anyway, I'll send a message to everyone correcting my mistake. And thanks for being a wonderful cultural informant. I learned 2 things today: all Kaurs are females and that teachers shouldn't make assumptions about gender in names when teaching online courses.

And then Rupinder replied,

> No worries . . . I would further mention here about one more thing, we all can have the same first names, for example, Rupinder can be both, males and females. But last name Kaur is definitely a female last name. Singh is mostly (ninety percent) last name for males but can be used for females or used as Mrs. Singh. But males cannot be called Mr. Kaur (Male dominated world, right?).

 See **Approaches to Fulfilling Your Role as Cultural Informant and Strategist** in the Classroom Best Practices section of this chapter.

NONNATIVE-ENGLISH-SPEAKING TEACHERS FROM OUTSIDE THE TARGET CULTURE

In many educational contexts, ESOL and English language development are increasingly taught by nonnative-English-speaking teachers (NNESTs) with varied cultural backgrounds. Though the linguistic boundaries of native and nonnative English speakers are no longer clear and even the notion of these two entities have become obsolete (Canagarajah, 2005), there is still the aspect of culture to consider. Indeed, English language teachers of other than Anglo-Saxon cultural backgrounds are more likely to be familiar with the role of a cultural informant in the classroom. They can often relate more directly to the experiences their students have in navigating multiple cultural meanings while learning to interpret cultural-and linguistic-specific clues in English. Through indirect modeling, NNESTs can share experiences of what it is like to be multilingual; to deal with culture shock, identity crises, and sense of belonging; and to communicate in a language other than one's first language. Kramsch (2009) reminds us that "our students learn as much from who we show ourselves to be and what we do, as from what we say in class" (p. 209). Research has also shown that NNESTs often show a deep sensitivity to their students' needs and are better able to develop an effective curriculum and pedagogy (Auerbach et al., 1996) than NESTs. Kamhi-Stein (2002) claims that NNESTs' self-identification as teachers, immigrants, and ESOL learners significantly affects their classroom instruction. She found that NNESTs bring together the commonalities among linguistic and ethnic groups represented in the class as a way to collaborate and create a community of students; they may apply instructional materials developed in countries outside the mainstream to offer a variety of perspectives and use their own and their students' experiences as sources of knowledge.

JUGGLING MORE THAN ONE CULTURE

Think of the years of experience some NNESTs have living and working in an English-speaking country, or conversely, that there are NESTs who have also lived and worked for periods of time in a culture apart from their English-speaking home country. These lived experiences influence greatly what such teachers bring to the role of cultural informant. Tuula (who is a NNEST and has immigrated to Canada from Finland) and Johanne (who is a NEST and has lived and worked in Zambia and Indonesia) have awareness of the important role of cultural knowledge in language learning: It is not just a benefit but an asset to have lived experiences **straddling two or more cultures**.

Having a native language in common with students or knowing another language is a source of strength in ESOL teaching. For example, teachers can rely on their native language as a wonderful resource to demonstrate how the phonology of another language influences speech, or they can select idioms and proverbs and compare them with those written in English. Learners often use their native language in the process of transitioning from one culture to another over a longer time than one would expect. Among the many benefits, using the first language allows for a full and deep expression of emotions, which is not easy to do in newly acquired English. Speaking one's own language also provides a means of maintaining identity in the new culturally/ linguistically unfamiliar and challenging phases of settlement. In that regard, when the teacher and learners communicate in a common language other than English, the teacher can affirm that identity and instill confidence their learners. In fact, it is a good idea for all English language teachers to acknowledge and share with their learners the deeper cultural meaning of their first languages as the connection to their ancestry and history.

Besides the benefits of common language, some NNESTs may unfortunately experience linguistic discrimination and credibility and competence issues as a result of their accent. However, they need to realize that the goal is not to sound like an "ideal" native

English speaker, especially in an increasingly globalized and multilingual society. When NNESTs develop a sense of legitimacy about themselves as multicompetent bilingual or trilingual professionals in the field, they pass on this asset to their learners. Nevertheless, the challenge is not language per se, but adding the cultural dimension to their teaching, especially if they have not been raised, educated, and socialized in the target culture. Without this socialization, how can NNESTs acquire the necessary sociocultural knowledge, pragmatic rules, and skills to promote students' acquisition of intercultural competence? Like their learners, NNESTs can also become cultural explorers by thoroughly immersing themselves in the target culture. They can, for example, attend cultural events, observe classrooms in public schools, read local newspapers, and form relationships and dialogue with NESTs and neighbors face-to-face and using social media. Through such participation, teachers can gradually acquire the knowledge, skills, and attitudes to become teachers of language *and* intercultural competence (Corbett, 2003; Ortaçtepe, 2015).

CULTURAL CONFLICTS IN THE CLASSROOM

Cultural conflicts can happen in the classroom, whether they are between teachers and learners or among learners who come from different cultural groups, some of them possibly at war back home or who have had a long history of conflict. We know that culture affects communication and communication affects culture. Cultural conflicts in the classroom occur when learners who have different cultural values, beliefs, and norms of behavior clash, resulting in antagonism, discord, and destabilization of the learning environment. Along with culture, the conflict could be based on one or more of the following prejudices: race, sexual orientation, gender, age, ability, socioeconomic status, religious and political beliefs, rural or urban demographic and so on. For example, while many learners come from cultures that value education and respect for teachers, these cultures may also have more traditionally defined gender roles and roles based on age. Some learners may feel uncomfortable addressing a teacher by their first name or they may openly challenge a teacher's authority because she is young and female (Johnson-Bailey & Cervero, 1998). It is not uncommon for some learners to show more respect for White, male NESTs, which can lead to a challenging classroom environment for a teacher who does not have one or more of those traits.

Cultural Conflicts: Teacher and Student

Cultural clashes can arise when a teacher's instructional style is not meeting the expectations of their learners. For example, pedagogical practices influenced by Chinese Confucianism tend to be teacher centered and authoritarian; as a result, adult ESOL learners who have been schooled in such an approach may find that their teacher's learner-centered, collaborative-based methodology is in conflict with how they wish to be taught. This conflict may be resolved when teachers take the time to first respectfully acknowledge their learners' pedagogical views and later explain why a particular strategy they are using will promote language learning.

CLASSROOM MANAGEMENT AND CULTURE

It is the second day of class and advanced-level ESOL learners are enrolled in a government sponsored program. There are 40 students on the attendance sheet, both male and female, from China, Libya, Saudi Arabia, Ukraine, Thailand, Korea, El Salvador, and Somalia. On the board, the teacher has written prompts, such as, "Have respect for each other's culture" and "Work together as a team." She asks the students to find a partner, preferably someone they don't know from a different culture and of the opposite gender. She asks them to sit together and discuss ways to create a positive learning environment for the rest of the term. Everyone begins to move about to find a partner except a small group of male Muslim students at the front of the room. When the teacher queries their behavior, they politely say that they cannot work with women and would rather work with each other. Another group of students from China remain seated, looking disoriented. They quietly chat among themselves in Mandarin.

No doubt, the teacher had sincere intentions of bringing students together and creating an inclusive classroom in a participatory fashion. Her philosophy of teaching adults was that students should share power and have input into the curriculum and their own learning. They should have the opportunity to explore issues that affect their lives and certainly the aforementioned scenario could foster a discussion of cultural attitudes and behaviors.

However, the teacher could approach the current situation several ways. She could, without prejudice, change the activity and put students in various multicultural groups to discuss cultural taboos and practices in classrooms in their home countries before entering into the originally planned activity. Another option is to carry on, offer no resistance, let students work with whom they choose, and focus on the English language learning inherent in the proposed discussion about classroom etiquette.

When teachers encounter cultural issues that may involve gender or disobedience, it is sometimes most efficient to return one's focus to precise language use unfettered by emotion, thereby lightening the atmosphere and reducing tension. Each situation demands original, insightful, and often on-the-spot responses and strategies.

(Adapted from Li, Myles, & Robinson, 2012)

Cultural Conflicts: Among Students

Cultural conflicts can take place among students from different countries, especially when they are involved in pair or group-oriented activities, because of differences in particular cultural behaviors (e.g., learners may react differently to being touched or kissed, or to having their hand shaken by a person of the opposite gender) or in communication style. What may be a normal, typical and even obligatory way of communicating in one culture can be totally different in another. As a result, when learners are working in pairs and discussing the solution to a problem as part of a language learning activity, for example, they may experience unexpected reactions to comments, or a partner's reaction may not be understood. One learner may appear to react too strongly or abruptly, while the other may appear too timid to voice their opinion in order to keep the relationship harmonious.

Conversational rules, such as how a student pauses in conversation or group discussions, may disrupt effective communication. In some cultures, pauses are very short, and if a person wants to voice an opinion, they have to be prepared to jump in quickly. In other cultures, the pause is significantly longer. People from such cultures, who are accustomed to lengthy pauses, may feel disrespected and perceive those who jump in quickly as pushy and controlling. The issue is that both parties are playing by different rules—rules that neither of them recognize or understand (McKay & Burt, 2010).

In addition, misunderstandings in language and different cultural approaches to providing feedback from teachers and peers, for example, can cloud learner expectations. Sometimes, this evolves into conflict where learners may feel criticisms are personal and negative instead of impartial and positively constructive, especially from their peers.

It may be easier to address a cultural conflict when it is overt; however, emotionally laden antagonisms can take place within a classroom and a teacher may be totally unaware of its occurrence, especially if students are communicating in their native languages. McKay and Burt (2010) share the story of an ESOL teacher who came upon a couple of female Khmer learners having a heated conversation in Khmer that led to a physical fight in the middle of the classroom. The teacher stepped in to separate them although she had the feeling they thought it was not her place to get involved. In retrospect, she realized that her involvement might have shamed them, because she never saw either woman in class again.

The Concept of Face

The concept of face plays a role in intercultural conflict. It is related to people's self-image or self-respect and their concern for how others perceive them in different social interactions, cultures, and contexts. Redmond (2015) explains that our faces are created according to the cultural environment in which we live, and its expectations of appropriate behavior related to common rituals. In other words, how people deal with ways of keeping or saving one's face differs across cultures. For example, if an ESOL customer started bargaining in a store in the United States to achieve a better price on a purchase (a common practice in their native culture), the sales clerk is likely to react with confusion and possibly hostility. As a result, the customer might not only feel embarrassed and confused, but also experience a loss of face due to their culturally inappropriate behavior. An apology from the customer would be in order to restore face and bring a healthy balance to the relationship between the customer and sales clerk.

Facework can be defined as the specific verbal and nonverbal behaviors that we use in interactions to maintain or restore loss of face. It is a term used by researchers to conceptualize and better understand interaction behavior. Intercultural facework proficiency refers to the optimal integration of knowledge and communication skills in effectively managing conflict (Ting-Toomey, 2004). Amarasinghe (2012) points out that

> to understand the intercultural conflict negotiation process, one has to first understand the diverse approaches that people bring with them from different cultures in expressing their different values and norms, their face-saving orientations, goal emphasis, and conflict styles in handling a conflict episode. (p. 176)

Other factors explaining intercultural facework behavior include age, gender, spirituality, language differences, educational level, and social and economic status.

Individual differences and other factors aside, various cultural dimensions have been used to explain behaviors. For example, facework depends on individualistic and collectivistic value tendencies. As you recall from previous chapters, individualistic cultures place a high value on independence, taking initiative, creativity, and authority in decision-making. Individuals are expected to take care of only themselves and their immediate families for their own perceived benefit. Collectivist cultures, on the other hand, value and are loyal to the group above the individual. Harmony, getting along and maintaining face are seen as all-important (Hofstede, Hofstede, & Minkov, 2010).

Power-Distance, the way a culture deals with status differences and social hierarchies, also plays a role in facework (Ting-Toomey, 2004). People in societies exhibiting a large degree of Power-Distance accept a hierarchical order in which everybody has a place and pleasing one's superior, whether they are a boss or teacher, is the best strategy for working harmoniously. In societies with low Power-Distance, people strive for equal distribution of power. With regards to managing conflict, collectivists from societies with high Power-Distance tend to engage in indirect styles of conflict negotiation, and individualists from societies with low Power-Distance display explicit verbal messages to convey personal thoughts, feelings, and opinions. For example, in East Asian cultures, conflicts tend to be avoided or they are resolved through mediators who are carefully selected by both parties, and in the United States, conflicts are generally dealt with more directly and right on the spot (Laroche & Yang, 2014).

CULTURAL CONFLICT IN GROUP WORK

Knapp (2011) provides a scenario of inappropriate behavior that took place during group work among three ESOL learners in an engineering course in which they were completing a project. The activity was competitive and high stakes as the group that produced the best results received the highest grades in the class. There was also a rule that students who did not adequately contribute to the project would be excluded from the high grade. The team leader of one of the groups had written a letter to the lecturer, complaining about three uncooperative students, one of whom was from India. Apparently, the conflict originated from a misunderstanding concerning the obligation to take part in an interaction that was not chaired by the lecturer (the authority) and, at the same time, from different assumptions about who was responsible for completing tasks and who was expected to take the initiative.

Knapp (2011) goes into some detail describing the behavior of the lecturer and how he reacted to the letter and the student from India who was not attending group meetings or taking any initiative, preferring to wait for others to give him direction. The lecturer wished to discuss the matter openly, to "make it public," which, as Knapp points out, did not bode well at all with the student from India who saw this as an enormous *face* threat. However, it would have been completely unthinkable for this student to criticize or contradict the lecturer's suggestions, so he remained silent. Such silence was then interpreted by the lecturer as agreement when it may ➜

How students from different cultures keep *face* when they are confronted with a disagreeable situation on the one hand, and a full-blown conflict on the other, varies according to their unique and engrained cultural behavior. Ting-Toomey (2009) describes a study in which a questionnaire was administered to individuals from China, Germany, Japan, and the United States asking them to recall and describe a recent interpersonal conflict. Briefly, the results revealed that cultural individualism-collectivism had a direct effect on conflict styles and saving face. German respondents reported frequent use of direct, confrontational strategies, while the Japanese mentioned the use of different pretending strategies to act as if the conflict was nonexistent. The Chinese participants claimed a variety of avoiding, obliging, and passive-aggressive tactics, and the Americans reported using upfront expression of feelings while remaining calm when handling a conflict situation.

TEACHER/STUDENT CONFLICT

When Johanne was teaching English for academic purposes in Indonesia, she had a student who was upset with her grade. The grade calculation was based on results from a final term exam and classwork assignments that were weighted according to their difficulty. Students required a grade of 70 or higher to continue postgraduate work in Australia, and this student received a 68. As a student, she worked hard, was conscientious, and participated nicely in class, so her grade came to her as a complete shock and, unbeknownst to Johanne, she was very angry. In retrospect, Johanne realized why.

Throughout the term, Johanne continually told students that she was happy to talk with them in her office if there were any problems or they needed extra help completing assignments. As a result, she had the expectation that students would talk directly to her in person if there were a conflict or misunderstanding. As it were, before leaving for the Christmas break, she had checked her box only to find a letter from this student. In the letter, the student's anger jumped off the page! In a most nasty tone, she wrote that Johanne had deceived her and that her grade was totally unfair. The whole time Johanne was reading it, she kept wondering why the student hadn't come to her in person to talk about her feelings. Johanne thought if she had talked directly to her, they could have arrived at a mutually agreeable solution to the problem, because Johanne also wanted the student to continue her studies. In the end, Johanne told the director about the issue, and he suggested finding a way to raise her mark as it was so close to the cut off. He also suggested that Johanne inform the student about the plan by writing a letter to her.

This was Johanne's first experience with receiving and writing letters to deal with a student-teacher conflict. She learned that writing letters is one way that students from particular cultures save *face*.

Managing Cultural Conflicts

English language teachers need to understand and apply their cultural knowledge and skills at mediation to address, navigate through, and diffuse culture-based conflicts as they arise. They need to be competent in intercultural facework. Clearly, it is *how* we work through the conflict that determines our success at resolving the issue. As mentioned before, culture is made up of values, beliefs, and practices that are shared by a group of people, and at times, misunderstandings and miscommunication, let alone competing interests for power, can arise and affect the classroom dynamic.

Though learning can still take place when there are disagreements (if managed appropriately and kept reasonable), it is when the power dynamic in the classroom becomes inequitable and mutual respect is no longer an underlying element to the learning process that problems can arise. At this point, the ESOL teacher must intervene and use conflict resolution skills to remedy the situation and make sure that highly charged emotions do not linger in the classroom. Restoration of harmony and the maintenance of relationships should be the primary goal (Satterlee, 2002).

Sometimes, conflicts can be prevented or at least minimized by the teacher becoming more aware of the diversity of cultural and individual experiences and the knowledge that learners can bring to share in the classroom—a very important element in teaching adults, especially. Recently, an adult student in Tuula's English for the Workplace course shared a criticism of another instructor he had had previously for having made him "feel like a child in the classroom." The instructor had been teaching the cultural custom of shaking hands. Because this student is an experienced businessman who has worked globally in many cultural contexts, he felt the teacher could have asked the group first about their experiences of greeting people instead of assuming that they knew nothing about the meaning of shaking hands in North America. Inviting students to share their knowledge and skills related to their own cultural behaviors before embarking on a topic affirms their identity and validates their position in class as adult students with life experiences.

 See **Collaborative Conflict Resolution Strategies With Adult Learners** in the Classroom Best Practices section of this chapter.

CLASSROOM BEST PRACTICES
Cultural Identity and Self-Reflection

The following suggestions are adapted from *Here Comes Everyone: Teaching in the Intercultural Classroom* (Alberta Teachers' Association, 2010).

Think about how your cultural identity shapes your thinking and guides your actions. To understand your learners' behaviors, reflect on your own beliefs, attitudes, biases, and prejudices, all of which may be affecting how you act in the classroom in sometimes overt and sometimes very subtle ways. The journey toward intercultural understanding begins with self-reflection and knowing yourself.

Activity: A step-by-step guide to understanding one's cultural identity

- **Shaping Identity:** Consider important events and experiences that have shaped your identity. What were your early family experiences, beliefs, and values? How did they change as you grew older? What lessons did you learn from school, work, travel, and relationships? What did you learn from your family, friends, and colleagues about people who were different from you? What experiences have altered your view of others or your own identity? How did your social, educational, and work experiences develop your perceptions of diversity?

- **Considering Differences:** Some people believe that diversity in our society raises problems that we must all try to solve, while others believe that diversity is an asset we should all embrace. There are several reasons for thinking about diversity as a strength.

  a. The more you learn about people and build relationships with them, the less you fear them or what they stand for. Learning about people you think of as different challenges preconceived notions and breaks down inappropriate stereotypes, often represented in the media. Understanding difference removes the threat and anxiety born of the fear of the unknown.

  b. Acknowledging different world views helps us develop better solutions for complex problems. The greater the exposure to contrasting viewpoints, the more likely we are to be flexible and creative. As schools, workplaces, and society in general face issues of increasing complexity, diverse approaches to problem-solving are essential. Differences can create a healthy tension and sometimes even conflict that enhance creativity and learning.

  c. People who respect diversity can be more self-confident and healthy. Positive social interactions make us feel better about ourselves, expand our horizons, and enhance our self-esteem.

- **Thinking About Words and Communication Style:** The words we say profoundly affect how others understand and respond to us. We, and our students, need to develop awareness of the nuances of the English language, as understanding is inextricably tied to context and cultural association. Connotations and associations depend entirely on a person's life experience. Think about terms that describe your own culture, race, language, and ethnicity, then do the same for your learners' cultures. For example, how would you refer to your Asian learners? Do you lump them all together as Asian or do you find out their ethnicities and indigenous languages? (Many ESOL learners can speak three, four, or more languages.) What about Roma learners or those from the Middle East? Be conscious of the language you use in general and of the terminology you use specifically when discussing people and issues related to diversity and culture.

Find out from your learners which words are respectful and which are not. For example, indigenous North Americans describe a person who is gay, lesbian, bisexual, or transgender as "two-spirited," which refers to a masculine and a feminine spirit. Consider the limitations of labeling groups, because it is easy to start stereotyping or generalizing. Also think about how you present yourself to others. What and how much do you self-disclose in public?

- **Recognizing How Personal Biases Can Affect Instruction:** It can be very difficult to identify our own biases. Consider how men behave in your classes. Do you give them preferential attention because they are more assertive or demanding than the women? Do you favor students who have come from countries to which you have traveled or spent time in or know more about? Think about your assumptions and, through contact and conversations with cultural informants and your own research, find out if they hold any merit. For example, is the reason your Chinese learners want to be accountants because they are all good at math? Is the reason a Syrian refugee is not progressing because she has been cooking and cleaning all her life? Is the reason the learner from Myanmar is not completing the online assignment in the computer lab because people in that country do not use computers? It is important to question your assumptions because they are often made out of ignorance.

Approaches to fulfilling your role as cultural informant and strategist

The specific context of teaching determines naturally the chosen content and approaches that a teacher uses to address sociocultural issues. The modality used—online, in person, or blended—also impacts curriculum planning, the activities chosen, and the way cultural expectations are incorporated. Strategies should always be aimed at trying to optimize the development of communicative competence to help our learners develop the much-needed skills for situation-specific communication.

Examples of the role as a cultural informant and strategist vary according to the context of teaching. In an academic study context, the emphasis may be more on selecting readings and resources that provide an opportunity to practice critical thinking skills. In a workplace English and communication skills context, the approach may include more about how to interact with superiors or colleagues in meetings or through correspondence. Whatever the context, students need to be made aware of and understand processes involved in current events, such as an upcoming election or changes made to municipal rules that will affect their lives.

Many of the examples here relate to several contexts, because the teacher is guiding and advising learners to gain knowledge through exposure to practices that are both cultural and linguistic:

- Teach other perspectives/viewpoints on social issues than just the views and opinions presented in the news or texts; help learners move beyond comprehension to a more critical analysis of information they read and listen to.

- Allow learners to develop analytical thinking skills to look beyond the surface meaning. Have them reflect on what others might think or how others might interpret world events and/or opinions.

- Offer strategies to handle conversations and interactions that require using tact, discretion, and diplomacy (e.g., how to provide/respond to criticism, become confident talking about oneself, express one's own ideas and opinions well, learn to agree/disagree with tact, and manage own emotions).

- Act as a trusted advisor when necessary with learners who have questions about cultural practices and turn to you for advice when they are unsure or experience difficulties.

- Encourage learners to develop their own network of contacts in the community that include experienced ESOL speakers and others who can provide mentoring and help with their intercultural adjustment process.

Collaborative Conflict Resolution Strategies With Adult Learners
(Adapted from Study Guides and Strategies, n.d.)

English language teachers can utilize the following collaborative conflict resolution strategies as they see fit given the specific context in which a misunderstanding occurs. Keep in mind the cultural backgrounds of learners and how they might perceive and contribute to the resolution process. In general terms:

The teacher

- gathers information (identifies key issues without making accusations);
- focuses on what the issues are, not who did what; and
- avoids making accusations and finding fault.
- **Individuals or group members** state their position and how it has affected them.

The teacher

- listens attentively and respectfully without interruption and in turn repeats or describes the other's position to the listener's satisfaction;
- tries to view the issue from other points of view besides the two conflicting ones;
- brainstorms to find the middle ground, a point of balance, creative solutions, and so on; and
- states what he or she can do to resolve the conflict or solve the problem.

In the end,

- an understanding is reached with agreed-upon actions for both parties;
- a procedure is identified should disagreement arise; and
- progress is monitored, rewarded, and celebrated.

Both teachers and learners should feel free to speak their mind. Students should feel listened to and know that they are a critical part of the solution. Try to understand their point of view and actively work toward a mutual decision. If the conflict cannot be resolved in this manner, mediation by a third, neutral party, such as director of the department or language institute, is an option.

CONFLICT RESOLUTION

Although the focus is on workplace teams, as opposed to learners in classrooms, Ford (2001) lists a set of recommendations for resolving conflicts with diverse individuals from unique cultural backgrounds.

Know Yourself and Your Own Culture

Starting with yourself, examine your own beliefs, values, biases, and prejudices. Being aware of our own cultures helps us to be open to different ideas because we are able to compare and contrast different approaches without being threatened. How do you behave? What are your hot buttons? How do you generally resolve conflicts? What makes you comfortable or uncomfortable?

Learn Others' Expectations

We should expect different expectations from our own culture, and one way of learning about those expectations is to find out about how conflict is resolved in other cultures. You can use a cultural informer, such as a settlement worker or cross-cultural liaison, or, if your students have a high enough English proficiency level, you can engage in a classroom discussion about resolving cultural conflicts.

Check Your Assumptions and Ask Questions

It is natural to make assumptions, but understanding the basis of our assumptions helps to avoid making stereotypes about specific cultural behaviors. One approach is to give specific feedback on the behavior you observe ("I noticed that you avoided eye contact when we were discussing the situation") and to seek clarification of your interpretations. Another variation is to give feedback on how you felt when the specified behavior occurred. ("I felt ignored when you avoided eye contact during our discussion. Can you tell me what was going on?")

Listen Carefully

Listening is widely acknowledged as a key conflict prevention and resolution skill. Effective listening enables new norms to emerge that reflect a deep knowledge for one another's ways. It is better to arrive at a compromise that respects both cultural orientations than impose the values of the dominant culture.

CASE IN POINT: CULTURE DOES MATTER

When we become more culturally conscious, we begin to develop an understanding of how important it is to allow for incidents of cross-cultural communication to take place in our teaching. Tuula calls these opportunities "cultural moments" that can occur naturally and spontaneously in our ESOL classrooms. In teaching and interacting with internationally educated immigrants in business communication skills courses, Tuula has discovered that she can develop greater rapport with the participants and learn more about them by allowing them to demonstrate customs that are intrinsic to their first cultures. Though as the instructor she is responsible for teaching the course curriculum, which is geared to helping newcomers develop and practice North American cultural and business etiquette, it is nevertheless equally important that the students can show attributes and cultural customs from their native cultures.

CULTURAL MOMENTS

Recently, in a community college career bridging program in project management, Tuula invited a guest speaker with international project management experience in a multitude of nongovernmental organizations around the world to address the class on human rights and diversity issues in Canada. William, a 72-year-old human rights activist, received a truly exceptional reception on a cold December afternoon when he stepped into the classroom. All the students present—both in the room and in two remote locations on video screen—stood up to welcome him. Bill was visibly taken aback by the gesture and mentioned to Tuula after class that he was deeply moved by the simple and spontaneous gesture. He immediately recognized it as a show of respect for him as an older professional with a lifetime of work experience. William also aptly pointed out how this reverence for the older person with life experience is disappearing from the mainstream North American culture.

William's response gave Tuula an opportunity to talk with the class not only about what they had learned from his talk but also about the intercultural communication that took place when the students stood up to show their respect. They were surprised as well as pleased to find out that William had been so moved by their standing ovation. The incident provided a welcome opportunity for the group to discuss other formal and informal social customs and to ask questions about the differences they have noted between their cultures and the customs in Canada.

As an English language instructor, Tuula reflected on what had taken place in the guest lecture as an example of how important it is to allow for cultural moments to play themselves out. The students had the opportunity to be intercultural speakers of English on an equal footing with their instructor and the guest lecturer, commonly perceived as the native speakers in the hierarchy of communication.

References

Alberta Teachers' Association. (2010). *Here comes everyone: Teaching in the intercultural classroom*. Retrieved from http://www.teachers.ab.ca/SiteCollectionDocuments/ATA/Publications/Human-Rights-Issues/MON-3%20Here%20comes%20everyone.pdf

Amarasinghe, A. (2012). Understanding intercultural facework behaviours. *Journal of International Communication, 18*(2), 175–188.

Auerbach, E., Barahona, B., Midy, J., Vaquerano, F., Zambrano, A., & Arnaud, J. (1996). *Adult ESL/literacy from the community to the community: A guidebook for participatory literacy training*. Mahwah, NJ: Lawrence Erlbaum Associates.

Canagarajah, A. (Ed.). (2005). *Reclaiming the local in language policy and practice*. Mahwah, NJ: Lawrence Erlbaum Associates.

Corbett, J. (2003). *An intercultural approach to English language teaching*. Bristol, England: Multilingual Matters.

Deardorff, D. (2006). The identification and assessment of intercultural competence as a student outcome of internationalization at institutions of higher education in the United States. *Journal of Studies in International Education, 10*, 241–266.

Ford, J. (2001). *Cross cultural conflict resolution in teams*. Retrieved from http://www .mediate.com/articles/ford5.cfm

Hawkins, M., & Norton, B. (2009). Critical language teacher education. In A. Burns & J. Richards (Eds.), *Cambridge guide to second language teacher education* (pp. 30–39) Cambridge, England: Cambridge University Press.

Hinkel, E. (2013). Culture and pragmatics in language teaching and learning. In M. Celce-Murcia, D. Brinton, & M. Snow (Eds.), *Teaching English as a second or foreign language* (4th ed., pp. 394–408) Boston, MA: National Geographic Learning/ Cengage Learning.

Hofstede, G. (1986). Cultural differences in teaching and learning. *International Journal of Intercultural Relations, 10*(3), 301–320.

Hofstede, G., Hofstede, G., & Minkov, G. (2010). *Cultures and organizations: Software of the mind* (3rd ed.). New York, NY: McGraw-Hill.

Johnson-Bailey, J. & Cervero, R. (1998). Power dynamics in teaching and learning practices: An examination of two adult education classrooms. *International Journal of Lifelong Education, 17*(6), 389–399.

Kamhi-Stein, L. (2002, April). *The construction of a non-native English speaker's classroom: Insights from a diary study.* Paper presented at the annual meeting of TESOL International Association, Salt Lake City, UT.

Kinginger, C. (Ed.). (2013). *Social and cultural aspects of language learning in study abroad.* Philadelphia, PA: Johns Benjamins.

Knapp, A. (2011). Using English as a lingua franca for (mis-)managing conflict in an international university context: An example from a course in engineering. *Journal of Pragmatics, 43*(4), 978–990.

Kramsch, C. (2009). *The multilingual subject*. Oxford, England: Oxford University Press.

Laroche, L. & Yang, C. (2014) *Danger and opportunity: Bridging cultural diversity for competitive advantage.* New York: Routledge.

Li, X., Myles, J., & Robinson, P. (2012). *Teaching ESL in Canada*. Toronto, ON: Oxford University.

McCurdy, D., Spradley, J., & Shandy, D. (2005). *The cultural experience. Ethnography in complex society* (2nd ed.). Long Grove, IL: Waveland Press.

McIntosh, P. (1989). *White privilege: Unpacking the invisible knapsack.* Retrieved from http://www.cirtl.net/files/PartI_CreatingAwareness_WhitePrivilegeUnpacking theInvisibleKnapsack.pdf

McKay, S., & Burt, M. (2010). *Culture shock in the classroom: Yours and theirs.* Retrieved from https://lincs.ed.gov/lincs/discussions/englishlanguage/10culture_full

Ortaçtepe, D. (2015). EFL teachers' identity (re)construction as teachers of intercultural competence: A language socialization approach. *Journal of Language, Identity and Education, 14,* 96–112.

Redmond, M. (2015). *Face and politeness theories* (English Technical Reports and White Papers 2). Retrieved from https://lib.dr.iastate.edu/cgi/viewcontent.cgi?referer=https://www.google.ca/&httpsredir=1&article=1006&context=engl_reports

Satterlee, A. (2002). *Conflict resolution strategies for the adult higher education student.* (ERIC Document Reproduction Service No. ED 462 055). Retrieved from http://files.eric.ed.gov/fulltext/ED462055.pdf

Scollon, R., Scollon, S., & Jones, R. (2012). *Intercultural communication: A discourse approach* (3rd ed.). Malden, MA: Wiley-Blackwell.

Study Guides and Strategies. (n.d.). Conflict resolution. Retrieved from http://www.studygs.net/conflres.htm

Ting-Toomey, S. (2004). Translating conflict face-negotiation theory into practice. In D. Landis, J. Bennet, & M. Bennett (Eds.), *Handbook of intercultural training* (pp. 217–248). Thousand Oaks, CA: Sage.

Ting-Toomey, S. (2009). Intercultural conflict competence as a facet of intercultural competence development. In D. Deardorff (Ed.), *The Sage book of intercultural competence* (pp. 100–120). Thousand Oaks, CA: Sage.

Widi Nugroho, B. (2008, August 19). Teaching critical thinking: A necessity born of diversity. *The Jakarta Post.* Retrieved from http://www.thejakartapost.com/news/2008/08/19/teaching-critical-thinking-a-necessity-born-diversity.html

ENGLISH FOR ACADEMIC PURPOSES PROGRAMS AND CULTURAL EXPECTATIONS

OVERVIEW

According to an *Open Doors* report from the Institute of International Education (Kerr, 2017), there are now 85% more international students studying in U.S. colleges and universities than there were a decade ago. The largest number of these students are from China (31.5%), India (15.9%), Saudi Arabia (5.9%), and South Korea (5.85%). In Canada, the trend is similar, with the international student population at Canadian universities growing by 88% from 2005 to 2014, while the comparable growth rate for Canadian students was 22% (Statistics Canada, 2016). As teaching staff in postsecondary education can attest, these students come from very different cultural and educational backgrounds than their North American classmates.

This chapter explores the challenges and opportunities that an intercultural English to speakers of other languages (ESOL) classroom presents to teachers and students alike in college and university programs. Integrating intercultural communicative competencies in the English for academic purposes (EAP) curriculum and in ESOL courses and programs is a complex process and, for most, still a new and untested challenge. In some colleges and universities, faculties, administrators, and instructors are increasingly supporting initiatives to foster the development of global citizenry. The objectives of these efforts are to integrate international students into postsecondary education and life on campuses and to provide opportunities for homegrown students to broaden their own cultural awareness and embrace a more internationalist mindset. Equally important are initiatives to involve faculty and staff in postsecondary education to develop intercultural communication competencies to teach and provide services to increasingly global and culturally diverse students.

THINKING ABOUT THE TOPIC

Among the many questions about cultural differences and perspectives that are likely to manifest in the classroom and on campus, the following may be included (Kerr, 2017; Hinkel, 2013):

- With regard to communication and the exchange of ideas, how appropriate is it to disagree with or challenge teachers?

- How great a risk can students take in expressing their opinions and ideas? Are they accustomed to taking initiative and willing to share their perspectives?

- How do international students appropriately handle conversations and interpersonal communication with college/university administration, faculty, and staff?

- What kind of relationship do international students have with their professors and classmates and other professionals perceived to hold positions of authority? What perception do students have of their professors? Are their professors put on a pedestal?

THEORETICAL PERSPECTIVES

Participation and Classroom Interaction

Risk-taking is a complex phenomenon that surfaces quickly when English language teachers begin to develop an understanding of how cultural factors influence communication. The preparedness to take risks or, conversely, aversion to risk-taking are culturally conditioned behaviors that affect the participation of students in the classroom and will most definitely influence their willingness to engage in the learning process. As mentioned in Chapter 1, the broader and more complex meaning of culture addressed in this book refers to the beliefs and value systems that are learned through socialization but often remain invisible as they become part of our identity. These beliefs and values are also embedded in classroom practices and assumptions about acceptable behavior or conduct that professors, for example, expect all students to show in their studies. With regards to international students and their communication preferences, Hinkel (2013) reminds us that "quite reasonably, learners first tend to apply the standards that exist in the first or native language (L1) communities where they were socialized" (p. 3). What is acceptable and appropriate or expected conduct in the classroom, such as raising one's hand to answer a question, is learned through culturally specific socialization: the beliefs, values, attitudes, and behavior individuals learn as part of the culture(s) in which they are first socialized (Scollon & Scollon, 2001).

In many Asian cultures, the role of authority in postsecondary education is securely deposited on the shoulders of the professors. Students from these cultural backgrounds seldom openly question authority. They may also be reluctant to discuss any perspective or idea that challenges the instructor's point of view. Because authority relationships are also culturally lived experiences and embedded in identity, they are invisible and seldom questioned or problematized. In most cultures in the world, the respect for teachers as authority figures who shape the development of children starts early in grade school and is reinforced in the family. Mostly, we all value educational achievements and respect the people whose work involves educating others. Many international students also come from cultures that place high value on the expertise and knowledge of their teachers and people who educate the next generation. Their hopes and dreams are often placed in the hands of teachers (and their families) who not only influence their students but also make decisions that affect the future of their lives and careers.

Culturally different behavior can inevitably challenge learned values, and reactions can vary. However, solutions to these challenges can involve making the academic expectations more explicit through the design of course content and learning tools that address intercultural communication concerns and how we interact and communicate across cultures. As English language teachers, however, we also need to acknowledge and understand that cultural differences present both to teachers and students formidable opportunities for growth and learning.

Practicing Intercultural Awareness: A Two-Way Process

A college student approached Tuula as his course instructor to ask for help writing a letter to the dean of his program to clarify a misunderstanding with another professor who had accused him of having cheated on a test in class. This student had turned his head toward another student during test taking, not intending to take a peek at a classmate's paper but simply to stretch his neck. Unfortunately for him, the professor opted for the drastic approach of failing him on the test. The allegation unnerved this recently arrived international student; he had no idea where or how to seek help to rectify the misunderstanding. His lack of knowledge of whom to contact and the fear of failing other tests caused unnecessary stress that could have been avoided.

In higher education, faculty members hold an authority position which requires careful consideration of the impact of any judgment they make on students and how they handle behavioral issues especially. Intercultural awareness works both ways; it necessitates all of us to take a closer look at how easily we can misunderstand others or be misunderstood in communication across cultures. Our example illustrates how the professor in the test situation needed to take a step back from his initial, reflexive reaction to the gesture he witnessed to reflect on what had actually happened and how the student may not have fully known the expectations. Simply talking to the student to clarify the procedures in test taking and providing friendly advice about the expectations of behavior during exams would have resolved the situation.

Contrastive Rhetoric in Intercultural Writing

Recent research on the impact of cultural differences and their influence on academic writing skills has reawakened the discussion of contrastive rhetoric, which is the study of how a person's native language and culture influence their writing in second or additional languages. The term was first coined by the American applied linguist Kaplan in 1966 and has been widely used by others, among them Finnish-born, U.S.-based applied linguist Connor.

The complex key question is: To what extent are linguistic elements transferable from the native language to additional languages? We will not elaborate here on this extensive and ongoing discussion, but it is useful to note that recent research suggests it is important to include both quantitative findings (e.g., using a large number of essay writing examples of ESOL and English first-language students) as well as qualitative methods (e.g., interviews with ESOL and English first-language writers) in the analysis of students' writing to view contrastive rhetoric in intercultural learning contexts. Other researchers also point out that increasing awareness of cultural customs and practices will impact writing in both ESOL and English first-language because writing—especially for academic purposes—is often taught differently in different cultural contexts (Connor, 1996; Uysal, 2008).

A useful example here is a study that involved 90 Chinese university students (Xing, Wang, & Spencer, 2008). The researchers outlined five features of contrastive rhetoric (English paired with East Asian style appearing first) that warrant consideration and could be used as a baseline for contrastive rhetoric research and classroom application in East Asia.

In simplified terms, the researchers claimed that from a Western perspective, East Asian academic writing

1. features a delayed thesis statement,

2. turns more to unrelated subjects or other angles than proceeding in a linear fashion,

3. contains fewer topic sentences but incorporates more topic changes,

4. uses more metaphor, and

5. employs fewer transition markers.

The interesting findings of this study illustrate that cultural socialization and early learning of writing skills in one's native language continue to have an impact on writing in ESOL, even if the students have taken courses in writing in English as part of their education.

Following is an excerpt from a first-year college international student essay on the topic of children and extracurricular activities. The student studies early childhood education in a 2-year program that prepares her to work as a kindergarten teacher. In the EAP writing course, she had practiced writing in paragraphs and developing parts of the essay to form a main argument or thesis that she was asked to defend in the essay.

INTERNATIONAL STUDENT ESSAY EXAMPLE: CHILDREN AND EXTRACURRICULAR ACTIVITIES

In today's world extracurricular activities such as music or sports are most important for children because with this they get knowledge about time management, self-exploration with the different talents as well as they can improve their self-confidence too. Only academic education is not enough sometimes. Main argument of my essay is "Should parents push their kids into extracurricular activities such as music or sports?" I am going to discuss about the advantages and disadvantages of my argument.   →

> First of all, I want to discuss some advantages from extracurricular activities such as time management, self-exploration, increase in confidence etc. Children should learn about time management which increases their self-confidence and they know how to balance between academic education and as well as extracurricular activities. In addition, to this, activities such as music increases creativity as well as imagination power in kids. Activities such as team sports increases in social comfort and relationship in kids because they get connected with different people every day. For e.g., when I was in school I was very shy. My teacher insists me to take part in sports activities in school but due to my shy nature I said no to her. After some days my parents insist me to join sports club and I started it. After that I realized that sports club helped me a lot in built up social relationships and after that I forgot my shy nature and I make many friends.

The student is forming her main argument as a question (a common feature in South Asian student essay writing) about the role of parents encouraging children to engage in extracurricular activities. However, what follows is a list of many activities and some benefits rather than the writer discussing more in-depth the main argument and how parents can become more involved in the development of activities. The writing also shows an overreliance on *after* as a marker to keep adding examples rather than discussing and developing the ideas more fully.

How useful can teaching contrastive rhetoric be in an intercultural EAP classroom? Walker (2011) addresses the importance of contrastive rhetoric in teaching writing to ESOL/English as a foreign language (EFL) students, discussing the efficacy of the following instructional techniques to promote using contrastive rhetoric in the writing classroom:

1. Situating students as ethnographers, with attention to, for example, indirectness and politeness as students make comparisons between writing in their native language and in English.

2. Utilizing e-learning, which raises cultural awareness by bringing students together online.

3. Using students' native language as a means to reinforce the meaning of culture in a consciousness-raising activity.

4. Teacher conferencing and peer response, to focus specifically on rhetorical differences in students' own writing.

Walker (2011) says that ESOL/EFL students at either secondary or postsecondary levels may benefit from various techniques for delivering intercultural rhetorically oriented writing. He believes that the increasing use of technology-mediated teaching in postsecondary education will continue to place importance on the use of contrastive rhetoric in teaching EAP writing. His discussion of how to use these techniques is especially useful for English language instructors who are teaching EAP blended and e-learning courses that allow for close collaboration among students and between the instructor and students using digital media. Though the use of students' native language may not be an option in many North American educational settings, knowledge and awareness of the cultural features that show up in our students' writing is of great significance.

Other intercultural research has explored the similarities in how academic writing is taught globally and whether contrastive rhetoric could be used to support the relationship between culture and writing. For example, Uysal (2008) has studied essays written by students from Turkey studying in the United States and the transfer of elements across languages. She found the essays to be similar in many respects (e.g., statement of claims, use of extensive examples, and other rhetoric devices) and mentioned that this result indicated the possibility of bidirectional transfer as most patterns were traced to both instructional contexts. For example, the common use of explicit and clear claims, location of thesis statements, use of rebuttals, and use of examples in the essays were features emphasized in English as well as in Turkish writing classes as major ways of making an effective argument. However, the researcher noticed that, similar to Japanese and Chinese writers, students tended to use obscure topic sentences or stand-alone examples, assuming that the reader would make connections between the example and the argument by themselves (Uysal, 2008, p. 194). She also commented that although cultural context should be taken into consideration when determining the factors that affect language transfer, such consideration is also rather complicated. For example, she claimed that knowledge and skills connected to organizational patterns and coherence were most likely transferred in both directions; however, example paragraph patterns were probably transferred from Turkish to English and frequent use of transition markers was probably transferred from English to Turkish (Uysal, 2008, p. 195). Certainly, both cultural and educational factors play an important role in second language writing processes and products.

CHALLENGING PEDAGOGY FROM A CULTURAL PERSPECTIVE

Though the numbers of international students continue to increase in our universities and colleges, programs commonly assume that pedagogy and content do not need to change despite the noticeable global shift in the composition of students and their background cultures. It seems that cultural differences do not appear to have an impact on the principles of pedagogy, although there are examples of various U.S. universities engaged in internationalizing their curricula and courses, through, for example, encouraging discussions and shared projects between American and international students (West, 2009). The assumption, however, is that most international students will accommodate and adjust to these cultural differences in their studies. Yet, such obvious academic expectations as the ability to think critically and to analyze research findings are rooted in traditional academic pedagogy. They are also specific to the local cultures in which the educational institutions operate.

DEFINITION OF CRITICAL THINKING

Critical thinking is the ability to understand the logical connections between ideas, resolve problems, communicate ideas, and contribute to discussions and decision-making; it may be conceptualized differently across disciplines and cultures. In learning, critical thinking is considered a competency that is necessary to analyze and comprehend new knowledge. In employment, critical thinking may be exercised more directly as the ability to use one's judgment in making a choice or a decision about a process or a course of action. In communication, critical thinking helps in decisions about how to communicate in a situation that involves others.

Adapted from Touchstone Institute (2018)

How can pedagogical practices, particularly critical thinking, be examined from an intercultural perspective? Turner (2006) uses a case study to illustrate the need to challenge or question Western-oriented teaching and learning practices. She discusses an example of Chinese students who participated in a U.K.-based postgraduate business management study program. She says that the group of visiting Chinese students became too quickly stereotyped as not being as proficient as other students in showing critical thinking—an important academic competency. According to research she elaborated on (e.g., McNamara & Harris, 1997), international students often have a more acute need to bridge the gap between different ways of knowing as they may express their knowledge differently from what is customary, in this case in the Anglo-Saxon academic tradition.

Turner (2006) points out that the Chinese students in the study had expressed their critical thinking differently in writing, which was partly misinterpreted as lack of critical thinking because it was viewed from only one perspective, specifically the one that required familiarity with the British academic system and its expectations. As most of this knowledge and expectations are implicit, the Chinese students who came from a very different academic system experienced a knowledge gap that was not recognized and, as a result, caused a great deal of stress and misunderstanding.

In Turner's (2006) findings, she discusses the students' experiences of the cultural differences, which they articulated while comparing the British and Chinese study methods and practices. They all discovered that most of the expectations in the British academic system were implicit and taken for granted as shared knowledge:

> The main focus of learning conversations was confined to techniques, rather than underlying intellectual processes beneath the declarative level. In addition, the students quickly saw that they suffered practical disadvantage compared to British or European classmates who had previously received training in these practices and who were better-versed in the kinds of cultural knowledge that contributed to student success. (p. 25)

The key expectations that lecturers had of them were academic performance, including problem-solving, frequent quoting of sources, evidence-based argumentation, and working independently. One of the students expressed this dilemma by saying that

> the lecturer gives you the case and you have to write some feeling about it. You have to read a lot of books and you have to read a lot of articles . . . but you have to put a lot of your own feeling in your essay, so it is really difficult I think. (Turner, 2006, p. 19)

Turner (2006) shows how the Chinese students had to quickly identify the differences in the construction of knowledge and how crucial this understanding was to their academic success.

COMMENTS BY VISITING CHINESE STUDENTS IN THE UNITED KINGDOM

Here, in a lecture, when sometime the lecturer tells something, then we are divided into groups and we discuss in the groups. But in university in China, the whole lecture is the teacher saying. (Turner, 2006, p. 17)

Although [the lecturer] tried to explain it to me and she tried her best to explain it, but I still can't get anything. I still can't get any information. I don't think I can connect to the things that she said, connected with the knowledge that I learned before. (Turner, 2006, p. 20)

In her conclusion of the study, Turner (2006) mentions that oddly enough, none of the participants explicitly discussed critical thinking or criticality as part of the skills they were gaining or of the expectations that lecturers articulated as necessary; they discussed group work, problem-solving, and essay argumentation. The students were made aware of the value placed on various other skills within the generic definitions of criticality, but because the expectations were largely implicit, the Chinese students were left feeling uncertain as to what competencies they were supposed to have shown in the classroom and in their assignments. Had their experiences of a different academic system been acknowledged, they would have had an opportunity to write essays and participate in group discussions with others to express their ideas and share their views about how their academic experiences were different in China.

CULTURAL VARIABLES AND ENGLISH FOR ACADEMIC PURPOSES: STYLE AND SUBSTANCE

It's necessary to change pedagogical practices to suit the cultural needs of international students, but are such changes necessary for students who may only be visiting? Clearly that is not realistic or necessary, but as Turner's (2006) case study illustrates, proficiency or performance may need to be problematized and measured with more understanding of the impact of cultural variables on content, teaching and learning practices, and the assessment of competencies. If the influence of cultural traditions and practices are far reaching and have an impact on outcomes, it makes sense to incorporate a variety of assignments that provide students more choices and ways to express their knowledge. If in postsecondary education, cultural factors affect learning performance, especially the perception of what constitutes successful performance, then the academic success of students can be directly influenced by assessment that fails to recognize the impact of said factors.

In EAP classrooms, English language proficiency is the catch-all category to assess abilities of students to use their critical reading and thinking skills and to acquire the language to express their point of view in presentations and writing. Understanding how cultural differences impact study conventions and English language teaching needs to remain an ongoing concern for practitioners as well as for anyone involved in curriculum design.

Cultural information and approaches to knowledge transfer seem to be most effective when they are incorporated both in the content of curriculum and in the types of assignments that allow for more accurate assessment of performance and progress. The following examples suggest strategies and ideas that embrace more open-minded or inclusionary perspectives in teaching and in the evaluation of international ESOL learners' performance (e.g., Turner, 2006; McNamara & Harris, 1997):

- **Scaffolding as a strategy to teach critical reading and thinking:** building of knowledge and competencies incrementally to promote reading comprehension as a process and allowing for step-by-step development of critical thinking skills and the ability to evaluate reading texts. Not all international students understand the complex meaning of critical thinking skills and how they are developed in academic studies.

- **Use of both instrumental and deeper critical thinking approaches:** using both in-depth and more surface level analyses that allow for expression of knowledge in a variety of ways, without one type dominating or being preferred. In the ESOL classroom, a variety of summarizing and paraphrasing exercises, reviews of books, and the use of videos (e.g., TED Talks) can complement more in-depth research and analysis of multiple and more extensive reading sources.

- **Presentations and group projects that complement individual performance tasks:** to allow for participatory learning experiences that support various styles of learning and help reduce performance anxiety.

- **Blogging, journals, discussion forums:** most educational learning management systems, such as Brightspace and Blackboard, include blogs, discussion boards, and journal features that can be used effectively to encourage students to write and experiment with different genres. Writing about travel and other personal experiences, paraphrasing and summarizing of a variety of texts, and blogging can be used well as platforms to experiment expressing opinions and formulating arguments.

- **Variety of assessment tools and assignments used in evaluation:** to recognize that writing skills are constantly developing and that learners need to make connections among reading, research, and writing to learn the required academic study skills that meet the expectations in postsecondary education. Instructors in their turn need to design a variety of assessment tools and approaches that recognize the process that is involved in developing ways to express opinions and write about research findings.

Academic Writing Instruction

Having taught writing skills in EAP and other study programs both in college and university programs, both of us, Johanne and Tuula, continue to discuss the challenges that our international students encounter in expressing their ideas in English in the genre most of us know as academic writing. We ask ourselves if it is enough that students acquire the use of language and the rhetorical devices to write essays and research papers using the acceptable standardized formula. After all, any textbook in the genre provides plenty of examples of how to form a thesis argument, write well-structured paragraphs, and present solid evidence to defend arguments.

Writing is, however, a more complex process than just mastering linguistic tools. Expression of ideas in another language is also a cultural process of adjustment and accommodation to a new culture that not only takes time but also involves self-reflection and awareness of cultural practices. International students are learners who are coping with multiple changes as part of acculturation. As Turner (2006) discusses in her case study, her Chinese students come from a collectivist culture in which postsecondary education is also anchored in more authoritarian traditions of learning known for not encouraging students to engage in open and free criticism. Critical thinking and writing are largely the traditions of academic work in the Western world and, therefore, may be culturally unfamiliar to some international students. This unfamiliarity with the process is often difficult to understand; we all make assumptions about learners having the same prior knowledge at the postsecondary level. Many international students experience this gap of knowledge as isolation and as differences that are hard to bridge, especially if these differences are left unrecognized.

International students are engaged in a process of changing their thinking and are, therefore, on a steep learning curve, and their instructors usually have to teach courses that are not only heavy in content but also cover a myriad of skills, including learning to use grammar, tone, style, and the mechanics of academic writing. It is probably safe to say that everyone in this process simply gets busy meeting the course expectations with a varying degree of success. As instructors, we are frequently held back by time restrictions imposed by the colleges and universities and the fast-paced course syllabi. As a result, we are often just doing our best with what we have and hope that the mixed group of international students get through the course and with luck avoid plagiarizing and landing themselves in hot water with the administration.

Plagiarism Unplugged

Tuula recently taught a course in critical reading and writing skills to a group of first-year college students, all of whom were international students. Despite the time and effort spent on teaching paraphrasing, quoting, and how to evaluate and reference resources—even after issuing repeated cautions about plagiarism, which were clearly spelled out in the course description—a few students blatantly plagiarized sections of their essays. Why do international students plagiarize knowing that educational institutions have strict policies that can ultimately lead to expulsion?

Over the years of teaching, instructors in higher education learn to better understand the performance anxiety that students experience, especially if they are ESOL writers. Why not lift beautifully written segments out of research when the original author expresses the ideas in much better language than the student can? The need to have a good grade and pass a course often outweighs the risk of getting caught. As English language teachers know, plagiarizing is not limited to international students or to ESOL courses. The alternative of putting a lot of work into learning to write their own ideas and score well is simply a daunting task for some ESOL learners who are juggling a myriad of both implicit and explicit expectations. Though many will argue, perhaps it is time we begin to loosen the strictness of genre definitions in academic writing.

Many college ESOL curricula recognize that teaching academic writing is a process that requires a great deal of work, preparation, and practice before students can acquire the skills to write essays and reports that abide by the Western rules of academic integrity.

Other Forms of Expressing Knowledge

It is of course important that the students are taught the style, content, and mechanics of writing an academic research essay if that is the requirement in their studies so that they learn to apply these skills to their course work. However, it is equally significant that all teachers begin to loosen up the genres of writing, especially in EAP curricula, and offer different options and ways to develop critical thinking and writing without feeding the anxiety to perform to a standard that may not apply fully to what the students are asked to do in their studies. Many of the programs taught in community colleges or even in universities do not require essay writing as the sole measurement of overall academic writing competencies. Following are a few other ways to assess these competencies.

- **Report writing and journalistic reporting** explore writing through storytelling and the sharing of personal narratives that can be combined with research and the reporting of findings. These types of assignments require analysis of facts and research, but they also allow for more imaginative expression of knowledge.

- **Writing reviews of books, films, and restaurants** is another way to express knowledge and ideas and to experiment formulating opinions. These forms of writing can serve as building blocks toward more extensive writing, such as expository or argumentative essays, which require more extensive research, analysis, and critical thinking.

- **Use internet-based resources to explore differences between facts and opinions.** The proliferation of blogging can create confusion among students about the credibility of sources to use in writing. Doing online research requires careful analysis of the multitude of types and purposes of writing in our time. Analyzing the all-too-frequent posting of opinions as credible facts—claims that are often not supported by reputable academic research—works toward learning the principles of critical thinking, which are necessary for differentiating between credible and dubitable arguments and choosing the best research sources for one's own writing (Brown, 1998).

- **Share narratives and intercultural experiences.** Instructors can also share stories from our own lives and international travel and work experiences to model ways to write intercultural narratives. Engaging students in storytelling helps to take them from speaking to written expression and bridge gaps that are often perceived as strict boundaries between various genres of writing. While students are engaged in writing more "free style" about their own thoughts and experiences, they also learn to reflect better on the changes they are experiencing, who their readers are, and how as writers they might want to reach their audience. This type of writing also helps to explore identity and to engage students in a process rather than immediately get them stressed out about writing using a strict standard or narrowly defined expectations that cause performance anxiety.

SOCIAL LIFE ON CAMPUS

Integration of international students in the broader social life on college campuses is a challenge. As English language teachers, we are bound to be aware of the unicultural student cliques that are formed. It is a natural human reaction to seek comfort in the company of others who are from the same cultural and language background. However, in the case of international students, this practice also has the effect of separation from the mainstream student population and from the contacts and activities that would help with social integration.

The following are comments collected from Tuula's first-year international students in a community college course survey about their feelings associated with integrating and fitting in as new students and newcomers in the college, which was located in Toronto, Canada.

STUDENT COMMENTS: SOCIAL LIFE ON CAMPUS

It's hard to build relationships here with other people—I stay with people in my own group.

I don't know how to build friendships here without being completely fluent in English and culture. I find it hard.

My challenges are making friends, meeting new people; I'd like to hang out with people from other places and countries.

I am afraid to fail and just study to keep up with the work load and all the courses I'm taking here.

Some community colleges and university programs have taken steps to address these issues more proactively. A dynamic and globally interactive approach to intercultural awareness and competency building is provided by internet-supported intercultural information portals, such as Aperian Global and Cultural Navigator. Such portals provide continually updated comprehensive research about cultural differences in numerous countries and regions in the world. These web-based resources offer well-documented information and assessment tools, including learning pathways, for the faculty and students to use in their curricula and assignments. Typically, these resources are more familiar to expats working in various global business roles and who have the need to understand the cultures and people in the countries where they are employed to do business internationally.

Offering courses to faculty and staff on intercultural communication or purchasing a license to make a learning portal available to students, faculty, and staff shows a commitment by educational institutions to making sure that the whole educational community is involved in developing intercultural awareness and to building intercultural competencies in practice. Using these intercultural web-based tools allows educators to bring together students, faculty, and staff to work as teams on intercultural issues and to resolve problems and avoid potential conflicts in communication.

CLASSROOM BEST PRACTICES

How can English language teachers tap into the range of literacies and language knowledge of our students? As we've discussed, if the measurement of student learning is based solely on criteria that fail to recognize the influence of cultural variables on learning outcomes, the students are then perceived to fail. In EAP, some of the most innovative research and practices today are beginning to embrace this plurality of cultural identities and the influence multiple literacies have on communication and on language teaching.

Digital Autobiographical Identity Texts

One example we are including here is Corcoran's (2017) digital autobiographical identity text (AIT).

> Over the past two years in my EAP classroom, I have substituted one of my major assignments (e.g. argumentative essay paper) with an Autobiographical Identity Text (AIT). An AIT is a multimodal, digital "text" constructed using various audio and video technologies (e.g., Screencast-o-matic; Prezi) allowing for a narrative description of students' language practices over time. This narrative, digital text allows students to represent their multiple, hybrid, evolving identities as language learners/university students in a comprehensive manner that provides a platform for the production and development of authentic academic language use. (Corcoran, 2017, pp. 1–2)

Corcoran (2017) suggests that AIT is a very useful tool because as instructors we often do not reflect enough on the central role of language(s) in the construction and negotiation of self. He also uses the concept of English as an additional language to draw attention to the presence of multiple literacies and the mix of languages that inform learning in EAP. He argues that AIT can easily be combined with more traditional forms of texts and approaches as a complementary tool that provides students options to express their knowledge using multimedia. AIT is particularly useful as a pedagogical tool in academic bridging programs with international students who are developing more advanced-level writing and critical thinking skills to pursue further postsecondary studies. In the practical work of ESOL teaching, Corcoran's (2017) AIT model is a great tool that allows teachers to reflect more on our own multiple social identities related to our teaching roles, such as coach, mentor, language teacher, classroom strategist, trusted advisor, and counselor.

 See Chapter 3, **Teacher as a Cultural Informant and Classroom Strategist**, for a more in-depth discussion of these roles.

Using TED Talks in ESOL Classrooms

Many English language teachers already use TED Talks in ESOL classrooms in a myriad of ways to encourage discussion, teach language and presentation skills, and introduce both young and adult students to varieties of English. Because the talks are global and cover an enormous range of subjects and themes, TED Talks are also a great way to introduce many intercultural perspectives and ways of seeing and interpreting the world. Following are just a few examples of ways to use TED talks in teaching EAP.

- **Complement reading texts with videos and transcripts.** TED Talks offer a video talk with a transcript of the speech, which can be used as reading and critical thinking analysis tools in the classroom. Tuula uses TED Talks to help students in college writing courses to brainstorm about essay topics and engage with a topic to clarify their own thinking.

- **Present a range of opinions, perspectives, and questions.** These can help stimulate discussion among students that can be transferred to discussion forums or chat rooms; TED Talks are informative and can be paired with research and reading online. Lee (2016) provides useful practical examples of how to use TED Talks in classroom teaching in *21st Century Communication 4: Listening, Speaking and Critical Thinking.*

- **Bring cultural inclusiveness into the classroom.** The versatility of inspiring speakers from around the globe offers teachers opportunities to choose presenters and topics of interest from various cultures, including issues and speakers from the home countries of ESOL learners. Choosing culturally appropriate and relevant TED Talks also helps teachers build intercultural learning communities in keeping with The 6 Principles of Exemplary Teaching of English Learners (TESOL International Association, 2018).

- **Enhance intercultural awareness and knowledge building.** ESOL classrooms in North America are multicultural, multilingual platforms of adult learning; most students do not know about each others' cultures or customs of origin as the focus is on learning English. Awareness of intercultural communication leads to learning how cultural differences actually impact behavior. In TED Talks, ESOL learners are exposed to communication and the competencies and skills that are involved in learning to practice public speaking and presentations in English in their new culture. These talks showcase effective use of language to persuade, inspire, and move audiences, using techniques of public speaking.

Sharing Narratives About Culture

> Narratives are event-centered and historically particular, located in a particular time and place. Stories concern action, more specifically human action, and particularly social interaction. Stories have plots. They have a beginning, middle and end, so that while they unfold in time, the order is more than mere sequence but reveal a "sense of the whole." Stories show how human actors do things in the world, how their actions shape events and instigate responses in other actors, changing the world (and often the actors themselves) in some way. (Mattingly & Lawlor, 2011, p. 6)

The preceding quote illustrates intercultural research that has been done in the education of health-care professionals on the importance of intercultural communication and the need to develop communication competencies. Health-care professionals provide services to an increasingly multicultural population and work in cross-functional teams with colleagues who come from diverse cultural backgrounds and occupations. The power of narrative interviewing patients to gain fuller understanding of their health and wellness issues is only one example of the type of communication repertoire that is now considered important in the training of future practitioners (Teal & Street, 2008). Teal and Street (2008) focus on critical elements of cultural competencies that they believe are important in the education of doctors and health-care practitioners:

1. communication repertoire

2. cultural situational awareness

3. adaptability

4. knowledge of core cultural issues

Proponents of narrative interviewing claim that patients from different cultural backgrounds are more likely to share useful and important information when they are engaged in talking about themselves and their life experiences. In ESOL pedagogy, storytelling, as pointed out earlier, has often been used as a tool to develop speaking and writing, particularly through journaling and keeping a diary. Using narratives is also a powerful way for learners to explore intercultural dilemmas and questions, not to mention sharing their stories about moving from one part of the world to another or growing up in a multicultural society.

 See Chapter 2, **Classroom Best Practices**, for more on storytelling and sharing of cultural identity.

Activity: Foreign Words That Convey Complex Meanings

Languages sometimes have expressions that are hard to translate precisely into another language. In *10 Breathtaking Foreign Words*, blogger Ticak (2016) describes 10 expressions that encapsulate more effectively the sounds of words in other languages than what the actual translation of the words into English can convey. For example, the Japanese expression *Shinrin-yoku*, which in English translates loosely to "forest bathing," gives a more demonstrative sense than its English translation of the feelings of being in a forest, hearing the wind in the trees, or walking in the grass and stepping through fallen leaves on the ground.

Sharing as teachers in our classrooms various expressions from our own and students' first languages offers an opportunity to explore the more complex connections between language use and cultures. This type of activity also provides more options when teaching vocabulary; students can explore words from other languages and have a chance to incorporate their first language in their writing, as long as they define that language for readers. Tuula has found this practice helpful as a strategy to break down cultural barriers in teaching writing. She often uses the example of the word *sisu* from her first language, Finnish. This expression has no one direct equivalent in English; it describes inner strength and resilience, the guts and gumption, if you like, that it takes to endure difficult experiences, such as an illness or a loss. In other words, *sisu* conveys a sense of energy, an attitude, and emotions that are all combined in one short phrase. Discussing with learners the use of foreign words can also open a window into the cultural experiences of the people who coined these unique phrases.

Using Discourses Appropriately

As English language teachers, we incorporate in teaching various communicative and cultural aspects of appropriate language use. Speakers of other languages require this knowledge and cultural awareness to develop the competencies to choose the phrases and expressions that fit the purpose of communication.

Sociocultural competency is an important part of this cultural learning. In general terms, it is the ability to understand the cultural rules and conventions of language use, the naturalness of language, including how native English speakers express themselves appropriately within the overall social and cultural context of communication. Learners need to discover and use this new knowledge, and they do so often under the constraints of real-time communication and interaction.

Critical cultural awareness suggests an ability to evaluate critically the communication situation in which we find ourselves, based on specific criteria, perspectives, and practices that are common in the culture in which we are living, studying, and working.

Activity: Making verbal requests

ESOL learners are often in situations that require them to ask for information or make requests in English. Given the immediacy of the interaction, they often end up using language that is too direct and may lack the finesse of expression that is desirable. The various types of requests elicit different responses, depending on the audience and the culturally specific situation of communication. As an example, share the following sentences with your students:

- Could/can/would you take a look at my ideas here?

- Do you have a moment to take a look at my paper?

- Take a look at my suggestions here and get back to me, will you?

- What do you think? Am I on the right track?

- Your thoughts please?

These examples can help students pinpoint the audiences and explore the various responses that these requests are likely to elicit. Though the more direct questions may work fine in interactions between peers, lack of politeness may result in an unfavorable response in an interaction between a professor and a student or a manager and employee. Here, critical cultural awareness is about understanding the differences in the positions people have in an organizational hierarchy and how the choice of language is affected by the social distance between individuals.

Activity: Culturally appropriate conversations: Making written requests

This activity can be done in a college or community writing course with adults who are learning about writing email and following the etiquette of online writing.

- ESOL learners are given a task to write an email to a supervisor to request a leave of absence from work for training purposes. Having learned about email and the ways it is used at work, they know that the first paragraph needs to express the purpose of the email as a culturally acceptable convention of writing direct communication in the workplace.

- However, though the students may know about the sociocultural context of the task, the language they often choose illustrates the difficulty of finding appropriate expressions. They do not yet have the cultural knowledge of workplace writing conventions of how to write the request in the way that elicits a favorable response from the supervisor.

- Here are a few student writing examples:

  —"I am taking some time off to attend training and ask you to give me permission . . ."

  —"OK if I don't show up and take some time off to take a training course next week?"

  —"Will you accept that I take a few days off for training?"

As these examples show, "directness" here is interpreted by the students as expressing their request as statements, often translations from their native language in the absence of knowing more appropriate target language. In the workplace environment, first lines such as these are likely to elicit a more negative response. The tone in the writing suggests a command or "telling the boss" rather than language that conveys a polite request for permission to take time off work.

Communicative discourses are complex in meaning and always require careful explanation of how language is used in specific circumstances within a culture and for which purposes. In this example, the level of formality that is required in a typically North American workplace situation would be the first issue to discuss with learners to illustrate how the relationship between the supervisor and the employees affects the choice of language in the email. Though in North American workplaces, employees and their supervisors call each other by first names and often behave in ways that appear to be casual and informal, the same level of informality does not as a rule apply to written workplace communication.

Teaching speaking or writing in these types of interactions needs to include, among other things, use of "softeners" (e.g., the modals *could/would/would you mind if I* . . .) and various forms of polite expressions that help students connect cultural knowledge of the interaction to the purpose of communicating a formal request.

CASE IN POINT: CRITICAL CULTURAL ENCOUNTERS

Developing awareness of how our interactions are culturally programmed in various communication situations is a competency that everyone benefits from, including students pursuing academic studies. International students also interact and communicate with administrative and support staff and will most likely encounter difficulties. Similarly, administrative and support staff in postsecondary educational contexts may not be familiar with the diversity of backgrounds of the students whose culturally different communication customs are bound to raise questions and cause misunderstandings.

Snow (2015) identifies and discusses critical cultural encounters and the importance of exercising "dual-process views of thinking" to develop habits of thought that he considers useful in intercultural communication situations. These habits include

- being consciously aware of the interpretation process in intercultural communication situations;

- consciously considering multiple interpretations of puzzling or problematic intercultural encounters;

- paying conscious attention to factors that may affect how one interprets problematic intercultural encounters, especially factors that affect feelings or interpretation rules; and

- paying conscious attention to the "benefit-of-the-doubt" question.

The following example illustrates an intercultural encounter between an international student who is talking to a college administrative staff member about registration procedures. The exchange between the individuals highlights intercultural differences that are largely unconscious and yet have a profound impact on the way the parties engage. A newcomer couple, Rahim and Rawan, is interacting with an intake officer, Candice, to enroll Rawan, the wife, in the college.

> **PROBLEMATIC INTERCULTURAL ENCOUNTER**
>
> Candice provides intake services at the Registrar's Office. A couple has arrived to get Rawan enrolled. The man, Rahim, continues speaking for his wife, Rawan, even though Candice has pointedly responded only to Rawan with her answers. At one point in the conversation, Candice asks, "Can't she speak?" in a condescending tone and blocks the husband from looking at the document she is showing Rawan. She doesn't spend the time she usually does providing extra helpful information.
>
> What could the people in this scenario do differently?
>
> How would you suggest Candice handle the encounter?
>
> (From Sorbera, 2017)

International students in educational institutions may encounter behavior and attitudes that challenge their own values and beliefs. Having staff and faculty trained in intercultural awareness and communication is probably the best investment that a college or university can make to benefit everyone. The scenario here was taken from a community college in Ontario, Canada. In this case, the Institute is offering faculty and staff intercultural training courses to help them develop an understanding of how they can handle communication, which requires intercultural sensitivity and knowledge of both one's own and others' ways of communicating when the parties are not from the same culture or do not share similar beliefs and values.

In an ESOL classroom, an instructor might want to use this type of scenario as an example for discussion about the meaning of culture and how both the couple and Candice approached this situation from their own different cultural perspectives. The purpose here would be to get the students to identify communication styles and customs that can be misinterpreted outside their own cultural practices and communities.

References

Brown, K. (1998). *Education, cultural and critical thinking*. Surrey, United Kingdom: Ashgate.

Connor, U. (1996). *Contrastive rhetoric: Cross-cultural aspects of second language writing*. New York, NY: Cambridge University Press.

Corcoran, J. (2017, Winter) Digital autobiographical identity texts in the EAP classroom. *College ESL Quarterly*, 1–7.

Hinkel, E. (2013). Culture and pragmatics in language teaching and learning. In M. Celce-Murcia, D. Brinton, & M. Snow (Eds.), *Teaching English as a second or foreign language* (pp. 394–408). Boston, MA: National Geographic Learning. Retrieved from http://www.elihinkel.org/downloads/Culture_and_Pragmatics.pdf

Kaplan, R. (1966). Cultural thought patterns in intercultural education. *Language Learning, 16*(1–2), 1–20.

Kerr, D. (2017, April 21). *Preparing foreign students for studying in the United States* [Blog post]. Retrieved from http://www.aperianglobal.com/preparing-students-for-studying-us/

Lee, C. (2016). *21st Century Communication 4: Listening, Speaking and Critical Thinking.* Boston, MA : National Geographic Learning.

Mattingly, C., & Lawlor, M. (2011). Learning from stories: Narrative interviewing in cross-cultural research. *Scandinavian Journal of Occupational Therapy, 7*(1), 4–14. Retrieved from https://www.ncbi.nlm.nih.gov/pmc/articles/PMC3051197/

McNamara, D., & Harris, R. (Eds.) (1997). *Overseas students in higher education: Issues in teaching and learning.* London, England: Routledge.

Scollon, R., & Scollon, S. W. (2001) *Intercultural communication: A discourse approach* Oxford, England: Blackwell.

Snow, D. (2015). Language teaching, intercultural competence and critical incident exercises. *Language and Intercultural Communication 15(2),* 285–299.

Sorbera, B. (2017, March 25). Intercultural awareness workshop. Humber Institute of Technology & Advanced Learning, Toronto, Canada.

Statistics Canada. (2016). Study: International students in Canadian universities 2004/05 to 2014. Retrieved from http://www.statcan.gc.ca/daily-quotidien/161020/dq161020e-eng.htm

Teal, C., & Street, R. (2008). Critical elements of culturally competent communication in the medical encounter: A review and notes. *Social Science & Medicine, 30,* 1–11.

TESOL International Association. (2018). *The 6 principles for exemplary teaching of English learners: Grades K–12.* Alexandria, VA: Author.

Ticak, M. (2016, September 29). 10 breathtaking foreign words [Blog post]. Retrieved from https://www.grammarly.com/blog/most-breathtaking-foreign-words/

Touchstone Institute. (2018). *Communicative competence at work: A framework for intercultural communication in the workplace.* 360° Project: View of Culture and Communication. Retrieved from https://360communication.ca/

Turner, Y. (2006). Students from mainland China and critical thinking in postgraduate business and management degrees: Teasing out tensions of culture, style and substance. *International Journal of Management Education, 5*(1), 1–31. Retrieved from https://openair.rgu.ac.uk/handle/10059/423

Uysal, H. (2008). Tracing the culture behind writing: Rhetorical patterns and bidirectional transfer in L1 and L2 essays of Turkish writers in relation to educational context. *Journal of Second Language Writing, 17*(3), 183–207.

Walker, D. (2011). How to teach contrastive (intercultural) rhetoric: Some ideas for pedagogical application. *New Horizons in Education, 59*(3), 71–81.

Xing, M., Wang, J., & Spencer, K. (2008). Raising students' awareness of cross-cultural contrastive rhetoric in English writing via an e-learning course. *Language Learning and Technology, 12*(2), 71–93.

EMPLOYMENT PREPARATION PROGRAMS AND CULTURAL INTEGRATION

CHAPTER 5

OVERVIEW

Given our increasingly global and culturally diverse landscape of work and professional development, the need to develop proficiency as intercultural communicators has perhaps never been so acute. The myriad of interactions and contact among people across the globe requires us to pay careful attention to how we exchange knowledge and information across cultural and social divides. As the needs of employers evolve, postsecondary education is also required to help meet the growing demand for graduates who have the knowledge and skills to work in local and global environments. It is now common to see communication, critical thinking skills, and intercultural competencies built into college and university curricula as desirable learning outcomes to prepare graduates for transition into employment. We can argue, therefore, that the enhancement of cultural communication skills is relevant not just to newcomers but to all of us.

Intercultural communication and competencies are often referred to in employment contexts as, simply, good communication or "people skills"—the ability to handle diversity and complex interactions that determine success in interpersonal relations. Though there are many descriptions of skills, knowledge, and competencies, most employers and professionals continue to talk about *hard skills* and *soft skills* (or social skills). This distinction illustrates the differences, respectively, between an individual's technical knowledge and qualifications and their ability to interact with others, communicate effectively, and build successful relationships at work. Intercultural communication and the competencies we discuss in this chapter involve the use of soft skills; we focus on how verbal and nonverbal communication are affected by cultural differences.

In this chapter, we demonstrate how language and its many functional and sociocultural uses are embedded in workplace and employment systems and practices. In the world of work, these practices and the art of fitting in as employees often remain hidden to English to speakers of other languages (ESOL) learners as they navigate their way through the hiring process, start a job, and become integrated in the workforce.

THINKING ABOUT THE TOPIC

Questions about the role and meaning of culture in employment may include:

- What are intercultural communicative competencies (ICCs) in employment?
- Why are cultural awareness and knowledge important in employment?
- What does it mean to have a workplace cultural or professional identity?
- What does emotional intelligence (EQ) have to do with culture?
- How do we develop ICCs and skills for the workplace?

THEORETICAL PERSPECTIVES

The evolution of competencies in our rapidly changing world is reflected in the current understanding of the aptitudes that make up what we commonly call soft skills. A 2015 U.S. study, *Workforce Connections: Key "Soft Skills" That Foster Youth Workforce Success* (Lippman, Ryberg, Carney, & Moore), provides a comprehensive definition that incorporates many intercultural competencies, including communication:

> Soft skills refer to a broad set of skills, competencies, behaviors, attitudes, and personal qualities that enable people to effectively navigate their environment, work well with others, perform well, and achieve their goals. These skills are broadly applicable and complement other skills such as technical, vocational, and academic skills. (p. 4)

Soft skills has become the ubiquitous term in many sectors to describe many noncognitive traits, in contrast with essential technical skills, defined differently in various industries and occupational sectors. In health care, these soft skills are usually characterized as *patient counseling* and *bedside manners* and are defined as professional communication competencies. In business, retail, and professional services, soft skills are commonly defined as *customer relations* or *service skills* and *client relationship management* competencies. Research that focuses on the changes in employment in the 21st century also suggests that some employers are reporting a "soft skills gap" that impacts human capital development and workforce success at large. The Manpower Group's report *The Value of Soft Skills to the UK Economy* (Development Economics, 2015) is an example of this trend.

SOFT SKILLS IN EMPLOYMENT

Malmborg (2015), creator of a role-play training app for organizations, posted the question, "What soft skills do trainers teach most?" to a human resources discussion group on LinkedIn.

> About 350 trainers specialized in everything from computer games and video to Improv Theater and board games answered my question. Actually, the result wasn't that surprising. The three most taught skills were Communication, Teamwork and Listening. These are all inherently social skills. ➔

> Teaching social skills makes a lot of sense in the world we live in. Companies increasingly need their employees to be able to talk and work with pretty much everyone. Simply being able to get along with Joe from accounting is no longer going to cut it. Companies in the 21th [*sic*] century have offshore subsidiaries, joint ventures and partners all over the world. Modern employees need to navigate a multitude of cultures and customs on a daily basis let alone handle Joe from accounting. (Malmborg, 2015)

A notion of *intercultural effectiveness*—though it may not necessarily be called by the same name in various employment sectors—illustrates the skills that employers would like to see in the workplace: the ability of employees to be flexible and adaptable and to accommodate various cultural differences. Salo-Lee (n.d.) points out that the studies on intercultural competence carried out over the last few decades indicate that the knowledge of any country and its culture, knowledge of the language of the culture, and intercultural communication skills are important in reaching intercultural effectiveness. For example, the Canadian government document, *A Profile of the Interculturally Effective Person* (Vulpe, Kealey, Protheroe, & Macdonald, 2001), lists these key qualities in the profile of an interculturally effective employee:

- an ability to communicate with people of another culture in a way that earns their respect and trust, thereby encouraging a cooperative and productive workplace that is conducive to the achievement of professional or assignment goals;

- the capacity to adapt his/her professional skills (both technical and managerial) to fit local conditions and constraints; and

- the capacity to adjust personally so that s/he is content and generally at ease in the host culture. (p. 6)

Adaptation, flexibility, modesty, respect, an ability to build relationships, and the knowledge of self and one's own culture are also often listed as the key components of intercultural effectiveness. Tolerance of ambiguity, ability to be nonjudgmental, and expression of empathy are further seen as important ingredients of intercultural competence in the workplace and as components in preparation for employment (Stahl, 2001).

INTERCULTURAL COMMUNICATIVE COMPETENCE IN WORKPLACE-FOCUSED LEARNING PROGRAMS

In the various employment preparation programs for ESOL learners that incorporate language and communication training, there are common features or themes in instruction. In North America, these features are built into community college and university programs as specific career-bridging initiatives or as particular government-sponsored and -funded learning programs in various communities. The programs can also take place within the workplace itself. Career pathway requirements are often expressed as learning outcomes in individual communication skills and ESOL language courses that focus on developing English language competencies for the workplace and in business.

In the United States, there is an increasing demand for an adult education system that focuses on the skills that adults need for work and viable, sustainable employment. Indeed, attention is placed on forming collaborative relationships between training providers, such as community colleges that offer career pathways, and adult education programs focused on ESOL instruction. Employers and members of workforce boards are encouraged to be involved as well. The U.S. Department of Education's Office of English Language Acquisition (OELA) provides programs and leadership to help ensure that immigrant learners attain English proficiency and levels that are expected in education and employment. Included in the many OELA programs is a National Professional Development (NDP) initiative that provides grants to organizations to implement development courses for English learners and newcomers (OELA, n.d.). *Preparing English Learners for Work and Career Pathways* explains that new immigrants and refugees may be unfamiliar with the culture of the U.S. workplace or the culture of career training (Literacy Information and Communication System, 2014)—hence the need to include ICC development in education and training programs.

A successful workplace-focused program in Canada is called Occupation-Specific Language Training (OSLT) and is offered in various occupational fields to internationally trained newcomers who have previous education and work experience in their professions abroad. Canadian immigration regulations allow for active recruitment of qualified and well-trained newcomers from abroad with university degrees and prior professional work experience. The OSLT curriculum (2010) expresses explicitly some of the key features of ICCs because the program specifically prepares learners for employment and integration into the workforce.

There are many other language learning and workplace preparation programs and approaches; however, this example illustrates well how learners need to understand workplace- and employment-oriented cultural practices as they learn the appropriate sociocultural and other competencies that enable them to prepare for work in a new culture. In the curriculum, any components to develop more cultural awareness and knowledge relate to the specific language and communication skills learning objectives.

Participants in these programs develop language and communication skills with the objectives to

- understand workplace culture in their occupation and sector;
- interact effectively with their colleagues, clients, and supervisors;
- give and receive information by email and telephone;
- interview and network effectively and manage self in employment; and
- develop soft skills (e.g., oral/written communication, critical thinking, interaction with others, diplomacy and tact, team working).

Because OSLT programs are provided to ESOL learners with high levels of English proficiency, the curriculum is designed to incorporate specific cultural knowledge and communicative practices common to practitioners in a specific occupation or profession. The following is a sample description of an OSLT course targeting interprofessional health care practitioners:

This practical and innovative course will help you

- understand health care workplaces in Ontario such as clinics, community agencies and hospitals.

- better communicate on interprofessional health care teams.

- accurately provide and collect information on a client's care.

- network with local employers, industry associations and employment resources.

Small-group exercises based on everyday communication tasks in health care will help you

- practise common interprofessional workplace communication skills.

- develop strong networking and career-building communication skills.

(OSLT, 2010)

Compared to other industries, intercultural competence in health care can be more complex and challenging. Health care involves services that are "intensely personal," often touching "the core of patients' and providers' culturally influenced values, beliefs, and attitudes" (Anand & Lahiri, 2009, p. 387). It is certainly important for providers to learn and, most importantly, respect the cultural beliefs and behaviors of all their patients. Furthermore, it is important for health-care systems to develop and implement long-term strategies that support both providers and patients by, for example, ensuring that all staff have the skills and tools they need to provide interculturally competent care (Anand & Lahiri, 2009, p. 401).

INTERCULTURAL VALUES AND BELIEFS

In all employment preparation programs that include language training, the overall curriculum will touch on cultural knowledge and information that include standard industry employment practices and information about workplace culture(s). In an increasingly globalized network of multinational organizations, native- and nonnative-English-speaking employees both are more likely to be working internationally with their counterparts on several continents and in multiple countries. With the rapid development of technology, employees in the IT industry and finance sectors are already working virtually around the globe in workplaces in which most communication takes place electronically, and people meet using videoconferencing. A clash of values and beliefs is inevitable when people of different backgrounds and cultures work closely together with the added complications inherent in technology-mediated interactions.

RESEARCH ON INTEGRATION

When Johanne was conducting interviews for her PhD thesis on the experiences of ESOL engineering students during their professional internships, all the interns mentioned that they were working in a very multicultural and multilingual workplace environment. In fact, many of their coworkers were ESOL speakers themselves from a variety of countries. Johanne also conversed with a director of a workplace and language training company who shared the following:

> It's not only language, in some cases, it's language and culture but then it is the organizational culture, too . . . New Canadians made a lot of assumptions about what the company would do for them based on their own work situation in their own country . . . in some cases, they were coming from [a] hierarchical, driven-type of organization and all of a sudden they are moving into an organization where people are expecting them to make independent decisions . . . so if they go to their boss and say, "This is what's happening, what should I do?" Well, [the boss says] "Solve the problem. You've got that information. You fix it. Don't expect me to do it." And the thought is, "Wow, my boss doesn't know anything." And so there is that kind of tension.

> There can also be a sense of credentialism that they have in a lot of cases, and their concept is, "Well, I have a PhD, therefore I am respected by everyone . . ." There isn't a sense of having to prove yourself. [However,] we all have to do that in a new job . . . and when we change companies, we are proving ourselves again. We have to play that game. The feeling is: I have this qualification. My boss knows I am well trained therefore I am a certain status. It doesn't work that way. (p. 151)

(Mednick Myles, 2005)

Learners in ESOL employment preparation programs need the guidance of instructors to navigate differences that can be challenging and often also require both attitude and behavioral adjustments. Integration is, therefore, a process that takes time and usually requires individuals to go through several phases of transformation. Though our working world may be global, workplace practices are usually anchored in local cultural customs. The following list of values and beliefs is useful in considering the scope of issues that are not just about communication and language but also about learning to develop intercultural competencies:

- Perceptions and attitudes concerning gender and other dimensions of diversity (e.g., glass ceiling, women in management, age, abilities)
- Work ethic and expectations of taking initiative
- Working independently without supervision and with others—independence vs. interdependence
- Understanding and dealing with conflicts and disagreements
- Building rapport and relationships in professional career development
- Marketing self and competencies/skills

- Expressing and responding to opinions
- Communicating "upward" and "downward"—understanding position in workplace hierarchy
- Understanding human rights principles, diversity, and inclusion practices—expectations of nondiscriminatory behavior in employment, services, and housing.

Connectedness of culture and communication in workplace contexts has generated a great deal of interest in the form of research and in the development of guidelines for curriculum and best practices that focus on the role of ICC in employment and on the integration of newcomers into the mainstream workforce. Among such recent initiatives is the Ontario Government–sponsored and funded 360° View of Culture and Communication, a project which involved Touchstone Institute (2018) conducting consultations over 2 years with multiple stakeholders, among them employers, to map out the full scope of communication needs and expectations for the successful integration of newcomers in the 21st-century workforce. The project has culminated in an online web-based intercultural workplace-focused curriculum framework. This framework includes intercultural knowledge and awareness and strategies and approaches recommended by organizations, groups, and individuals who wish to implement programs and provide intercultural employment-focused training. The website also provides resources tailored for use by multiple stakeholders, among them English language teachers and ESOL learners, curriculum developers, and administrators of adult ESOL and employment preparation programs. According to their website,

> The 360° approach is rooted in the understanding that, like communication, knowledge building is a multifaceted and co-constructed phenomenon. Lead [*sic*] by the Project 360° team, we engaged experts in the realm of workplace communication to create an inclusive and multi-stakeholder methodology.

> Built from relevant and current theory in linguistics, intercultural communication, and language assessment, the competencies included in our framework were robustly vetted through multi-step, broad-reaching consultations to capture perspectives from language and communication professionals, competency experts, employers, employees, integration professionals, HR professionals, and trainers. This iterative and inclusive process comprises our unique 360° approach—made most unique by the contributions of our many collaborators. (Touchstone Institute, 2018)

INTERCULTURAL WORK EXPERIENCE

Tuula worked for a few years as a senior manager of a communication training division in a large professional services firm in India. Though the work procedures and practices were distinctly North American, the workforce was predominantly Indian. As an instructional designer and trainer, she had to discuss the training needs with directors and managers of the firm's taxation, audit, and business consulting services. Among the many differences she remembers from the time, she recalls her Indian colleagues' need to establish personal rapport first before they could directly address business, such as talking about a training program, who should participate, or the logistics.

She later participated in intercultural training in which she learned more about the collectivist nature of Indian culture and how in that tradition it is important to exchange information about families and to socialize with colleagues even in the business context. North America, in contrast, is known to be a predominantly individualistic culture in which business people focus more on getting the work done first before they socialize. If and when to share information about family is also a personal choice, and individuals are generally more willing to share details about their personal life after they get to know their colleagues better.

CULTURALLY INFLUENCED WORKPLACE COMMUNICATION

What, then, are some of the interactional competencies in the workplace that require cultural learning? The objectives of any learning program naturally determine the focus; most employment preparation and ESOL business communication skills courses include many of these curriculum components:

- preparing for/practicing job interviews
- networking for employment to develop presence in social media and the community
- small talk; expression of empathy and socializing related to work; diplomacy and tact
- nonverbal communication (eye contact, gestures, personal distance)
- telephone etiquette (communication related to fostering business relationships)
- ways to express/manage emotions (understanding self-management at work)
- use of time and space that fits employer expectations
- email etiquette; writing work correspondence (knowledge of writing conventions)
- providing and receiving constructive feedback
- participation in teams and meetings
- presentation and negotiation skills

Chapter 1 introduces research in ICC and the models that provide guidance to teaching ICCs. The goal of intercultural competence in language learning as it is understood today represents a marked shift from the idealized native speaker model used in the past. To reiterate, culture is no longer understood narrowly as a description of ethnic or nation-specific characteristics, but as a dynamic, pluralistic, and global composite of intercultural interactions. The term *intercultural speaker* (referred to in Chapters 1 and 2) is used in the literature to demonstrate how none of us has a single identity but in fact belong to multiple social groups, and we each therefore have more than one cultural and social identity (Byram, 2011). We bring to interactions with others a complex sense of these identities, which in turn influence the communication and exchange of information.

As English language teachers, we are in fact intercultural speakers who teach how language and social skills are used in communication in general and in specific contexts, including in the workplace. Our learners need to have key information about employers' performance expectations, but there is no one uniform or ideal form of English used in the various multicultural and multiethnic workplaces in today's global world. Though communication as a key soft skill continues to involve language, it is equally important to teach teamwork, positive attitude, and networking. As ESOL teachers, we bring to our work our own social identities, which are formed by our education, membership in professional associations, ethnic and family backgrounds, and work and life experiences. When we interact with students in the classroom, we are acting in the role of a trusted advisor; we share our life and work experiences and invite students to share theirs. Teaching offers, therefore, a great opportunity to develop both the awareness and the practice of intercultural communication.

The knowledge we as English language teachers have of various workplace and employment cultures needs to be as much part of our curriculum and teaching as language skills in communication. Language is, after all, embedded in cultural and social practices. Conversely, our learners bring to the classroom their knowledge and cultural and social identities, which provide us with rich resources to draw on in the exchange. Cultural awareness in the context of employment preparation programs is clearly a two-way street that involves both instructors and ESOL learners actively participating in the exchange and transfer of cultural knowledge and information.

CULTURAL CONVERSATION: THE ART OF SMALL TALK

An internationally educated surgeon and his North American colleague are having a consultation with the parents of a teenage boy in a hospital; they are suggesting that the boy needs to undergo surgery to deal with a damaged disc in his spine. While the surgeon is a highly skilled specialist, his English skills are still developing, and he makes an abrupt comment to the parents, "No surgery, he will not walk." The parents are visibly shocked to hear the news. Later, after the consultation, the colleague points out to the surgeon that he should have rephrased the comment to the parents and refrained from making statements that are too direct, which can upset patients and their family.

The example shows a situation in which small talk could have helped the surgeon to develop better rapport with the patient's parents. Small talk is used to build relationships with people with the purpose of establishing rapport and understanding. Engaging in small talk helps to build a relationship and often to soften the mood or atmosphere before starting a meeting or participating in an event. In counseling and coaching, small talk helps both parties feel more relaxed before they get into a more serious discussion about issues.

Why Is Small Talk Difficult?

Small talk is an essential component of communication, and the topics are culturally specific. Most native English speakers know how to choose a topic to fit the situation. People from other cultures and language backgrounds may feel apprehensive about small talk because they may lack the vocabulary, often colloquial, and knowledge of appropriate topics. Confusion about what to say and to whom may also lead to loss of self-confidence. Because it is impossible to know how others will react, trying out small talk feels like risking embarrassment by saying or doing something wrong.

One of the reasons ESOL newcomers find small talk so challenging is that they do not "live" in English. They likely have spouses and friends who stem from their own language and cultural groups. For some, the only opportunity they have for conversing in English is in the workplace.

CULTURAL SMALL TALK

An ESOL intern Johanne interviewed for her research on ESOL engineering students on professional internships mentioned that, in her internship, speaking English was the most challenging for her, especially small talk. For example, before a team meeting, there was about 15–30 minutes of chit-chat—social time. During that time, she only answered questions and most of the time didn't know what to say to people to maintain a conversation. Her boss would ask her how she was doing, and she would say, "I'm doing fine," without elaborating or asking him a question.

Before a meeting, workers may talk about the weather, sports, a television program or movie, or a news item, in fact a range of issues depending on common interests. Indeed, finding a common topic is a concern; however, it is only half the battle. Difficulties can occur as a consequence of more subtle issues, such as when ESOL learners mispronounce words or use awkward expressions that impart a sense of otherness. The conversation stops because it is not quite right. No doubt, cultural meaning and communicative styles interconnect in any act of verbal communication.

(Mednick Myles, 2005, p. 210)

Expressing Empathy

As the earlier example of the surgeon shows, in particular, people working in health care and service sectors are required to develop an ability to express empathy with people as patients who in North America are also considered consumers of health services. In the English-speaking world, empathy is most effectively expressed verbally and in body language.

> **PHARMACISTS COUNSELING AND ADVISING PATIENTS**
>
> Tuula worked as an English communication skills instructor in a career bridging initiative to train internationally educated pharmacists, most of them from Middle Eastern countries, to prepare them for their accreditation exams. The course curriculum included role-play activities between a pharmacist and a patient, who was picking up a prescription or consulting for advice on which over-the-counter medication to use.
>
> The pharmacists in the training program were assessed weekly on the progress of their counseling skills by a panel of licensed native-English-speaking pharmacists. Though they handled well explaining the dosage, they fell short in showing empathy. Many of the students felt it was a waste of their time to listen to the patients' complaints or small talk; they were quickly corrected by their Canadian professional peers, who explained the importance of showing empathy to all patients—who are also pharmacy customers. Listening and rapport-building skills were challenges for most of these internationally well-educated pharmacists who had seldom been required to engage in social talk with patients in their countries of origin.

NETWORKING IN THE DIGITAL AGE

An example from an employment preparation program illustrates the pivotal role that technology plays in today's ESOL teaching. As an instructor in a career and skills bridging program in a Francophone community college in Toronto, Canada, Tuula teaches English and work-related communication skills, which range from public speaking and presentation to customer service skills and writing for workplace purposes. Early on, with the program's first intake of students, it became clear that the students, mostly Francophone African and Middle Eastern professionals, had very little or no experience in networking to develop local employment contacts through social media.

LinkedIn (www.linkedin.com) is a popular employment and professional networking site used predominantly by English-speaking professionals and multilingual technologically savvy internationalists. However, because the career bridging and employment preparation program also offers a bilingual internship opportunity with employers, developing an online profile in English became an additional skill to add to the curriculum. It is also a good idea to discuss in the classroom other social media networks, such as WeChat in China, which the students may have used in their own language and culture.

 See Chapter 6, **Technology and Computer-Mediated Intercultural Communication**, for further discussion on multiliteracies.

Students in the program find out how quickly they can make contacts through LinkedIn and how often recruiters and employers use the site to scout for talent globally. A LinkedIn profile is best described as an interactive electronic résumé. Here are a few tips to help ESOL learners create their networking profiles:

- **Develop a branding statement:** Social media networking is based on the use of keywords and phrases which pop up in online searching. Students need to develop short descriptors of their skills and qualifications, often known as branding in marketing. The instructor should provide the details on how students can design their own unique statement of skills and backgrounds.

- **Write a full history of experience:** It is a great learning experience to acquire the sector-specific use of terms and phrases and the appropriate language to fit the cultural context. Teach students to research other LinkedIn profiles and external resources to learn to describe their work and volunteer experiences using language that garners attention.

- **Develop skills to market self:** This is a more North American–specific cultural competency that provides an excellent opportunity to teach intercultural competencies and to have students present and talk about their own qualifications and skills with confidence.

- **Introduce the concept of a whole person:** The various categories in LinkedIn provide a great opportunity to remind ESOL learners that employers are not only looking for education and technical qualifications, but that they also want to know about the candidate's personality, interests, and volunteer activities. The categories inform learners about the cultural dimensions of hiring and integrating employees in the workforce.

- **Posting of identity:** Though LinkedIn works on the principle of profiles and the posting of a personal photo to identify self, some users may not wish to post a personal photo. It is important to acknowledge this choice as appropriate and legitimate; alternatives to posting a blank photo frame can include a graphic design feature to illustrate the person.

USING EMOTIONAL INTELLIGENCE IN THE CLASSROOM

Emotional intelligence (referred to as EQ or EI) can mean either knowledge or a learning framework. When referring to knowledge, EQ assessment is often given to new hires to measure their social skills and aptitudes to fit in the workplace and in an organizational structure. When referring to a framework, the EQ framework includes strategies that have been implemented in many different forms in education and workplace cultures as useful principles to understand and interpret human behavior. The place of EQ in ESOL classroom teaching is not about whether instructors need to or even can *teach* EQ. Rather, it is about giving our learners an opportunity to understand how EQ competencies are viewed and valued by employers.

One of the many useful key concepts in EQ is the ability to manage one's own emotions—to understand not only one's own emotions but also the reactions that we have to others and their emotions. While our emotional makeup may be similar or vastly different, we all need to manage our emotions and associated impulses and behavior socially in workplaces, schools, and communities.

Cultures, as we have learned, also differ in the emphasis that is placed on demonstration of emotions. It only takes the experience of watching people in the arrivals and departure areas of an international airport to realize the variety of ways emotions are expressed in different cultures. Including new ways to teach that understanding, handling, and showing of emotions are cultural and not just individual behaviors in ESOL pedagogy and in the classroom is often difficult. Perhaps many teachers avoid the subject because it may require having to challenge the commonly held stereotypes and the images displayed in the media about people of different ethnic, cultural, religious, and national backgrounds. Are all Japanese reserved, and are all Brazilians outwardly emotional? As mentioned in Chapter 1, stereotyping fails to acknowledge diversity and that we are also individuals with distinct identities. Both teachers and learners will find that developing critical cultural awareness adds value to the learning experience. Including EQ in classroom discussions in employment preparation programs also provides a great opportunity to discuss various workplace values and cultural practices that are not necessarily visible or not often openly talked about.

EMOTIONAL INTELLIGENCE AS A DEAL BREAKER

"The rules for work are changing. We're being judged by a new yardstick: not just by how smart we are, or by our training and expertise, but also by how well we handle ourselves and each other. This yardstick is increasingly applied in choosing who will be hired and who will not, who will be let go and who retained, who passed over and who promoted." (Goleman, n.d.-a)

The rules that Goleman (n.d.-b) discusses in his work have little to do with what we may have been told was important in school or later read on our own. The new measures to which he refers take for granted that we all have enough intellectual ability and technical expertise to do our jobs. EQ focuses instead on personal attributes, such as initiative, empathy, adaptability, and persuasiveness.

There is a myriad of ways educators can use EQ in the classroom and in ESOL pedagogy. Goleman's own blogs on various aspects of emotional and social intelligence are accessible as good reading resources for students. (See www.danielgoleman.info for general information of courses and resources.) His ideas and strategies are always thought provoking and offer great opportunities to learn about self and others. He writes extensively about the wisdom of using EQ successfully in organizations and in learning.

Here are a few suggestions based on how we (Tuula and Johanne) as authors and teachers have integrated EQ in teaching and in classroom practices:

- **Model compassion and empathy for ESOL learners:** Role modeling is always the best way to show in practice how we use language in communication that respects the feelings of others. You can teach empathy and compassion when providing feedback and constructive criticism to learners.

- **Teach learners to develop awareness of how others view them:** For example, have learners develop a professional profile on LinkedIn that includes information about their own passions, visions, and interests—not just a list of their jobs and employers.

- **Include EQ case studies and successes and use EQ self-assessment tools:** Research and present scenarios that show how using EQ leads to success in interactions with others, in job searching as well as at work dealing with people from different backgrounds and cultures. The internet also provides access to many free and well-designed EQ assessment tools and surveys that give learners information about their own EQ strengths and weaknesses and information to better understand the emotions that regulate human behavior.

- **Show how to take initiative and influence others:** Teaching language and culture means integrating into classroom practice opportunities for learners to take initiative and gain confidence to have conversations with experts in their fields and to exchange ideas and perspectives that can help them develop abilities to influence others. Teachers can organize role-play activities to simulate conversations learners have with professional networking contacts and employers. Tuula has found it most useful to have students participate in career fairs in which they approach employers to inquire about job opportunities and have conversations to talk about their own qualifications and backgrounds.

MENTORING IN ESOL EMPLOYMENT PROGRAMS

The gap between different types of language proficiency—in our context between ICCs in general and the occupation/profession-specific language and customs—is not easy to bridge. Most employment preparation programs and career bridging curricula address the sociocultural, functional, and strategic uses of language required in the workplace. These communicative competencies include, among others, social networking, preparing for and participating in job interviews, writing emails and reports, and handling workplace conversations.

Providing mentoring to ESOL learners in employment preparation programs is a strategy that has been found very successful. Mentoring already has a long tradition in the business world to develop management and leadership skills: Experienced employees are expected to share their expertise and help foster the growth of the younger generation that follow them. Coaching internationally educated learners and immigrants complements this tradition of sharing knowledge and experience with those who are inexperienced in a new culture. In addition to mentoring, job shadowing and internships are often provided in employment preparation programs to expose students to real-life work situations and give them the opportunity to learn hands-on skills. Job shadowing and internships also provide the much-needed practical experience of learning to communicate with others of different cultural and social backgrounds within an organization.

One of the most successful mentoring models has been to use professionals as volunteer mentors of skilled immigrants; immigrants benefit greatly from a peer mentor in their own industry sector who can guide and advise them about the employment practices and cultural customs and who can provide personal support. Volunteer mentors also gain experience as counselors and are often rewarded by their employers for their participation in a state-of-the-art coaching of individuals who are engaged in cultural and employment transition.

MENTORING PARTNERSHIP MODEL

The Mentoring Partnership program is one of Toronto Region Immigrant Employment Council's proudest accomplishments. It is a proven successful strategy that helps skilled immigrants connect to meaningful employment. Employers report that when their staff sign up as mentors, this can be the catalyst for real organizational change.

People who volunteer as mentors gain management, leadership, and essential cultural competency skills. Meanwhile, their mentees get support with their job search and a deeper insight into the Canadian labor market.

The program matches recently arrived skilled immigrants with mentors in their own field or with similar work and educational backgrounds. The mentor develops an action plan with specific goals in collaboration with the mentee based on their most immediate needs. On this list of content and objectives are usually job searching techniques; interview preparation; review of résumé; writing email and cover letters; and discussions about job postings, employers, and the importance of the internet as a versatile tool to do research about opportunities and to gather information. Experienced mentors share not only their employment experience but also valuable information about workplaces and which strategies and techniques to use in handling contact with employers.

Having operated since 2004 in the Toronto region, the Mentoring Partnership has facilitated more than 10,000 mentoring relationships between skilled immigrants and established Canadian professionals.

(Adapted from Toronto Region Immigrant Employment Council, n.d.)

Employers who partner with mentoring programs can also form relationships with immigrant service delivery agencies or education partners in the communities to recruit volunteer mentors. This sharing of responsibilities model has worked well; service delivery partners match mentors with skilled immigrants and support the mentoring relationship over a specific time period. Mentors are also offered training to ensure that they understand the commitment to a program that fosters integration of skilled newcomers in the workforce.

 See **Appendix E: Communication in the Workplace** for a schematic representation of the issues and challenges in workplace communication.

CLASSROOM BEST PRACTICES

Cultural Conversation: Preparing for Job Interviews

How can we teach ESOL learners to do well in a culturally demanding job interview? Most of the information that is associated with performance in job interviews is culturally specific. In the organizational hiring context, the employer screens and shortlists applicants and makes the final hiring decision through an interview process. The expectations employers have of someone "interviewing well" are not necessarily the same as the candidates.

There is a Chinese saying that we are all reflected in *three mirrors*. The first mirror reflects what we think of ourselves, the second of how others see us. The third mirror is about the truth. This is a useful analogy to keep in mind when preparing students to do practice mock interviews and role-plays. It would also be a good idea for teachers to explore interview protocols from other countries and cultures so that they can make comparisons with their ESOL learners.

A few ideas to consider in teaching both content and strategies:

- **Focus on communicative use of language:** Have everyone create a mini branding statement of their own skills and work experience; include industry-specific keywords and phrases in the answers to questions; help learners understand the rationale for the questions; explain the necessity to show appropriate body language (smile, posture, tone of voice).

- **Cultural knowledge:** Research the internet and screen interview techniques and videos that show how to answer questions well, what applicants wear to interviews, and how candidates can make a good first impression.

Classroom activity: Tips on holding mock interviews

- **Create mock interview panels** in which learners take turns playing specific roles as interviewers and candidates to get a feel of both roles and the differences.

- **Incorporate peer feedback suggestions** on how to improve in addition to instructor-led debriefing and corrections.

- **Videotape interviews and practice phone interviews**; replay and discuss results with learners and encourage constructive criticism of self and peer feedback.

- **Ask learners to visit job fairs and trade shows** and practice their quick elevator pitches (succinct and persuasive sales pitches) in conversations with real-life employers.

- **Arrange learners to have "information interviews"** with native-English-speaking professionals and employer representatives to get more authentic practice.

Tips on building an online profile and on job search preparation

- **Have learners develop a LinkedIn profile** with keywords and language that employers can understand and use in their search of candidates; explain how this profile helps develop a more active network of contacts in their occupations.

- **Have learners do their own research of practices** used in their professional fields; involve them in taking more active ownership for finding employers and jobs that match their skills and knowledge.

- **Provide trustworthy advice on résumé writing practices** and strategies that help learners present themselves professionally in the job market; help dispel any myths and misconceptions about the job search process.

- **Invite guest speakers** (employers, recruiters, etc.) to provide learners opportunities to interact with real-life people, ask questions, and get to know the practices that help them become more confident as job seekers.

Classroom activity: Interview questions, "Tell me about yourself"

Prepare students for this activity by providing them with the following context:

Sumara is getting ready to have an interview for an internship opportunity with a local bank as an assistant to the financial advisor. She worked as a client service officer and as a financial advisor in a large commercial bank in New Delhi before she moved to the United States. She will be interviewed by a panel of representatives, including a human resources manager, the branch manager, and the financial advisor. How should she summarize her skills and knowledge to make a good impression?

What do the employers expect to hear and see when they say to Sumara, "Tell us about yourself"?

- A very short summary of who she is and what her experience and skills are related to the job

- A glimpse of her personality—a smile, pleasant voice, and a good positive attitude

- A demonstration of confidence about herself and enthusiasm about the work

What should she *not* say about herself in her quick elevator pitch?

- List all the education and jobs she has had (the interviewers can read her résumé)
- Weaknesses that she may have (they will likely ask about this in a different question)
- Personal information about her marital/family status, religion, or age

What could Sumara do before the interview?

- Practice doing her 30-second elevator pitch about herself in front of a mirror
- Get feedback from friends about her delivery
- Be herself, take deep breaths, and relax as much as she can

What you need for teaching

- A job ad for a financial advisor role in a commercial bank—requirements, attributes, skills
- Web link to the bank's website to review its mission statement, operational principles, etc.
- List of keywords, phrases, and banking jargon from websites, job ads, blogs, LinkedIn, etc.

Examples of tasks and activities

- **Reading and Vocabulary:** Review a job ad for a financial advisor posting from the bank; explain terminology and keywords and concepts used in the ad; research and study the bank's main website page to review a mission statement and other key features about the bank's operations.

- **Writing Practice:** Have each student draft an elevator pitch for Sumara based on the profile and then compare their version with a classmate; you can discuss a few examples in class and then have students start creating their own profiles.

- **Debrief and Discussion:** Get learners to share examples and give feedback; debriefing should include a list of the points that are important to include in a statement or elevator pitch to show the candidate has understood the internship opportunity and what the bank is about: work experience in a nutshell, passion about the work, and what aspects of the work are most important to the candidate.

- **Job Interview Videos:** Share with students a collection of videos that are good examples on how to answer popular job interview questions. Though most real-life interviews are very interactive, videos like these are scripted and tend to show multiple examples to provide the viewer with useful information that can be applied directly to a job interview; they also contain text comments to explain why some phrases and language are recommended or to be avoided.

See "Examples of Good Job Interview Answers" (DenhamResources, 2016) on YouTube and videos from the Toronto Region Immigrant Employment Council's (2010) Finding Talent, which explore different cultural values and how they influence the way in which newcomers understand and answer questions in job interviews.

Cultural Conversation: Negotiating

Learning about cultural variables

In ESOL teaching, we are primarily concerned with learners developing the ability to master the language required to hold their own in interactions with others in speaking and writing. We are trained to focus on the output of language with the goal of accuracy and fluency. In teaching cultural information, however, we need to focus more on providing the context and cultural variables—the situations of language use; the influence of age, gender, and social positions; and the various circumstances in which communication occurs. Without understanding of the impact of these variables on communication, ESOL learners use language that may be inadequate or inappropriate. The choice of language also goes hand in hand with behavior that fits the specific sociocultural context.

Teaching sociocultural aspects of language becomes more obvious when we are teaching specific skills, such as negotiating, which involves cultural knowledge of customs and practices. Tuula recently coached a civil engineer who was a green building construction company owner. Having been educated in China, he had trouble in negotiating arrangements with suppliers of construction materials in North America. His English, which was formal and sounded academic, resulted in misunderstandings with salespeople who had different education levels and were accustomed to speaking in more colloquial vernacular with construction industry representatives. Fluency in this intercultural context required developing an ability to switch between varieties of English to communicate with different sociocultural groups.

Classroom activity: Negotiating arrangements

We know from teaching speech acts in pragmatics that that there are many levels of formality and phrases and expressions in English that ESOL learners often find confusing. Anchoring language in its sociocultural context provides learners the examples they need to avoid making too many faux pas. The language used to make appointments provides a typical example of the varieties of language that convey multiple levels of formality:

- I need to make an appointment to see the doctor . . .

- Would you have an opening to see the doctor next Tuesday?

- I'd really appreciate if the doctor could see me sooner than later . . .

- Would next week Tuesday work for an appointment?

- What about Tuesday? Is the doc in then?

ESOL learners often work in customer service and in administrative positions and meet people who use many of these varieties of English. In workplace-oriented or English for specific purposes programs it is important to teach colloquial English vernacular and to demonstrate the behaviors our students are likely to encounter in real-life work situations. YouTube and other video materials available on customer service training are good resources to add to classroom work as they illustrate both communication and behavior.

Building relationships

Negotiating is a process that includes asking questions, stating needs, and proposing and exploring ideas and issues with others, for example, involved in a sale or purchase. In the business context, negotiations involve bargaining, making/rejecting offers, and closing deals. Experienced negotiators often use language of persuasion and summarizing of information as they build rapport with customers, suppliers, and vendors.

Here are some examples of negotiation phrases and expressions in a business context (adapted from Emmerson, 2009).

Bargaining

- We'll be prepared to lower the price, but only if you order a larger quantity.
- Would you be willing to accept a compromise? We could offer you a 20% discount on the price if you . . .

Accepting/Rejecting Offers

- That sounds like a reasonable offer. I think we can work with that
- We will agree to your offer. That's a deal!
- That's not a viable option, really.
- It would be difficult for us to accept your offer as it is.
- We're sorry but we can't accept your offer.

Summarizing

- Let's just take a minute to review what we've been discussing.
- Can we just go through the offer again, please?
- We would like to take some time to go over the details of your offer again.

Strategies and language skills

Returning to the example of the civil engineer/green building company owner: He asked to have communication skills coaching to help improve his English to negotiate better with his customers. On further discussion, he and Tuula agreed that he also needed to listen more carefully to his customers to learn more about their needs. Developing his products and services depended on his knowing his customers so that he could work with them to find solutions to their many varied home building needs. In the process, this engineer found that he could also provide advice on energy conservation to homeowners and use the company website to write regular blogs for his clients.

Active listening skills are not just about comprehension of language but also about learning to listen "between the lines" for information that is unsaid or implied. It requires awareness of cultural practices and behaviors, which in our example include the civil engineer learning to ask more questions and to listen more attentively. As a result, he realized he could expand his business by offering his expertise on other green building and conservation issues. Active listening, as Zuker (2005) points out in her informative book about creating rapport, comprises many attributes:

Listening Without Advising
Being present—simply "being there"—is often enough. It is sometimes important to listen but not to jump in to give advice or think we need to resolve the issue right away with correct answers; we can help others tell their story and get through their frustration, anger, resentment, or feelings of powerlessness by having them feel heard and by remaining silent to listen. Often, a solution emerges in the discussion that ensues.

Listening to Promote Understanding
"Being all ears" also means paying attention when our mind wanders or when we lose focus and can't concentrate. An active listener restates the content of what is being said by putting it into their own words, using phrases such as, "So what I'm hearing you say is . . ." and "Correct me if I'm wrong, but what I hear is that you would like to . . ."

Asking Good Questions
What and *how* are used in open-ended questions that work better than *why* questions because they won't make others feel defensive or ask them to explain their motivations. "What is your understanding?," "What would you like to see happen?," or "How would you like to resolve this problem?"

Cultural Conversation: Providing Critical Feedback
Constructive criticism
How is providing critical feedback influenced by cultural differences? Research suggests that ESOL learners may provide constructive criticism differently than native English speakers, mostly by using less softening and more direct language. As a result, they often run the risk of coming across as rude or aggressive to the person receiving the feedback. Some researchers claim that ESOL speakers also tend to use more intensifiers, such as *too* and *very*, and modals, such as *must* and *should*, more frequently when they give advice to others (Nguyen & Basturkmen, 2010).

Providing feedback on performance—in education or at work—is inevitable and built into the procedures used in schools, universities, and employment. However, what may not be obvious to many ESOL learners is the kind of language spoken or written in these interactions and the choice of strategies that are commonly employed in giving feedback. Providing feedback to anyone who is from a different culture and holds a different position in a social hierarchy requires particular awareness and tactfulness. Responding appropriately to constructive criticism by others, including peers, also involves cultural know-how and careful use of language.

Classroom activity: Practicing the art of criticism

Though critical feedback by definition refers to providing critical (i.e., negative) comments about someone's performance, the actual process of identifying a problem and providing advice are linguistically complex acts of discretion and diplomacy. Discretion because the wording of the criticism has direct impact on the person whose performance is evaluated, and diplomacy because the verbal and nonverbal elements also convey emotions and attitudes. Because most of us are not adept at providing critical feedback, it is not surprising that we often talk about the "art" of criticism.

In *Teaching Constructive Critical Feedback*, Nguyen and Basturkmen (2010) provide excellent examples of strategies and mitigation devices (softeners that can reduce potential offense). For example, the following "markers of uncertainty" can be taught to ESOL learners to help them offer appropriate constructive feedback to their peers:

- Making statements such as

  —I'm not sure . . .

  —maybe . . .

  —I don't know that I agree with everything you say . . .

  —I am not so sure what I think about . . .

- Using modals and adverbs (e.g., *may, might, could, possibly, probably*) help convey criticism but without the full weight of certainty.

- Using questions to avoid bold statements or imperatives that often convey harsh judgment, for example:

  —Could you say it differently?

  —Have you summarized the main ideas well, do you think?

- Using conditional verb tense forms:

  —If you used a few more examples, you would strengthen your argument considerably.

  —I would like to hear more details about . . .

- Other linguistic expressions used as softeners:

  —*I think* you need more facts here . . .

  —*It seems* to me that you have a good understanding. A few more examples *would be good* to have . . .

  —You need to be *a little* less direct and subtler here . . .

"When you . . . I feel" feedback model: Practicing inclusion

The situation-behavior-impact model, created by the Center for Creative Leadership (2018), is used in communication and business coaching in particular to provide feedback that is related to real-life communication situations. It is effective anywhere because it can be applied immediately to respond to specific behavior or comments. When we can outline the impact of behavior on others, we actually provide the chance to reflect on their actions and think about what they need to change.

> **Situation:** Describe the situation, being specific about when and where it occurred. (E.g., "When you gave your presentation in class yesterday . . .")

> **Behavior:** Describe the observable behavior. (E.g., "When you gave your presentation in class yesterday, and you completely forgot to mention the contribution of your group members to the research . . .")

> **Impact (I statements):** Describe what you thought or felt in reaction to the behavior. (E.g., "When you gave your presentation in class yesterday, and you completely forgot to mention the contribution of your group members to the research, I actually felt really embarrassed for you.")

The functions of language refer to the specific discourses that we use in situations that require discretion and diplomacy. Using "I" statements helps as a strategy to keep the flow of conversation going without offending others or putting them on the defensive, and it precludes assuming what the other person is thinking.

The pronoun *you* can be perceived as accusatory rather than as an invitation to collaborate and solve the problem. Use of pronouns *I/we* and *you* in the right contexts is an important part of inclusive communication. For example, most ESOL learners will appreciate knowing that *I* is used in business correspondence to indicate the writer taking responsibility for any actions in the message, whereas *we* is used to refer to the organization or business collectively, sometimes to deflect responsibility. Learning to use both pronouns appropriately and correctly in conversations with colleagues and in emails and letters is part of teaching effective workplace writing skills to learners.

Sandwich technique

The sandwich method or technique, sometimes also called the hamburger method, is probably the most familiar approach used to provide constructive criticism. In this metaphor, the pieces of bread represent positive feedback/compliments and the meat of the sandwich represents constructive or negative feedback. The negative is couched between two positive observations because criticism and advice are easier to receive when also receiving compliments or praise for having done something well. For example, "I really liked your examples in the presentation; they illustrated the problem well. However, I would have liked more evidence of how the problem could be resolved . . . that would make your talk even stronger in content."

SMALL TALK STARTERS

The weather

- Beautiful day, isn't it?
- Looks like it might rain . . .
- Sure, would be nice to be out there . . .
- Couldn't ask for a nicer day, right?

Current Events

- Did you hear the news about . . . ?
- The forest fires out West are scary . . .
- I read the new subway line will cost millions . . .

Office/Work

- Looking forward to the weekend?
- You look like you could use a cup of coffee . . .
- Have your worked here long?

Social Events

- How do you know [name of person]?
- Have you tried the chocolate mousse?
- Pretty amazing gathering, don't you think?

Small Talk Worksheet: Tips for Teaching

The topics that are *not* suitable for small talk in North American multicultural contexts include politics, religion, sexuality, and gender and race/ethnicity issues.

It is important that our learners understand why these emotionally charged and often highly divisive issues are best left out of small talk conversations. Always good to remember that small talk is used to develop rapport and build social relationships with people who are otherwise strangers to each other. Topics that are neutral are most suitable.

Body Language

Small talk is a social activity and meant to relax people and to put them at ease with each other. It is always good to remember to smile and make direct eye contact while still respecting the comfortable distance between the speakers. Although in many cultures, people feel comfortable touching the shoulder or arm of the other person, in the English-speaking world a handshake is more customary.

Naturally, people who already know each other may give each other a hug or embrace briefly, but this is only done after the two have gotten to know each other well or are friends or close acquaintances.

Keeping the Conversation Going

- I agree with you completely about that . . .
- Glad to know that we share similar interests.
- That's a really good point you're making.
- How fascinating . . . I'm going to share this with my colleagues.
- What a great idea! I really like what you're saying . . .
- I might look at what you said a bit differently, but it's great we can talk about it.

Ending the Conversation

- It was great to talk you.
- Hope to see you again.

CASE IN POINT: LANGUAGE IN SOCIOCULTURAL CONTEXTS

The sociocultural context in the following scenario is an engineering firm in North America. The clients of the firm may include a mix of people working in the construction industry, civil engineering, and architecture as suppliers, customers, and contractors. The conversations that Zachary as an employee has with them regularly require him to build rapport as he holds conversations on the phone or meets with project stakeholders in person.

SMALL TALK IN THE WORKPLACE

Zachary is a civil engineer by training and currently working as an architectural design technician in a busy engineering firm. He emigrated from Algeria 2 years ago and managed to get this position as an engineer in training, an interim status provided by the licencing authority to internationally trained engineers who are pursuing professional certification in Canada.

Zachary had his first performance review with his supervisor, who told him that he needed to do better in his dealings with clients on the phone and in meetings. The reason he had not made much progress was because his strategies were too direct. He felt confused and mentioned he didn't understand why he had to discuss how he or the clients were doing any given day or to listen to clients talk about the weather or how their kids were doing. He simply wanted to talk about the actual job. He asked his supervisor, "Why can't I just tell them that the measurements of the beam were not quite correct and need to be redone?"

Here, the sociocultural and functional elements of learning to use language appropriately also require understanding more fully the engineering workplace culture. For Zachary, it is important that he understand how an engineering firm functions and how he is required to communicate in English to do his job as an architectural design technician. Though he can handle all the technical requirements on the job, he has been asked to work on how he communicates with his colleagues and the firm's clients. Not only is work small talk culturally new to Zachary, but he also lacks the comfort in English to engage in this type of communication, which presupposes knowledge about exercising tact. The questions about how he and his family are doing seem to him to be irrelevant to the job duties he has in the firm. In fact, this lack of soft skills is one of the greatest challenges that newcomers face when they first start working in a new culture and workplace. Though Zachary will benefit from taking language and other training courses, he may also need to have a more experienced mentor/coach who can help him develop and fine tune his people skills.

There are a number of ways to teach small talk and to help ESOL learners attain a high comfort level in engaging in it. To begin with, providing the full cultural "picture" helps students understand the strategic uses of language in situations that require tact and discretion. When teaching skills to build rapport and interpersonal communication, English language teachers may find it useful to explore with learners the dimensions of workplace culture—in our case study, the customs, traditions, and practices that are common in most engineering firms. Often, these practices are expressed in the mission statement of the company and in the values considered important: punctuality, teamwork, taking initiative to lead projects, and providing quality customer service.

- **Explore workplace culture** through examples of cultural practices and customs in engineering firms—websites, job profiles, articles, and videos.

- **Discuss soft skills** using examples from Zachary's workplace: communication with customers; building rapport with clients; and handling inquiries, concerns, and complaints.

- **Study social functions and events**, such as softball games, workplace social events, and conferences—situations in which employees are networking and meeting others and likely to use small talk.

In a workplace cultural context, engaging in small talk on the phone or in meetings is the most common strategy used to interact with people and put them at ease. We often call this breaking the ice. Sometimes, small talk is necessary to allow people who meet for the first time to get to know each other. At other times, it is simply used as a polite way to have conversations with people who already know each other from a work context. Inquiring about the well-being of the person and family and talking about the weather or sports are among the more common ways to engage people in light superficial conversation.

References

Anand, R., & Lahiri, I. (2009). Intercultural competence in health care: Developing skills for interculturally competent care. In D. Deardorff (Ed.), *The Sage handbook of intercultural competence* (pp. 387–402). Thousand Oaks, CA: Sage.

Byram, M. (2011). *Teaching and assessing intercultural communicative competence.* Clevedon, England: Multilingual Matters.

Center for Creative Leadership. (2018). The key to immediately improve your talent development. Retrieved from https://www.ccl.org/articles/leading-effectively-articles/hr-pipeline-a-quick-win-to-improve-your-talent-development-process/

DenhamResources. (2016, March 4). *Examples of good job interview answers* [Video file]. Retrieved from https://www.youtube.com/playlist?list=PLCB126B2811B2ADFE&feature=plpp

Development Economics. (2015). *The value of soft skills to the UK economy.* England, United Kingdom: Development Economics.

Emmerson, P. (2009). *Business vocabulary builder.* Oxford, England: Macmillan Education.

Finding talent. (2010, June 24). Retrieved from http://www.hireimmigrants.ca/resources-tools/videos/finding-talent

Goleman, D. (n.d.-a). Measures of emotional intelligence. Retrieved from http://www.danielgoleman.info/ei-assessments/

Goleman, D. (n.d.-b). Workplace. Retrieved from http://www.danielgoleman.info/topics/workplace/

Lippman, L., Ryberg, R., Carney, R., & Moore, K. (2015). *Workforce connections: Key "soft skills" that foster youth workforce success: Toward a consensus across fields.* Retrieved from https://www.childtrends.org/publications/key-soft-skills-that-foster-youth-workforce -success-toward-a-consensus-across-fields

Literacy Information and Communication System. (2014). *Preparing English learners for work and career pathways.* Retrieved from https://lincs.ed.gov/sites/default/files/ELL _Context_Instruction_508.pdf

Malmborg, S. (2015). *The shocking truth about soft skills training.* Outcome Simulations. Retrieved from https://outcomesimulations.com/shocking-truth-soft-skills-training/

Mednick Myles, J. (2005). *Communicative competence in the workplace: A look at the experiences of English second language engineering students during their professional internships* (Unpublished doctoral dissertation). Queen's University, Kingston, Ontario Canada.

Nguyen, T., & Basturkmen, H. (2010). Teaching constructive critical feedback. In D. H. Tatsuki & N. R. Houck (Eds.), *Pragmatics: Teaching speech acts* (pp. 125–140). Alexandria, VA: TESOL International Association.

Occupation-Specific Language Training. (2010). Colleges Ontario. Retrieved from http://co-oslt.org/en/

Office of English Language Acquisition. (n.d.). OELA. Retrieved from https://www2.ed .gov/about/offices/list/oela/index.html

Salo-Lee, L. (n.d.) *Communicating with "the Finns": From national characterizations to effective intercultural interactions.* Retrieved from https://www.jyu.fi/viesti /verkkotuotanto/kp/vf/liisa.shtml

Stahl, G. (2001). Using assessment centers as tools for global leadership development. An exploratory study. In M. Mendenhall, T. Kühlmann, & G. Stahl (Eds.), *Developing global business leaders, policies, processes and innovations* (pp. 197–210). Westport, CT: Quorum Books.

Toronto Region Immigrant Employment Council. (n.d.) *Mentoring.* Retrieved from http://triec.ca/our-initiatives/mentoring

Touchstone Institute. (2018). *Communicative competence at work: A framework for intercultural communication in the workplace.* Retrieved from https://360communication .ca/

Vulpe, T., Kealey, D., Protheroe, D. & Macdonald, D. (2001). *A profile of the culturally effective person.* Retrieved from https://blogs.rrc.ca/diversity/wp-content/uploads /2015/01/interculturally-effective.pdf

Zuker, E. (2005). *Creating rapport: Using personal power to influence without control.* Boston, MA: Thomson Course Technology.w

TECHNOLOGY AND COMPUTER-MEDIATED INTERCULTURAL COMMUNICATION

CHAPTER 6

OVERVIEW

New electronic and social media is influencing all aspects of our lives. Whether one is living in the United States or a small village in India, most people have access to technology at least at some point during the day and can communicate with each other in a virtual space. Electronic and social media include Facebook, Twitter, LinkedIn, Blogs, YouTube, Instagram, iTalk, MySpace, not to mention email and a host of other internet technologies. We use these platforms to interconnect, express our opinions, and participate in dialogue for social, educational, and work-related purposes. These technologies can improve the learning experience of English to speakers of other languages (ESOL) learners through community engagement; information exchange; collaborative creation of knowledge; and negotiation of meaning, which forces participants to check and clarify utterances before the flow of meaningful communication can proceed. All these activities are necessary for enhancing English language skills and acquiring intercultural sensitivity.

Still, English language skills and intercultural communicative competence (ICC) go hand in hand and both are especially important to online communication because nonverbal cues in the form of body language (e.g., grimaces, furrowed eyebrows, hand gestures) and even breathing patterns (e.g., a bored sigh or yawn) are generally absent. The video component in a call is helpful, but even that medium is constrained. In other words, what has become the norm in communication can also be extremely challenging for ESOL learners, who are vulnerable to misunderstandings and confusion. It is paramount that English language teachers include communication through internet technologies when incorporating ICC into their lessons and curriculum.

This chapter presents the concept of multiliteracies and the likely benefits and possible challenges ESOL learners have using and navigating various forms of electronic and social media, in relation to ICC. Attention is given to ways English language teachers can address these challenges and provide learners with the knowledge and skills to communicate effectively in various platforms.

THINKING ABOUT THE TOPIC

- What challenges do ESOL learners have communicating with individuals online for various purposes?

- What types of support, guidance, and activities can English language teachers offer to ensure the kinds of participation and linguistic interaction that can lead to language development and ICC?

- How effective are specific language learning social network sites (LLSNSs) in providing ESOL learners the practice and skills they need for effective online communication?

- In what capacity can electronic and social media be used to help ESOL learners acculturate to their new environment?

- How can electronic and social media foster sustainable intercultural communication and dialogue and hence English language acquisition?

THEORETICAL PERSPECTIVES: MULTILITERACIES AND THEIR CONNECTION TO ESOL AND INTERCULTURAL COMMUNICATIVE COMPETENCE DEVELOPMENT

To be literate in the world today involves much more than reading and writing skills on paper; indeed, we need to be able to navigate among different forms of writing, or *genres*, and, most importantly, to do it quickly. Literacy is not only about language itself, but also about the effects and communicative consequences that particular texts can have for different audiences. The result is that we have a much broader and more comprehensive understanding of language, culture, and communication especially now that we read, write, connect, interact, and share knowledge in ever changing online environments in significant ways (Kern, 2015). Technologies in the form of computer-mediated communication have obviously changed the ways in which language is used and how information is presented and received.

Taking the concept of literacy further is the idea of multiliteracies, which refer to variations in language use according to different social and cultural situations, and our ability to negotiate meaning in different social and cultural domains, such as digital media (Kalantzis & Cope, n.d.). Online technology sites provide a common medium for intercultural dialogue whereby individuals from different parts of the world exchange messages, collaborate, and retrieve information. All these activities require multiliteracy skills.

First, we need to be able to figure out differences in patterns of meaning from one context to another, which are influenced by a host of factors, such as culture, gender, life experience, and subject matter. With these factors in mind, we can safely say that every oral and written exchange is intercultural to a certain extent.

Second, meaning is presented in ways that are increasingly multimodal, that is, written-linguistic modes of meaning interface with visual, audio, and spatial patterns (Kern, 2015). As a result, the ability to mode-switch has become the norm. For example, the asynchronous nature of email messages can provide valuable opportunities for reflection and representation of cultural understandings. When ESOL learners compose emails, they have the chance to consider features of their own cultural background and those who will be receiving their message. They have the time to think about how best to represent their own understanding of the target culture. Alternatively, a synchronous connection, such as an online chat, relies on short, spontaneous responses.

If the ESOL student is to develop ICC, they must be able to notice salient features of the culture and context online with reduced cues. As Levy (2007) points out, "A learner's access to digital cultures is largely determined by their ability to manage the special modes of interaction that predominate in the online environment" (p. 117). Using various online modes of communication requires complex skills and much practice in navigating and negotiating meaning, both linguistically and interculturally.

Kalantzis and Cope (2008) suggest that teachers go beyond thinking of literacy as merely alphabetical forms of written communication. They argue that grammar should be considered open ended, flexible, and functional to help students be aware of language differences, which are steeped in cultural, context-specific, and multimodal channels or representations of meaning typical of new digital media. All in all, the combination of direct instruction with an appropriate level of facilitation is essential to helping ESOL learners navigate the sites and engage in appropriate and effective online communication.

What do these changes in the meaning of literacy, particularly multiliteracies, mean for ICC development?

ONLINE LITERACY

Kern's (2015) seven principles, stemming from a sociocognitive view of literacy, are relevant to understanding ICC teaching and development in relation to online technologies. Online literacy involves communication that includes the following components:

- **Interpretation**: The writers interpret events, experiences, and ideas, and readers interpret the writers' interpretation based on their own socialization and culture orientation.

- **Collaboration:** Writers write for an audience. Their decisions about what to say and what "goes without saying" are based on their understanding of who they are writing to. A reader's understanding of the text of reference is based on their own cultural knowledge and experience.

- **Conventions:** How people read is dictated by cultural conventions that change through use and are modified for individual purposes (e.g., a restaurant menu on a website).

- **Cultural knowledge:** Reading and writing occur within particular cultural systems of beliefs, attitudes, customs, ideals, and values. When readers and writers function outside a given cultural system, they risk misunderstanding or being misunderstood by those who are living inside the cultural system. Intercultural pragmatics plays a role here. →

- **Problem-solving:** Words are embedded in linguistic and situational contexts, and so reading and writing involves figuring out the meaning of words based on predictions and guessing.
- **Reflection and self-reflection:** Readers and writers think about language, both consciously and unconsciously, and its relation to the world and themselves.
- **Language use:** Understanding comes with knowledge about writing systems, vocabulary, and grammar as well as knowledge about how language is used in spoken and written contexts.

When ESOL learners read and write online in virtual communities (e.g., collaborating on a wiki document, participating in a blog, or communicating via email or Facebook Messenger with an e-pal), they learn to deal with uncertainties and ambiguities and new ways of organizing and expressing thoughts and ideas which, as we well know, go beyond learning factual information about their new cultural environment. These exchanges provide students with the opportunity to both 1) learn online literacy skills necessary to socializing, learning, and working in today's technological society, and 2) develop linguistic and intercultural competence by increasing their awareness of cultural differences in how people express themselves. When using social media, "individuals must mediate complex encounters among interlocutors [who have] different language capacities and cultural imaginations, who have different social and political memories, and who don't necessarily share a common understanding of the social reality they are living in" (Kramsch &White- side, 2008, p. 646, as cited in Warner & Chen, 2017, p. 123). For ESOL learners, communi- cating with people online requires entry into understanding those "cultural imaginations" in order to express themselves in a way that is effective and appropriate to an English- speaking audience. Through online exchanges with native English speakers, ESOL learners can also receive personalized information and advice, in other words, an insider perspec- tive from real informants about life in the United States, Canada, Australia, and elsewhere.

Analysis of language use in computer-mediated communication can help us under- stand how particular language behaviors function in intercultural online email commu- nication. In her interviews and text analysis of exchanges between Chinese international students studying business administration in the United States and their U.S. mentors, Xia (2007) determined four patterns of the Chinese participants' English language use: 1) Other's Oriented Talk, as revealed by their "extreme politeness, consideration of oth- ers as the priority, and talk about others [as opposed to themselves] in communication" (p. 67); 2) Mentor-Mentee Talk with Limited Relationship Development, which was illustrated by the topics the Chinese students chose to discuss, all of which were general in scope (e.g., weather, clothes, and housing), leaving little opportunities for fostering friendships; 3) Adaptation of Others Talk, which was a way for the Chinese participants to improve their English skills by using unfamiliar English expressions and the fact that learn- ing "unique online discourse" was facilitated by their "Chinese culture underlining solidar- ity and integration with others" (pp. 69–70); and 4) Icebreaker Talk, which relates to the way the Chinese participants kept the exchange to general, surface topics, never going into specific details. The participants felt that the lack of context cues in such communication was a constraint to deeper interaction. Xia (2007) explains that the Chinese participants communicated with their U.S. mentors from a code of honor; they kept to their official role as mentees. However, the U.S. mentors communicated with their mentees from a code of dignity, in which "communication functions to express individual intent and will" comprising "personal hobbies, personal interests, and personal plans" (Xia, 2007, p. 73). A text analysis of this sort reveals that rules and meanings regarding language are grounded in our cultural backgrounds and that mutual understanding can be enhanced by knowledge of cultural resources that play out in online communication.

USING SOCIAL MEDIA TO AID THE ACCULTURATION PROCESS AND FOSTER INTERCULTURAL COMMUNICATIVE COMPETENCE

The use of social media can be a real benefit to help ESOL learners—both new immigrants and international newcomers—maintain links with their home countries and, most importantly, adjust to their new social, academic, or workplace environment. Through interactions on social media, these learners have the opportunity to feel part of an intercultural online community. Participation on Facebook, for example, has the potential to foster students' pragmatic use in English (Chen, 2013), which is essential to ICC development. For international students, Facebook, as an online space for socializing, has been a popular medium to help them acclimatize to college life, build friendships with native English speakers, and practice and experiment with their English language skills in a positive way (Mitchell, 2012). For example, Chen's (2013) case study of two international graduate students studying in the United States illustrated the potential of using Facebook for acquiring pragmatic use in English. Interestingly, Lee and Ranta (2014) found a high correlation between frequent Facebook use among international students at a Canadian university and improvement in their speaking skills and oral fluency development, according to their self-assessment questionnaire. However, people from different cultures can also have different ways of presenting themselves and of perceiving others on social networking sites; in other words, they may have different ways of managing their online communicative behaviors. These differences can make it difficult for international students to make friends online with native English speakers because, similar to face-to-face interactions, establishing and maintaining personal relationships involves unwritten rules of behavior.

As newcomers, the advantage for ESOL learners is that they can build strong relationships with other English speakers offline and manage those relationships online as they acculturate to their new surroundings. Online communication allows them to receive information and emotional support in a timely fashion. When Sawyer (2011) examined the effects social media usage on the adaption process of a small number of international students studying at an American university, she found that most of the participants used these sites, especially Facebook, multiple times a day to communicate with family and friends in their home countries as well as others in their new setting. These international students also talked about culture shock and how social media helped them, with mailing lists and online social groups, become more integrated into the new culture. They also utilized social media sites not only to better understand cultural differences and local, everyday life (especially seen through photos of social events), but also to improve their English language skills, particularly slang and common phrases.

Despite these advantages, the students also discussed the addictive quality of sustained online interactions and that social media sites can actually present an obstacle to communication because students are unable to gauge emotions, feelings, and facial expressions during communication. They are not able to tell how others deliver or react to messages nor can they hear tones of voice that can convey emotions. All in all, the international students felt they were able to maintain a sense of community through social media in the United States through groups on social media sites that reflected their interests. They could communicate online with people they had met at the university and use social media to build relationships and feel part of the university community, along with maintaining connections and updates about what was happening in their home countries.

Clearly, Facebook is an excellent tool that can provide substantial benefits to students adapting to a culturally unfamiliar country. Sustained participation online can promote interconnectedness and understanding among people from different countries and cultures. Nevertheless, cultural differences can also influence communication, and one way of understanding these differences is through the individualism/collectivism dimension (Hofstede, Hofstede, & Minkov, 2010). For example, people from cultures scoring high on the individualistic scale may focus on meeting new people and ensuring maximum visibility on a social media site, as opposed to people from collectivist cultures, who would be inclined to already existing relationships with a small number of people (Rosen, Stefanone, & Lackaff, 2010). In a study of cross-cultural communication that looked at how university students born in Britain and international students from China studying in Britain used Facebook to communicate with friends from different cultural groups, Jiang and de Bruijn (2014) found that observing (reading posts but not responding), communicating (exchanging messages), and grouping (getting involved in a Facebook group) were the prime types of Facebook interactions. The authors concluded that there were differences between the Chinese (collectivist) and British (individualistic) participants at various levels. For the Chinese, relationship building and providing mutual support was a priority, whereas the British participants were more focused on managing their friendship network for personal goals.

Social Media and Classroom Practice

It is important for English language teachers to become more aware of how culture plays a role in the way their learners communicate on Facebook and other social media sites. Though misunderstandings can occur, the benefits of connecting ESOL learners with native English speakers gives both parties opportunities to negotiate meaning in an online format. Lee and Ranta (2014) maintain that teachers should encourage but *ease* their learners into participating on social media. They suggest that teachers and learners use Facebook as a source of authentic language for analysis by observing various speech acts, such as greetings, requests, apologies, refusals, and complaints, made by native English speakers in other Facebook groups. Once ESOL learners have become familiar with and competent in the culturally embedded etiquette of such online communication, they can be buddied with native-English-speaking students they have possibly met in person to engage in online social conversation and discuss topics of mutual interest.

One word of caution: Although classroom Facebook use has been demonstrated to enable sociopragmatic awareness and encourage participatory learning, outside of pedagogical applications the possibilities for participation and access are shifting and often unequally distributed (Warner & Chen, 2017). It is still unclear whether Facebook interactions enhance communicative competence, and more specifically ICC, in other online or face-to-face contexts. For maximum benefit, English language teachers need to include online communication that addresses intercultural pragmatics, the exploration of cultural norms and issues, and the development of ICC into their curriculum.

Email Correspondence, Video Calls, and Chats

Email communication is a highly used form of communication for social, educational, and business purposes. For example, it is now common practice for job applicants to submit their résumés as email attachments and cover letters as email body messages to employers. Despite email's frequency of use, however, ESOL learners can lack the necessary email etiquette and, we argue, ICC, to communicate effectively and meet the expectations of an English-speaking audience raised in Western cultural traditions (Biesenbach-Lucas, 2007) as opposed to individuals from their native culture and language background. Misunderstandings can surface, especially in hierarchical relationships and in situations in which email recipients are requested to do something that might be an imposition upon them. Writing emails to authority figures requires a high level of English language intercultural pragmatic competence and awareness of politeness conventions (Economidou-Kogetsidis, 2015).

In postsecondary education, for instance, it is important for ESOL students to understand and use indirect and polite language when they are writing emails to their professors. Research has found that in student-to-professor email communication, native English students are more adept at expressing themselves in a way that addresses the power distance between themselves, as students, and their professors, as professionals with authority within the academy (Hendriks, 2010). Indeed, adjusting the level of politeness to variations in power distance may be challenging for ESOL learners who need to spend time planning and composing such emails, especially when face-threatening acts are involved (Chen, 2006).

Besides checking for correct spelling and grammar, ESOL learners need to make sure their requests are reasonable, the tone is polite, and the language is formal enough (yet not *too* formal or even flowery) given that they are communicating with a person in authority. Although recipients may judge ESOL senders less harshly than if they were native speakers (Hendriks, 2010), ESOL learners tend to be more direct in requesting information, for example about course materials, or action, such as arranging a face-to-face meeting (e.g., using *please* plus an imperative, which can make the request sound like an instruction, order, or demand), as opposed to indirect and deferential (e.g., "Would you mind?" or "I would be grateful if you could . . ."; Economidou-Kogetsidis, 2011). Using language that is too direct implies that the speaker does not assign the professor the degree of respect that they would normally expect from a student email. Even when learners give reasons or justifications for their request (to possibly mitigate the direct language) and close without a salutation or with such expressions as "thank you in advance," they invite further negative miscommunication. Besides language and culture, however, Economidou-Kogetsidis (2011) claims that

> the preference for directness, insufficient mitigation and lack of acknowledgment of the degree of imposition might not be typical of non-native speaker communication but typical of email communication among young people who grow up in an instant messaging culture where speed and directness are particularly valued. (p. 3208)

If there is some truth in her argument, then both native English and ESOL speakers would be in the same boat regarding email communication to authority figures. Economidou-Kogetsidis (2011) also found, however, that if basic politeness features are included as part of the emails, then some lecturers actually view the brevity of the messages positively. That aside, we want to emphasize that it would benefit ESOL learners to have explicit instruction and practice in email communication to a variety of people (of both high and low power distance) that specifically addresses ICC and intercultural pragmatic awareness. Without instruction, it is possible that ESOL learners' email messages will differ from native-English-speaker norms and expectations (Biesenbach-Lucas, 2007). Such differences can result in negative assessments of their personalities, stereotyping of cultural groups, and, most importantly, miscommunication that leads to a rejected job application or failed grade.

EMAIL COMMUNICATION CHALLENGES

The notion of audience and the rhetorical conventions inherent in texts are very much connected to ESOL students' understanding of the cultural aspects of communication. With regards to email communication in an IT workplace, an instructor explained to Johanne the following:

> People can't understand their [ESOL newcomers'] email messages because they lack all the things that we know [intuitively] as native speakers of English. This would be how to abbreviate things, or knowing when to use such phrases as "Hi, how are you doing" and "How is it going with the project?" These kinds of things and they would go directly into very, very heavy duty technical information. They have no salutations, no greetings, no nothing . . . and so it may be very abrupt, or it sometimes may come across as rude or lacking in terms of clarity . . . They think that formal writing means using a lot of clichés and that would make their writing better if they just used very complicated clichés. On the other hand, taken from a business writing textbook, they might give you all those very awkward stilted expressions, such as "Please do find attached." I think it is very much an indication of cultural translation to me. You don't feel comfortable in the everyday English environment and so you end up using that stilted, formal language because it may be the only way you think you should write. And nobody tells you the difference. (Mednick Myles, 2005, p. 236)

It would seem that one of the challenges for ESOL learners is to get beyond the crutch of modeling textbook language that may be inappropriate to the conversational style of an email message. Modeling an incoming email may be a more effective strategy to take when they are composing a response. Certainly, corresponding with native English speakers and paying attention to the initial tone and style and "filling in the blanks" with their own content are ways students can begin to modify their writing so that they approximate appropriate cultural and rhetorical norms for these types of texts.

In addition to email correspondence, computer-mediated communication can also take place through real-time video calls and chats. Though chat messages are based solely on written text, there are certainly advantages to communication and comprehension for ESOL learners when they can see their partner's image on the screen and hear their voices through video calls. In the chat medium, students are anonymous; they also have time to put their thoughts together in writing. However, with video, although there are important nonverbal cues, students assume a greater social presence, which means that issues involving politeness may come into play, especially when completing a task. In both cases, students may be reluctant to ask for explanations, both linguistic and/or cultural, because they feel they are disrupting and slowing down the conversation.

Negotiation of meaning in online exchanges has been shown to be beneficial to second language acquisition (see Yanguas, 2010), and we would argue, ICC, especially when confusion is due to cultural issues. Nevertheless, van der Zwaard and Bannink (2014) remind us that in many situations, ESOL student participants actually prefer to wait for their interlocutor to solve the problem rather than ask for clarification, which is related to the concept of face, discussed in Chapter 3. In their study of real-time video and chat communication between eight native speakers of English and eight ESOL speakers of Dutch completing a collaborative task, the researchers found that these undergraduate students made different discourse decisions during the video and chat calls. Without visual and auditory cues, the ESOL learners were not so concerned about face issues and communicated more freely in the chat medium. Despite only pretending to understand the task at hand, they actually completed it successfully. However, during the video call, the ESOL learners' loss of face and the native-English-speaking students' politeness and solidarity with them resulted in unfinished work. The researchers concluded that if the participants (ESOL students interacting with native English speakers) do not see or hear each other during live interaction, the ESOL learners "seem less inhibited to indicate non-understanding, and hence start up negotiation of meaning more often and more successfully" (van der Zwaard & Bannink, 2014, p. 146). Their findings indicate that English language teachers should be aware that loss of face issues may indeed affect the way their learners communicate in real-time online formats in which interlocuters can see or hear each other during the interaction.

Language Learning Social Network Sites

Language learning social network sites (LLSNSs) are online communities that are specifically designed to bring together computer-assisted language learning instruction and communication. They provide students with structured tutorials and the opportunity to apply what they have learned through collaboration with other language learners and authentic communication with native speakers around the world. Specialized websites for language learning include Lang-8, a language exchange social-networking website based in Japan, and iTalk, which connects language learners and teachers and exchange partners through video chat. Research on the effectiveness of using LLSNSs for language learning focuses on learner attitudes, how often they accessed the sites, and aspects of learner progress, namely identity construction and development, socialization and the development of pragmatic competence, and language improvement. Most recently, in a large survey of language learners using Livemocha (which closed in the spring of 2016), Lin, Warschauer, & Blake (2016) found that most participants felt that they had gained self-confidence in using the target language and motivation to learn more. Part of the reason for their enthusiasm may be that they could practice their skills and socially engage online with native speakers, a format into which they felt perfectly natural entering. They also experienced greater perceived progress in speaking and listening, as opposed to reading and writing. According to the authors of the study, this result may be due to relationship-building opportunities and the site's intention to integrate community through online interactions with native speakers.

Although there are challenges of attrition and identifying learner errors and mistakes, the advantage of these LLSNSs is that they offer both instruction through tutorials and the opportunity for language learners to converse with native speakers online. The questions are: Are they also able to foster ICC development? And what role does culture play in the online interactions? Our view is that these sites may be beneficial for linguistic purposes, specifically grammar and vocabulary, and only for ESOL learners at beginner to intermediate levels of English language proficiency. They are more likely to gain social and cultural insights, along with listening skills, from watching Hollywood films and American television programs, which are readily available on the internet (Trinder, 2017). ESOL learners might already access and watch these films and programs informally; however, for focused ICC development, teacher-guided, interculturally focused activities and exercises that include a reflection component are most valuable for classroom use.

In sum, when it comes to computer-mediated communication, ESOL learners undoubtedly "need the guidance and informed insight of their teachers to create their own online correspondence and to interpret and respond to the messages, blog posts and video recordings that they receive from their partners" (O'Dowd, 2011, p. 355). Through classroom discussions, discourse analysis, and modeling of authentic texts, students can develop the skills necessary to have effective intercultural online interactions in English.

CLASSROOM BEST PRACTICES

Buddy System With Native English Speakers Using Social Media

Telecollaboration refers to using online communication tools, such as a combination of email and video conferencing, to connect people in different locations and often with different linguistic and cultural backgrounds so that they can engage in collaborative project work and intercultural exchanges (Hockly, 2015). If ESOL classes are taking place in a college or university setting, English language teachers can partner ESOL learners with volunteers from other classes to act as online buddies who provide cultural information, answer questions, and model effective language. The medium for communication could be email, Facebook, Skype, or any other online platform, depending on the English language proficiency of students and their comfort level with synchronous or asynchronous communication. However, ICC will not happen automatically; both parties may also need classroom instruction on how to make cultural comparisons that go beyond food, fashion, and festivals. Through a set of guidelines, they can be asked to interpret and critically analyze the cultural content they receive in their online interaction.

ONLINE BUDDY SYSTEM

As an ESOL teacher, you have the following roles to play in setting up an online buddy system:

- **Organizer:** Find appropriate partner classes that use volunteers or learners who will receive credit for their participation. Set up the online buddies; outline appropriate topics for discussion; and create prompt questions, ground rules for the exchanges (e.g., required number of posts per week), and opportunities for individual and classroom reflections (e.g., journals).

- **Intercultural Partner:** Establish a professional relationship with teachers from other classes. Make sure they are on board and in touch with their learners who are participating in the exchanges. Those learners could be required to keep journals to reflect on their learning as well.

- **Model and Coach:** Arrange classroom sessions to model appropriate language and offer instruction in analyzing the interactions. Sessions can include instruction in asking and answering questions, using formal and informal language, and other specific features of online communication.

(Adapted from O'Dowd, 2007)

Online Communication and Collaboration

Learning management systems (LMSs), such as Blackboard and Brightspace, have evolved over the years into sophisticated multimedia platforms that allow instructors and students several innovative ways to collaborate and communicate. More obvious examples of these collaborative tools are discussion forums, blogs, wikis, and journals. Most of the platforms also include webinar and online teaching software and tools for versatile classroom teaching. LMSs can be used to provide discussion forums and chat rooms on intercultural communication and language learning issues and to present case studies and problem-solving scenarios for commentary and practice. Posting of videos, articles, links to blogs, games, and surveys also provide students information and networking connections to a variety of resources both locally and globally. Collaborative social learning platforms also foster and encourage learners to take more ownership of their participation and break the isolation that many international students and new immigrants experience in a new culture.

Telecollaborative chats between ESOL learners and native English speakers (as cultural informants) can also be used in class as materials for ICC development and training. Ryshina-Pankova (2018) suggests that chat excerpts can be analyzed with students for pragmatic and functional aspects, language patterns, and their purpose in enhancing ICC development (p. 235). For example, teachers can show students the kind of language they can use that doesn't appear too confrontational when disagreeing with someone or that doesn't appear too direct when asking questions. Students can also be required to expand and elaborate on their ideas by manipulating the chat excerpts to more fully express their opinions in culturally appropriate ways. It is always valuable to utilize concrete examples of text in this regard.

Specific Instruction in Email Communication

Teachers can offer explicit instruction in email etiquette that specifically focuses on ICC along with other linguistic and metalinguistic elements. Learners first examine and analyze model email messages before writing their own. They receive feedback on their own messages, and such feedback should address intercultural considerations and expectations. To begin with, ESOL learners need to increase their pragmatic awareness through consciousness-raising activities, which can help them become aware of the different politeness norms and tones that occur in an English text. Economidou-Kogetsidis (2015) highlights that misunderstandings are often caused by pragmatic transfer from the learners' native language and culture, and so such awareness is most important. She also emphasizes that teachers should prevent unintentional rudeness or subservience in the messages ESOL learners compose, so it is vital not to be too prescriptive or didactic in enforcing Anglo-Saxon standards of behavior. We still want students to have the skills to freely express themselves, while being mindful of email etiquette and cultural protocols.

Activity: Tips for Teaching Email Messaging

Biesenbach-Lucas (2007) provides the following outline for teaching student-professor email requests as part of an advanced English for academic purposes course for ESOL learners intending to attend American universities, but the steps can be adapted to include instruction for any email message crafted for a variety of purposes:

1. In a warm-up, students examine actual request examples—some appropriate, some not—and then, in an initial consciousness-raising lesson, discuss the reasons for pragmatic success and failure. You can provide prompt questions, such as, "Why is this email effective?" and "What is the problem with this email?" Ask students to consider the context, directness choices, address forms, and modification choices according to specific sociological and contextual factors (e.g., participants' relationships, degree of imposition involved, degree of formality, possible urgency, power differences, rights and obligations) and then do revisions on pragmatically inappropriate emails. You can also compare emails written in students' native languages with those in English, discussing politeness

norms that exist in their culture. Take one such email and translate it into English using Google translate, for example, and then discuss its efficacy in both cultures.

2. Students read several email messages and examine the layout of the messages on paper and on the screen. Discuss what an imposition is and how a professor may react to one. The messages they read should differ in terms of imposition (e.g., requesting feedback on one attached assignment is less imposing than requesting feedback on more than one).

3. Students divide each email message into its component parts and uncover the standard elements (e.g., subject line, salutation, mention of attachment, request, expression of gratitude, student's name).

4. Students focus on the actual request language and how it differs depending on the degree of imposition. Discuss language use and how words can be interpreted according to one's cultural orientation (e.g., Western versus Eastern).

5. Finally, students practice writing email requests for feedback, first in controlled fill-in-the-speech-act activities on worksheets and eventually on their own in the computer lab or on individual laptops, where they send actual email messages to their professor (or to another native-English-speaking person, depending on the nature of the email and its intended audience).

CASE IN POINT: CULTURALLY ORIENTED COMMUNICATION

As English language teachers, we are trained in the theory of second language acquisition and in the art and practice of teaching language, such as discourse, lexis, grammar, and sociolinguistic elements of language use. Developing intercultural reading or interpretation of our students' work is not necessarily something we view as an obvious part of teaching. Teachers often take it for granted that learners make certain types of errors; our role is to teach the correct forms and usage of language.

The following excerpts from email correspondence of students with their professor illustrate not only typical language errors English language teachers are familiar with but also other cultural information that is useful to know about and reflect on.

EMAIL MESSAGES FROM LEARNERS

Respected mam,

Could please recheck my essay. I am kind of thinking of better grade for the last one, if possible please forward me feedback for my essay. Please let me know where i was week.

Your's faithfully

_____   →

> Dear Ms. Tuula,
>
> I am very thankful to you for giving me second chance for the essay assignment. Please find attached herewith essay assignment and obliged. I'm not sure I pass hope so.

In teaching how to use email and the appropriate netiquette includes, of course, information and examples about how to address readers, organize the content, and close a message and create a signature line. *Respected Mam* is a salutation that we would advise the student to replace with the more conventional *Dear Madam* or *Dear Ms. X*. This student's writing could also be a loose translation from the first language and comes across rather bossy while it also makes us smile because we can see here the attempt made by the student to try to influence the professor about marking the essay.

Nevertheless, the email also shows respect for a professor by a student who sees the teacher in a much higher authority/power position. The content of the message reveals the student's own view of his or her position as someone who is "weak" and in need of feedback and help. The writing here reveals clearly a perception of positions in a hierarchy that reflects the cultural values the learner has grown up with in a society that is much more socially stratified. This is not surprising, as this writer is originally from India. It is not uncommon in India for families to attempt to use connections with people in positions of authority who can help them affect the outcome of their children's education or get access to coveted university and college positions. Though some of us have grown up with cultural values that condemn bribery and nepotism, we need to recognize that these practices are commonplace in many other cultures and countries in the world.

In the second email excerpt, we have evidence of an attempt at formal English used to thank the professor for a second chance to improve an essay. Here, the attempted formality is expressed with words such as *herewith* and *obliged*. We often see cumbersome efforts by students to find words that they think will fit the purpose of formal writing. If anything, as teachers we need to teach the styles of writing along with registers of language that capture the levels of formality that are used to convey more complex meanings. In short, teaching writing involves culturally specific practices and knowledge that is often tacit and not necessarily as easily accessible to international students in our classrooms as we assume them to be.

References

Biesenbach-Lucas, S. (2007). Students writing e-mails to faculty: An examination of e-politeness among native and non-native speakers of English. *Language Learning and Technology 11*(2), 59–81.

Chen, C. (2006). The development of e-mail literacy: From writing to peers to writing to authority figures. *Language Learning & Technology, 10*(2), 35–55. Retrieved from http://llt.msu.edu/vol10num2/chen/

Chen, H. (2013). Identity practices of multilingual writers in social networking spaces. *Language Learning & Technology* 17(2), 143–170. Retrieved from http://llt.msu.edu/issues/june2013/chen.pdf

Economidou-Kogetsidis, M. (2011). "Please answer me as soon as possible": Pragmatic failure in non-native speakers' e-mail requests to faculty. *Journal of Pragmatics* 43(13), 3193–3215.

Economidou-Kogetsidis, M. (2015). Teaching email politeness in the EFL/ESL classroom. *ELT Journal,* 69(4), 415–424.

Hendriks, B. (2010). An experimental study of native speaker perceptions of non-native request modification in e-mails in English. *Intercultural Pragmatics,* 7(2), 221–255.

Hockly, N. (2015). Online intercultural exchanges. *ELT Journal* 69(1), 81–85.

Hofstede, G., Hofstede, G. J., & Minkov, M. (2010). *Cultures and organizations: Software of the mind.* New York, NY: McGraw-Hill.

Jiang, Y., & de Bruijn, O. (2014). Facebook helps: A case study of cross-cultural social networking and social capital. *Information, Communication & Society* 17(6), 732–749.

Kalantzis, M., & Cope, B. (n.d.). *Multiliteracies.* Retrieved from http://newlearningonline.com/multiliteracies

Kalantzis, M., & Cope, B. (2008). Language education and multiliteracies. In S. May & N. Hornberger (Eds.), *Encyclopedia of language and education* (Vol. 1, pp. 195–211). Berlin, Germany: Springer Science+Business Media.

Kern, R. (2015). *Language, literacy and technology.* New York, NY: Cambridge University Press.

Lee, K., & Ranta, L. (2014). Facebook: Facilitating social access and language acquisition for international students? *TESL Canada Journal,* 31(2), 22–50.

Levy, M. (2007). Culture, culture learning and new technologies: Toward a pedagogical framework. *Language Learning & Technology,* 11(2), 104–127.

Lin, C., Warschauer, M., & Blake, R. (2016). Language learning through social networks: Perceptions and reality. *Language Learning & Technology,* 20(1), 124–147. Retrieved from http://llt.msu.edu/issues/february2016/linwarschauerblake.pdf

Mednick Myles, J. (2005). *Communicative competence in the workplace: A look at the experiences of English second language engineering students during their professional internships* (Unpublished doctoral dissertation). Queen's University, Kingston, Ontario Canada.

Mitchell, K. (2012). A social tool: Why and how ESOL students use Facebook. *CALICO Journal,* 29(3), 471–493.

O'Dowd, R. (2007). Evaluating the outcomes of online intercultural exchange. *ELT Journal,* 61(2), 144–152.

O'Dowd, R. (2011). Intercultural communicative competence through telecollaboration. In J. Jackson (Ed.), *The Routledge handbook of language and intercultural communication* (pp. 342–358). New York, NY: Routledge.

Rosen, D., Stefanone, M., & Lackaff, D. (2010). Online and offline social networks: Investigating culturally-specific behavior and satisfaction. In *Proceedings of the 43rd Hawai'i International Conference on System Sciences*. New Brunswick: Institute of Electrical and Electronics Engineers, Inc. (IEEE). Retrieved from http://citeseerx.ist .psu.edu/viewdoc/download?doi=10.1.1.458.380&rep=rep1&type=pdf

Ryshina-Pankova, M. (2018). Discourse moves and intercultural communicative competence in telecollaborative chats. *Language Learning & Technology, 22*(1), 218–239.

Sawyer, R. (2011). *The impact of new social media on intercultural adaptation*. Senior Honors Projects. Paper 242. Retrieved from http://digitalcommons.uri.edu/cgi/viewcontent .cgi?article=1230&context=srhonorsprog

Trinder, R. (2017). Informal and deliberate learning with new technologies. *ELT Journal, 71*(4), 401–412.

van der Zwaard, R., & Bannink, A. (2014). Video call or chat? Negotiation of meaning and issues of face in telecollaboration. *System, 44,* 137–148.

Warner, C., & Chen, H. (2017). Designing talk in social networks. What Facebook teaches about conversation. *Language Learning & Technology, 21*(2), 121–138. Retrieved from http://llt.msu.edu/issues/june2017/warnerchen.pdf

Xia, Y. (2007). Intercultural computer-mediated communication between Chinese and U.S. college students. In K. St. Amant (Ed.), *Linguistic and cultural online communication issues in the global age* (pp. 63–77). Hershey, PA: Information Science Reference.

Yanguas, I. (2010). Oral computer-mediated interaction between L2 learners: It's about time! *Language Learning & Technology, 14*(3), 72–93.

CONCLUSION

We have written a book that seeks to go beyond a discussion of the importance of inter-cultural communicative competence (ICC) and its related components. Instead, we have attempted to tackle the complex issues of how to integrate ICC into English to speakers of other languages (ESOL) teaching practice. Language practice is traditionally concep-tualized in terms of concrete knowledge and skills, such as grammar structures, speech acts, and vocabulary development, while intercultural goals are conceptualized in abstract terms, such as intercultural awareness, attitudes, and sensitivity. Our aim was to bring the two together. With the idea that theory informs practice—which in turn informs policy—we have outlined theoretical perspectives, made concrete suggestions, and shared ideas that address the importance of fostering inclusiveness and embracing diversity within our classroom walls and the community beyond. It is now time to turn ICC development into policy by specifically placing it as an objective or learning outcome in curriculum guide-lines, not only for ESOL programs, but also for teacher education programs that prepare individuals for teaching newcomers in a host of English language and English in the work-place programs.

That said, integrating intercultural goals and competencies into ESOL education requires more than an understanding of theory and a revision of curricula; it involves a complete reconceptualization of the nature of ESOL teaching and learning. Not only are knowledge and skills involved; such integration demands a change in *mindset* and a rethinking about our role as cultural informants and strategists in the classroom. It means that we are to consider *most communication situations* in terms of their cultural messages. For example, why might there be poor attendance at a Casino-themed, free-beer social for ESOL students primarily from Saudi Arabia? Why might a student be complaining about a stomachache when her real problem is anxiety and homesickness? Why might a student continue to copy verbatim out of a textbook or model essay when he knows well enough that plagiarism is unacceptable, and that the consequences may be a university suspension? Why might students prioritize family over career goals? Why might, in all these incidences, the students not tell you what they are really thinking?

As ESOL teachers, we should always ask ourselves the questions, "Is there something intercultural going on here?" and "What are my assumptions?" We should remind our students to do the same—describe, interpret, evaluate, or, in other words, stand back and reflect on what is happening from an *intercultural* perspective.

Developing ICC is a process of inner growth and of raising awareness—for both students and teachers. No doubt, ESOL students are learning English and ICC to be able to function and ultimately thrive in their new linguistic and cultural environments. But what does ICC mean for ESOL teachers? To be effective ESOL teachers, it is paramount that we engage in ongoing self-reflection, to see and understand ourselves as cultural beings. We must look within for a deeper understanding of who we are before we can adequately address the needs of our diverse group of students.

As authors and as ESOL teachers, we believe that integrating ICC into our teaching means that we are helping to build and maintain new diversity and inclusion practices that take into account the needs of learners to fully understand the ways in which culture informs and influences communication.

APPENDIX A: UNDERSTANDING CULTURAL PREFERENCES

Cultural preferences are manifested as values, attitudes, and behaviors that we all have learned as part of socialization in a particular culture. They are not cast in stone but are dynamic and subject to change in our lifetime. Though we may have been socialized in one culture, association with other cultures and membership in various social groups impact how we communicate with others. It is important to consider the influence of cultural dimensions, examples of which are listed here, on communication because our own preferences affect the sense of comfort we feel when we are in contact with others who do not share our own cultural backgrounds.

Appendix A: Understanding Cultural Preferences

Cultural Dimensions (those that influence attitudes, practices, and behavior)	Culture-Based Values	Perceptions, Expectations, Types of Behavior	Culture-Influenced Practices	Examples of Cultural Preferences
Time Perceptions of time and its use; concept of time is a basic cultural value and experience, informed mostly by cultural upbringing	**Fixed:** Punctuality, "time is money" (use it well); time is discipline **Fluid:** Flexibility, punctuality not the top priority, mediated by other social behaviors and other factors	**Single-focused:** One task at a time, commitment to schedules and deadlines **Multifocused:** Multitasking, focused on multiple simultaneous tasks	Variety of preferences based on individual and organizational practices and sociocultural traditions	**Fixed:** Showing preference for managing own time and being punctual; arriving on time to work and to appointments is viewed as a way to demonstrate respect for others and their time. **Fluid:** Showing preference for social behavior that considers lateness acceptable; being late to work and to appointments is considered acceptable behavior.
Space Comfort level with personal space; both physical space and preferences about personal boundaries	**Private:** Value placed on distance and clearly marked boundaries **Public:** Value placed on proximity, more permeable boundaries with others	**Privacy:** A "circle" around self, closed door policy **Public preference:** Sharing space and information more comfortably, open door policy	Influences understanding and interpretation of body language and nonverbal signals in communication	**Privacy:** Showing preference for guardedness in meeting new people and sharing personal information; wanting to maintain a distance physically and socially **Public:** Showing preference for openness and readiness to share personal information with new contacts; feeling comfortable with physical proximity.
Actions Importance placed on interactions in social or business/workplace or other institutional contexts	**Doing:** Focus on accomplishing tasks, emphasis on actions and results **Being:** Relationship-centered, building connections and trust, process oriented	**Bias for action:** Organizational cultures may favor "doing" vs. "being" (e.g., doing is rewarded more than building of trust and focusing on relationships)	Business and corporate cultural norms and practices, not-for-profit and other organizations (e.g., mission statements)	**Doing:** Showing preference for taking initiative and focusing on taking action as ways of interacting socially and building relations with others. **Being:** Showing preference for building rapport; keeping a low profile and listening to others as a preferred means of building trust.

Appendix A *(continued)*

Cultural Dimensions (those that influence attitudes, practices, and behavior)	Culture-Based Values	Perceptions, Expectations, Types of Behavior	Culture-Influenced Practices	Examples of Cultural Preferences
Communication Ways of expressing needs, ideas, and opinions to others; handling conflicts	**Low context:** Explicit and precise communication of meaning **High context:** Implicit, tacit communication of meaning	**Directness:** Straightforward handling of conflicts **Indirectness:** Implicit and mediated handling of conflicts, "saving face"	Conflict-averse approaches (not saying "no" to save face) vs. direct, "get to the point" approach to talking with others.	**Low context:** Showing preference for using explicit, direct language in communication and interactions with others and getting to the point quickly, e.g., business. **High context:** Showing preference for indirect forms of communication; focusing on protective and face-saving ways of communicating to avoid confrontation, e.g., social work, counseling, and therapy.
Formality in Communication Styles of speaking and the forms of expression and presenting of information	**Expressive:** Eloquence and emotional content valued **Instrumental:** Factual, detached, dispassionate style preferred	**Formality:** Adhering to rules, protocol, and customs **Informality:** Willingness to dispense with formality, spontaneity	Complexity of situational communication in an organization or field of study may influence levels of formality	**Expressive:** Individuals in public relations and marketing may prefer a more emotional and expressive approach to communication. **Instrumental:** Individuals in engineering and technology fields may prefer more factual and detached forms of communication.
Power Relations Differentiated power relationships; perceptions of status and prestige within a social structure	**Hierarchy:** Stratified structure with clearly marked power differences **Equality:** Minimized stratification, egalitarian power structures	Influences how people see themselves and interact and relate to each other within a workplace or an organization (e.g., pyramids vs. flattened organizational structures)	Power relations are "lived" learned experiences and influence behaviors and how people interact with each other	**Hierarchy:** Showing preference for authoritarian or more commanding styles of communication, common in contexts with clearly defined power relations. **Equality:** Showing preference for more egalitarian ways of communicating in accordance with expectations in less stratified contexts, e.g., community groups.

Appendix A *(continued)*

Cultural Dimensions (those that influence attitudes, practices, and behavior)	Culture-Based Values	Perceptions, Expectations, Types of Behavior	Culture-Influenced Practices	Examples of Cultural Preferences
Individualism vs. Collectivism Identity established as an individual or through association with and/or membership in a larger group	**Individualistic:** Focus on self, independent "I" dominates over "we," the rugged individual **Collectivistic:** Focus on affiliation, value placed more on "we" over "I"; the team is only as good as all of its members	In collectivist cultures, "the nail that sticks out is hammered down"; behaviors are more entrenched and show in attitudes; preferences influence behavior (e.g., marketing self and skills in employment)	Business practices, such as willingness to take initiative, speak up, and market own skills	**Individualism:** Showing preference for individual accountability and quick decision making; focusing on personal development and own interests. **Collectivism:** Showing preference for consensus building, team support, and focusing on loyalty to a group or collective.
Competitiveness Source of motivation; importance placed on rewards through achievements or through building successful relationships	**Competitive:** Value placed on achievements and assertiveness **Cooperative:** Value placed on interdependence and working together	Competitive and cooperative styles will often clash as perceptions are different; competitive styles may be rewarded more than cooperative, and such opportunities for reward will influence behaviors	Often results in stereotyping of groups or individuals based on perceptions, e.g., women are not as competitive, or men are better managers	**Competitive:** Showing preference for individual performance and achievements that may clash with the communication style of others. **Collaborative:** Showing preference for developing collegiality with others rather than focusing on winning an argument. Focusing on involving others in communication.

Appendix A (continued)

Cultural Dimensions (those that influence attitudes, practices, and behavior)	Culture-Based Values	Perceptions, Expectations, Types of Behavior	Culture-Influenced Practices	Examples of Cultural Preferences
Thinking How we conceptualize and process ideas and tasks; based on educational practices and other cultural influences	**Deductive and systemic:** Prefers theory and concepts, moves from abstract to details, focus on the big picture **Inductive and linear:** Prefers examples, experience; relies on inference; focus on the analysis of individual points more than the whole	Deductive and systemic thinking dominate in higher education; carried over to workplace practices as expectations that are unspoken or implied	Thinking preferences are not often understood as culturally informed or influenced practices.	**Deductive and systemic:** Showing preference for considering facts and figures as reliable information over other forms of knowledge; focusing on theory and concepts. **Inductive and linear:** Showing preference for examples and experience as reliable information; focusing more on inference of meaning and the importance of details.

The examples in the chart are drawn from multiple research sources and studies and adapted from the work of several anthropologists and international business consultants, including those in the reference list.

References

Hall, E. T. (1976). *Beyond culture.* New York, NY: Anchor/Doubleday.

Hampden, C., Turner, C., & Trompenaars, A. (1995). *The seven cultures of capitalism: Value systems for creating wealth in the United States, Japan, Germany, France, Britain, Sweden, and the Netherlands.* London, England: Piatkus.

Hofstede, G. (1980). *Culture's consequences: International differences in work-related values.* London, England: Sage.

Rhinesmith, S. (2006). *A manager's guide to globalization: Six skills for success in a changing world.* New York, NY: McGraw Hill.

Rockwood Kluckhohn, F., Strodtbeck, F. L., Milton Roberts, J. (1976). *Variations in value orientations.* Westport, CT: Greenwood Press.

Stewart, E., & Bennett, M. J. (1991). *American cultural patterns: A cross-cultural perspective.* London, England: Nicholas Brealey.

APPENDIX B: MODELS OF INTERCULTURAL COMPETENCE

Intercultural competence is a developmental process. Several models of intercultural competence have been put forward, in all their complexity, by academics and researchers from various fields; however, social psychology, anthropology, and education are known to be the prime movers in this area. In fact, Byram (2014) reminds us that there has been a long tradition of psychologists working within the areas of work and commerce in cross-cultural training; however, they have yet to turn their attention to the classroom and to language learning in particular. In addition, much of the research has focused on cultural exchanges, whereby U.S. college students sojourn to other parts of the world for work/study abroad programs, staying with host families or college dormitories. The challenge seems to be in whether we conceptualize competencies as a list of possible characteristics (compositional), as components representative of the interaction (co-orientational), as a process through which individuals progress and obtain competencies over time (developmental), and so on.

For our purposes, we briefly introduce you to three models of intercultural competence (IC). Although these models have been developed by Western academics and practitioners in the field, all four can be adapted nicely into an English to speakers of other languages curriculum framework.

1. Deardorff's Pyramid Model of Intercultural Competence

From the field of international education, Deardorff (2006) presents a pyramid schematic with "requisite attitudes" at the bottom, acting as the foundation, below "knowledge and comprehension" and "skills." "Desired internal outcomes" is above this, and "desired external outcomes" is at the top, representing thinking, behavior and communication. Components at the lower or personal levels inform or enhance those at the higher interpersonal/interactive levels. For example, attitudes (respect for cultural diversity, openness to learning, curiosity, and a willingness to take risks and move beyond one's comfort zone); cultural self-awareness; understanding the world from others' perspectives; and observing, listening, interpreting, analyzing, evaluating, and relating skills lead to a *shift* in thinking.

This shift involves adapting to different communication styles and behaviors, adjusting to new cultural environments, and flexibility in selecting and using appropriate communication styles; these skills are, in turn, manifested through observable *effective* and *appropriate* behavior and communication in intercultural contexts.

The advantage of this model is that Deardorff (2006) distinguishes performance from competence where external outcomes, such as the ability to carry out an appropriate intervention when there is a misunderstanding, are separate from internal outcomes, such as the desire to find opportunities to engage with otherness (Borghetti, 2017). Along with acquiring cultural self-awareness, a deep understanding and knowledge of culture (including contexts, role, and impact of culture and others' world views), and culture-specific information, sociolinguistic awareness is also a component, included under the knowledge and comprehension section. Indeed, in this model, having the language skills to function in a variety of social situations is a prerequisite for adapting to a new cultural environment.

What is effective and appropriate communication is often interpreted subjectively by the participants involved in the interaction. Deardorff (2008) points out that "effectiveness can be determined by the individual while appropriateness can only be determined by the other person—with appropriateness being directly related to cultural sensitivity and the adherence to cultural norms of that person" (para. 6). She also emphasizes the fact that intercultural competence is a dynamic, lifelong process, and, as such, it is important to understand how individuals acquire these necessary attitudes, knowledge, and skills. In addition, the skills acquired foster further understanding not only of other cultures, but also one's own culture. From an educational standpoint, critical, ongoing reflection becomes a powerful tool as learners document their development toward intercultural competence and acculturation, taking into account both language skills and culture.

Positioning is a term often used in cultural studies that calls attention to the relationship between power and knowledge. It refers to an understanding of who can speak and who is silenced, whose language is spoken and whose language is trivialized or denied, and whose actions are privileged and recognized over others. Sorrells (2014) explains that

> reflection that incorporates critical analyses of intercultural issues on micro and macro levels, that considers multiple cultural frames of reference, and that recognizes our own and others' positioning, enables us to act in the world in meaningful, effective, and socially responsible ways. (pp. 160–161)

2. Bennett's Developmental Model of Intercultural Sensitivity

Another model of interest is the developmental model of intercultural sensitivity, developed by Bennett (2004, 2014). The model is based on years of observing how people in both academic and business settings become more competent intercultural communicators. Unlike Deardorff's (2006) framework, the developmental model of intercultural sensitivity is not a model of changes in attitudes or behaviors; its focus is on cognition and how individuals become increasingly sensitive to cultural differences. Each stage represents a new way of experiencing cultural difference. The continuum moves from *ethnocentricicism*, the experience of one's own culture as central to reality in some way, to *ethnorelativism*, meaning that one's own culture is experienced in the context of other cultures. Intercultural misunderstanding is rooted in our ethnocentric projection of our own worldview onto others.

Components of the ethnocentric stage include the following:

- **Denial:** People are likely to think that their way of living is the correct way; they impose their value system upon others, believing that they are right and that others who are different are simply confused. They are not threatened by cultural differences because they refuse to accept them.

- **Defense:** People feel hostile and threatened by cultural differences; they refuse to acculturate, organizing culture into "us and them," where the "us" is superior and the "them" is inferior; they prefer to be with members of their own culture.

- **Minimization:** Superficial cultural differences in customs and rituals are acknowledged but there is the assumption that we all think in the same way, just like the Disney slogan, "it's a small world after all." According to Bennett (2014), minimization promotes "colour blindness"; it hides deep cultural differences, "including the masking of dominant culture privilege by a false assumption of equal opportunity," an important assumption of which English to speakers of other languages instructors need to be aware, particularly when preparing students for the workplace.

Acceptance, adaptation, and integration are components of the ethnorelativism stage:

- **Acceptance of cultural differences:** People are curious about and respectful toward cultural difference, but their knowledge does not yet allow them to easily adapt their behavior to the different cultural context. They no longer see other cultures as threatening, wrong, or inferior.

- **Adaptation to cultural differences:** People are able to behave appropriately in the different cultural context, or at least they have "feelings of appropriateness" and intercultural sensitivity, which help them to adapt their behaviors to the different cultural norms of their environment.

- **Integration:** Integration is concerned with cultural identity; in this case, people are already bicultural or multicultural in their worldviews and are able to move between and among different cultural contexts (not always in positive ways as they can become stuck between cultures and actually perform inappropriately in different cultural contexts). Once integrated, people can effortlessly and even unconsciously shift between worldviews and cultural frames of reference. Though they maintain their own cultural identity, they naturally integrate aspects of other cultures into it.

Through learning and experience, people become interculturally competent by going through these developmental stages from ethnocentric to ethnorelative. Although the model has been revised over the years and is well utilized in intercultural training programs, stages in the intercultural competence development process can appear rather stilted because in reality, newcomers may not experience change in exactly the same way. For example, an immigrant may feel that the custom of dropping in on people unannounced as he does in his home country is much more convenient than having to call ahead and make plans, as is the common custom in North America and other English-dominant countries. Or what about the international student who feels that the night life in their home town is far superior to the one in which his university in Canada is situated, especially when his university is located in a small city or town? Both of these individuals may appear to be ethnocentric in their attitudes, but whether they are placed at the defense stage of intercultural sensitivity is debatable. Furthermore, the issue of language proficiency is not mentioned; surely language skills would affect how well an individual can move from denial to adaptation or integration, or from ethnic psychological captivity to multiethnicity or global competency (which assumes an individual can communicate in several languages) to become interculturally sensitive and competent.

3. Arasaratnam: Model of Intercultural Communication Competence

Arasaratnam (2009) has focused primarily on the development of a theoretical framework to test the existing ICC models with the goal of developing a more pluralistic and integrated model of measuring intercultural effectiveness. Analysis of ICC is based on semantics and language-based studies; the key practical components of ICC in this model include, among others,

- knowledge and motivation,
- listening skills,
- prior cross-cultural experience,
- global outlook vs. ethnocentric viewpoints, and
- styles of communication.

Arasaratnam (2009) focuses on the development of a measuring tool she calls the integrated model of intercultural communication competence, with the goal of incorporating multiple cultural perspectives into one perspective and with the purpose of providing a critique of other ICC models. According to Arasaratnam and Doerfel's (2005) findings, those who were identified as competent intercultural communicators (from the other's point of view) all possessed five qualities in common, namely (1) empathy, (2) intercultural experience/training, (3) motivation, (4) global attitude, and (5) ability to listen well in conversation. Arasaratnam and Doerfel (2005) arrived at these findings by interviewing participants from 15 different countries. Participants were asked, among other questions, to describe a competent intercultural communicator. In this way, Arasaratnam and Doerfel (2005) were able to explore the concept of whether there are identifiable variables in a competent intercultural communicator that transcend cultural context and cultural identity of the perceiver. Based on their findings, therefore, it is not unreasonable to develop an instrument of ICC that relies on self-reported data, given there is evidence to suggest that variables inherent in a person contribute to perceived ICC from the perspective of the other (Arasaratnam, 2009).

References

Arasaratnam, L. A. (2009). The development of a new instrument of intercultural communication competence. *Journal of Intercultural Communication, 20,* 2.

Arasaratnam, L. A., & Doerfel, M. L. (2005). Intercultural communication competence: Identifying key components from multicultural perspectives. *International Journal of Intercultural Relations, 29*(2), 137–163.

Bennett, M. J. (2004). Developing intercultural sensitivity: An integrative approach to global and domestic diversity. In D. Landis, J. Bennett, & M. Bennett (Eds.), *Handbook of intercultural training* (pp. 147–165). Thousand Oaks, CA: Sage.

Bennett, M. J. (2014). The development model of intercultural sensitivity. IDR Institute. Retrieved from http://www.idrinstitute.org/page.asp?menu1=15

Borghetti, C. (2017). Is there really a need for assessing intercultural competence? *Journal of Intercultural Communication, 44.* Retrieved from https://immi.se/intercultural/nr44/borghetti.html

Byram, M. (2014). Twenty-five years on: From cultural studies to intercultural citizenship. *Language, Culture and Curriculum, 27*(3), 209–225.

Deardorff, D. (2006). The identification and assessment of intercultural competence as a student outcome of internationalization at institutions of higher education in the United States. *Journal of Studies in International Education, 10,* 241–266.

Deardorff, D. (2008). Theory reflections: Intercultural competence framework/model. NAFSA. Retrieved from https://www.nafsa.org/_/File/_/theory_connections_intercultural_competence.pdf

Sorrells, K. (2014). Intercultural praxis: Transforming intercultural competence for the 21st century. In X. Dai & G. Chen (Eds.), *Intercultural communication competence: Conceptualization and its development in cultural contexts and interactions* (pp. 144–168). Newcastle upon Tyne: Cambridge Scholars.

APPENDIX C: SIX PRINCIPLES OF CULTURE

The following principles are based on Atkinson (1999).

Principle 1: All humans are individuals

For a full understanding of culture, it is important to recognize individual heterogeneity and differences that exist among cultural groups. For example, such commonplace items like knowledge of traffic rules and how to drive, ordering fast food, or assuming the role of a teacher or student in a classroom are the result of conditioning within a specific cultural context.

Principle 2: Individuality is also cultural

Individuals do not exist separately from their cultural roots and social worlds. When teachers get to know their students as individuals, they also know them as cultural beings. Once that knowledge is obtained, it is the teacher's responsibility to develop pedagogy that addresses their unique, culturally embedded ways of learning and teaching.

Principle 3: Social group membership and identity are multiple, contradictory, and dynamic

All human beings exist in multiple social worlds, have multiple social allegiances, and play multiple social roles—all of which, additionally, are continuously changing. The acknowledgment and acceptance of multiple, complex cultural identities—which must have its foundation in really knowing one's students individually, culturally, should be the first principle of English as a second language teaching and teacher preparation.

Principle 4: Social group membership is consequential

Social life and social enculturation is never neutral; it is the result of one's history and position in society. The unequal distribution of power and resources should also be addressed.

Principle 5: Methods of studying cultural knowledge and behavior are unlikely to fit a positivist paradigm

A positivist paradigm assumes that there is an objective reality. Questionnaires, experiments, statistics, and other quantitative tools are characteristic of the research. On the other hand, ethnographic, qualitative research allows for interpretation, flexibility, and context-sensitive exploration of classroom practices as cultural constructs that may also take into account experiences in the wider community.

Principle 6: Language (learning and teaching) are mutually implicated, but culture is multiple and complex

Knowledge of language—including, centrally, how to use it—cannot be developed without simultaneously developing knowledge of the sociocultural contexts in which that language occurs and how and why it exists. The language-culture question is complex. The explicit teaching of culture often, if not always, depends on stereotypes and simplifications of behaviors. Language learners can be encouraged to do their own cultural research; however, in some cases, cultural informants may not be able to provide adequate insight and guidance in this regard.

In a more recent discussion about culture, Atkinson (2013) points out that language practice has been influenced by a host of disciplines from all over the world. However, he draws his favourite definition of culture from anthropology, which states that culture is "that planless hodgepodge, that thing of shreds and patches (Louie, 1920, as cited in Atkinson & Matsuda, 2013, p. 234). Given the context, a time in which anthropologists went into villages and studied small-scale cultures, Atkinson explains that from their perspective, culture was a

> blending, a fusion of diverse influences coming from other people over the hill, across the river . . . so in fact culture was an amazing sort of hodgepodge of different kinds of influences that had stabilized perhaps for the moment, perhaps ideologically, enough so that it influenced people's behaviors, but was by no means a monolithic, single sort of unchanging structure. (p. 234)

What is interesting is that the simple definition is not much different from the one teachers of English language learners refer to today.

References

Atkinson, D. (1999). TESOL and culture. *TESOL Quarterly, 33*, 625–654.

Atkinson, D., & Matsuda, P. K. (2013). Intercultural rhetoric: A conversation—the sequel. In D. Belcher & G. Nelson (Eds.), *Critical and corpus-based approaches to intercultural rhetoric* (pp. 227–242). Ann Arbor, MI: University of Michigan Press.

APPENDIX D: OBSERVING AND ANALYZING CULTURAL BEHAVIORS

Provide activities that give ESOL learners the opportunity to analyze their observations of cultural differences. The goal for them is to develop the skills of interpreting behaviors and paying attention to alternative cultural behaviors and perspectives. ESOL teachers can do the following to foster intercultural communicative competence development in their students based on observations, reflections, and attention to cultural details. These suggestions are adapted from the Massachusetts Department of Education, Adult and Community Learning Services (2005) and Alberta Teachers of English as a Second Language (2009).

- Analyze everyday behaviors in Western cultures (American, Canadian, Australian, etc.) and compare and contrast these with the students' own culture.

— Have ESOL students conduct interviews of native English speakers or experienced ESOL students to receive real-life stories of their observations and experiences (Hinkel, 2013). The first step is to formulate questions focusing on basic information that deal with concepts not easily observable. After students have the information, they can make presentations or complete a writing assignment. The following questions are suggestions:

- Why do some people I meet on the street ask the question, "How are you?" or "How's it going?" but do not wait for the answer?

- Why do strangers sometimes say hello to me when I walk past them?

- When and why is it okay to call teachers and professors by their first name?

- When is it appropriate to hug a person, when we first meet each other or when we leave?

- When is it polite to take off my shoes when I enter a house and when is it not necessary?

— Show pictures in which students discuss their assumptions about what is going on (e.g., two men walking arm-in-arm in New York vs. two men walking arm-in-arm in Jakarta).

— Use short film clips or podcasts to focus on cultural conventions associated with greetings, farewells, daily routines, personal hygiene, shopping, dating, marriage, going to work, and so on. Select clips that align with the students' level of English language proficiency because you don't want them to be frustrated with language items and vocabulary. Preteach new vocabulary and expressions before playing the clips or podcasts. Have students complete a chart, diagram, or outline with question prompts while they listen to a dialogue or watch a video. Then, lead a discussion of the cultural norms represented in the clip(s) and what these norms might say about the values of the culture(s). Discussion topics might include how people in different social roles relate to each other, considering aspects of communication such as conversational timing and turn-taking. Students describe the behaviors they observe, write about similarities and differences with their own cultures, and determine strategies for more effective communication.

- Identify culturally influenced behavior patterns in small talk, taboo topics, telephone protocol, degrees of familiarity, ways to express emotions, eye contact, use of time and space, and other dimensions of culture.

— Use role-plays to provide students with opportunities to practice various politeness strategies (and related grammar, e.g., modals and the conditional) and explore how these strategies reflect different degrees of familiarity. Include miscommunication scenarios. For example, after practicing greeting someone of the same age versus someone older, students might role-play a situation in which an inappropriate greeting or intonation is used. "Hello, nice to see you. How are you doing?" versus "Yo, what's up, man?" Students listening to the role-plays might be asked to identify the reason for the misunderstanding. (Also, it is probably a good idea to give more subtle examples than the one provided here.)

— Students are required to observe conversations on the street and various nonverbal behaviors, such as degree of proximity and hand gestures. Alternatively, they could observe a meeting and the ways in which people get the floor, take turns, and achieve consensus. Later, these behaviors can be role-played.

— Write a chart on the board showing characteristics of highly individualistic cultures (value freedom and independence) on one side and highly collectivist cultures (value group harmony and consensus) on the other (shown as a continuum with arrows), ideally using the students' home countries as examples. Ask students to think of phrases, expressions, or situations that illustrate the characteristics (adapted from Wintergerst & McVeigh, 2011). For example, children in collectivist cultures are likely to feel a strong obligation to care for elderly parents.

NONVERBAL COMMUNICATION—GUIDED PEOPLE-WATCHING ACTIVITIES

There are many components of nonverbal communication that are culture specific, such as body posture, eye contact, social distance, how people look at each other, expressions of emotion, greetings, and leave-takings.

The following activity can help students separate individual behaviors from those that are culturally determined, that is, acceptable in a particular community or context. Language complexity can be modified according to the proficiency level of the class.

- Explain what nonverbal communication means and demonstrate various examples with individual students at the front of the class (e.g., shaking hands and commenting that both men and women will shake hands with each other and make eye contact in a formal greeting).

- Write a selection of the following headings on the board and ask students to individually write down appropriate nonverbal behaviors under the headings common to their native cultures. In pairs or small groups, students share these cultural behaviors with their classmates, noting similarities and differences.

  — Formal greetings and leave-takings

  — Informal greetings and leave-takings (hellos and goodbyes)

  — Expressing gratitude or thanks

  — Getting someone's attention

  — Showing understanding or misunderstanding

  — Use of eye contact

  — Gestures showing approval and disapproval

  — Comfort with silence

  — Texting and cell phone etiquette

- Show a film clip or excerpt from a television program (e.g., *Friends, Mr. Bean*) that demonstrates examples of nonverbal communication in English-dominant countries and/or assign students the task of observing and documenting people's patterns of common nonverbal behaviors in various contexts (e.g., in a restaurant, at the supermarket, walking along the street, driving). Provide prompts, such as observing nonverbal behaviors among women and men, noting age differences, professions, and social status.

- Ask students to reflect on the reasons why people might behave in the way they do from a cultural perspective and discuss comparisons of nonverbal behaviors with ones from their native countries (whole class or groups).
- Encourage students to keep a personal log of their observations that includes strategies they can apply to their own interactions.

FOCUSING ON THE USE OF LANGUAGE IN CONTEXT: INTERCULTURAL PRAGMATICS

Write a list of speech acts: thanking, apologizing, refusing, inviting, complimenting etc. Have students discuss which ones they find particularly difficult or confusing to understand in English (adapted from Cohen & Ishihara, 2009). Choose a particular speech act, such as "giving and responding to compliments." Write discussion prompts or questions on a worksheet for ESOL learners to consider. Here are some suggestions:

- How would you compare how often you give, receive, or overhear compliments in English and in your native language?
- Are you comfortable and confident in giving and responding to compliments in English? What issues, if any, do you have? What do you want to know about complimenting and responding in English?
- What do people say in giving and responding to compliments in English? Write a few dialogues illustrating giving and responding to compliments.
- What do people say in giving and responding to compliments in your native country? Write a few dialogues in that language and provide a literal translation into English. (Cross-cultural examples raise students' awareness, prompting them to notice that literal translations do not always communicate the same pragmatic meaning in English.)
- What do people compliment others on? Is it about their clothing, cooking, teaching, writing, etc.?
- Who is giving and responding to the following compliments in English? Pay attention to what they say and imagine who they are and what their relationship may be.

  —"Nice haircut!"—"Thanks!"

  —"That's a nice tie you're wearing."—"Really? I just grabbed it off the rack without thinking about it this morning."

  —"I learned a lot in your class."—"Oh, it's nice of you to say that. Glad you enjoyed my class."

  —"Hey, sweetheart. I like the color of your lipstick."—"Gee, thanks. I'll wear it more often." (This is a flirtatious remark that may be more accepted in some cultures than others.)

After the discussion, you can introduce the multiple functions of compliments, adjectives commonly appearing in them, and grammatical structures. The intention, as in the culture learning approach (see Chapter 2), is for students to become adept at *noticing*: intently observing how the language of complimenting, as a cultural behavior, is utilized in various contexts and scenarios (adapted from Cohen & Ishihara, 2009).

References

Alberta Teachers of English as a Second Language. (2009). *Adult ESL curriculum framework: Intercultural communicative competence.* Retrieved from https://www.atesl.ca /resources/atesl-adult-esl-curriculum-framework/

Cohen, A., & Ishihara, N. (2009, March). *New insights into teaching pragmatics in the ESL/ EFL classroom.* Paper presented at the meeting of TESOL International Association, Convention, Denver.

Hinkel, E. (2013). Culture and pragmatics in language teaching and learning. In M. Celce-Murcia, D. Brinton, & M. Snow (Eds). *Teaching English as a second or foreign Language* (4th ed., pp. 394–408). Boston, MA: National Geographic Learning.

Massachusetts Department of Education, Adult and Community Learning Services. (2005). *Massachusetts adult education curriculum framework for English for speakers of other languages (ESOL).* Retrieved from http://www.doe.mass.edu/acls/frameworks /esol.pdf

Wintergerst, A., & McVeigh, J. (2011). *Tips for teaching culture: Practical approaches to intercultural communication.* White Plains, NY: Pearson Longman.

APPENDIX E: COMMUNICATION IN THE WORKPLACE

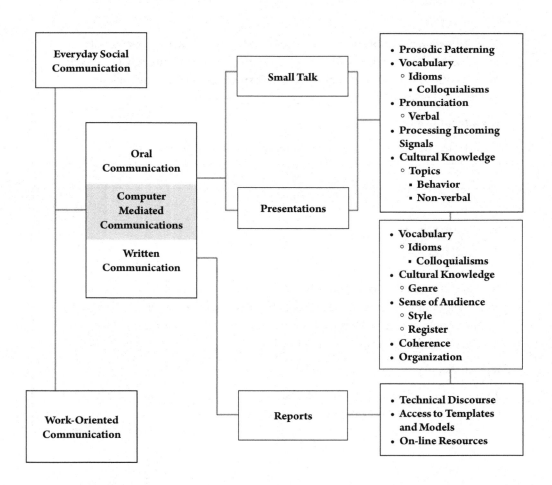

Reprinted from *Communicative Competence in the Workplace: A Look at the Experiences of English Second Language Engineering Students During their Professional Internships* (Unpublished doctoral dissertation), by J. Mednick Myles, 2005, Queen's University, Kingston, Ontario Canada.

This book is a copublication of TESOL International Association and NAFSA: Association of International Educators.

tesol press

TESOL is an international association of professionals advancing the quality of English language teaching through professional development, research, standards, and advocacy.

TESOL Press, the publishing division of **TESOL International Association**, supports excellence in the field of English language teaching through a full range of publications. TESOL authors are leading experts in the field and include experienced researchers, classroom teachers, and students.

www.tesol.org

To order this and other TESOL Press publications: bookstore.tesol.org

NAFSA: Association of International Educators believes that international education advances learning and scholarship, fosters understanding and respect among people of diverse backgrounds and perspectives, and is essential for developing globally competent individuals.

www.nafsa.org

To order this and other NAFSA publications:
Call **1.866.538.1927** | Online **shop.nafsa.org**